Pupil Book 4B

Series Editor: Peter Clarke

Authors: Elizabeth Jurgensen, Jeanette Mumford, Sandra Roberts

Contents

Ordering numbers beyond 1000 (2)

Order and compare numbers beyond 1000

Challenge 1

1 Order each set of numbers, smallest to largest.

a 3871, 2356, 1736, 5197   b 5812, 3982, 2645, 1836

c 4876, 1088, 3721, 2677   d 5222, 3121, 1889, 2776

2 Order each set of numbers, smallest to largest. Look at the 100s digits to help you.

Example
3185, 3288, 3346, 3409

a 1487, 1289, 1578, 1065   b 3825, 3166, 3498, 3255

c 5538, 5216, 5754, 5111   d 4622, 4826, 4286, 4166

Challenge 2

1 Order each set of numbers, smallest to largest.

a 4879, 2789, 4791, 2178   b 6372, 6187, 4277, 4722

c 3981, 3521, 3734, 3143   d 8256, 7256, 8454, 7454

2 For each number on these whiteboards, write one 4-digit number that is smaller and one that is larger.

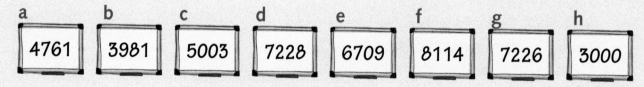

a 4761 b 3981 c 5003 d 7228 e 6709 f 8114 g 7226 h 3000

Challenge 3

1 Write a set of instructions for ordering 4-digit numbers.

2 Using the cards, make two 4-digit numbers that are smaller and two 4-digit numbers that are larger than each of the numbers on the whiteboards above.

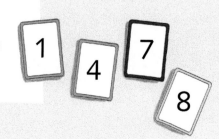

Place value problems

Solve number and practical problems that involve place value

Using the 1–3 spinner, reduce each 3-digit number to 0 in ten spins or fewer. Write the numbers you subtract and record your new number each time. You can subtract 100s, 10s or 1s.

You will need:
- Resource 7: 1–3 spinner

a 647   b 586   c 739   d 578   e 483

I spun 2 so I can subtract 200 or 20 or 2.

1 Using the 1–3 spinner, reduce each 4-digit number to 0 in ten spins or fewer. Write the numbers you subtract and record your new number each time. You can subtract 1000s, 100s, 10s or 1s.

a 3562   b 4271   c 4854   d 5311   e 5924

Example
4257
− 200
4057
− 3000
1057
− 2
1055

2 Explain how you chose which digit to reduce each time.

I hope I spin 1 so I can change the 1000s digit to 0.

1 Using a 1–6 dice, reduce each number to 0 in ten rolls or fewer. Write the numbers you subtract and record your new number each time. You can subtract 1000s, 100s, 10s or 1s.

You will need:
- 1–6 dice

a 5734   b 6483   c 8657   d 9248   e 7835

2 Play this game with a partner.

- You and your partner choose the same 4-digit start number and write it down.
- Take turns to roll the dice.
- Choose the 1000s, 100s, 10s or 1s digit and reduce your number.
- The first to reduce their number to 0 is the winner.

Rounding to the nearest 10 or 100

Round any number to the nearest 10 or 100

Challenge 1

1 Write the two multiples of 10 that each number comes between on either side of the number.

| a | 147 | b | 189 | c | 231 | d | 358 |
| e | 725 | f | 866 | g | 673 | h | 744 |

Example

460 ← 468 → 470

460 ← 468 → (470)

2 Now look at the 1s digit and decide whether the number should be rounded up or down. Circle the correct multiple of 10.

Challenge 2

1 Write the two multiples of 10 that each number comes between on either side of the number.

| a | 875 | b | 749 | c | 1837 | d | 2568 | e | 2371 |

2 Now look at the 1s digit and decide whether the number should be rounded up or down. Circle the correct multiple of 10.

3 Write the two multiples of 100 that each number comes between on either side of the number.

| a | 765 | b | 353 | c | 287 | d | 915 | e | 1528 |

Example

400 ← 468 → 500

400 ← 468 → (500)

4 Look at the 10s digit and decide whether the number should be rounded up or down. Circle the correct multiple of 100.

Challenge 3

1 Write the multiples of 10 and 100 that these numbers come between on either side of the number. Then circle the multiple of 10 and 100 that the number rounds to.

Example

(5470) ↖   ↗ 5480
            5473
5400 ↙   ↘ (5500)

| a | 2716 | b | 3569 | c | 3248 | d | 4635 | e | 7482 | f | 7255 |

2 Explain the rules for rounding numbers.

6

Negative numbers (1)

Count backwards through 0 to include negative numbers

llenge 1

Write the missing numbers.

a   –5, _____ , –3, _____ , _____ , 0, 1, _____ , 3, _____

b   –8, _____ , _____ , –5, _____ , –3, _____ , _____ , 0, _____

c   –10, _____ , _____ , _____ , –6, _____ , _____ , –3, _____ , –1

d   –15, _____ , –13, _____ , _____ , _____ , –9, _____ , _____ , –6

e   –19, _____ , _____ , _____ , –15, _____ , _____ , –12, _____ , _____

f   –25, _____ , –23, _____ , _____ , _____ , –19, _____ , –17

g   –28, _____ , _____ , _____ , –24, _____ , _____ , _____ , –20, _____

llenge 2

1 Counting backwards, write the next number after:

a –7   b –1   c –4   d –10   e –13   f –17   g –21   h –29

2 Start at these numbers and count back 5 numbers.
Record your numbers on a number line.

a –20   b –18   c –21   d –24   e –33   f –39   g –46   h –50

llenge 3

1 Counting backwards, write the next number after:

a –38   b –42   c –47   d –50   e –56   f –59   g –64   h –71

2 Start at these numbers and count back 5 numbers.
Record your numbers on a number line.

a –69   b –75   c –79   d –86   e –93   f –99   g –105

Subtraction chains

Use mental methods for subtraction

Copy the number chain, writing the start number at the beginning. Try to work out all the calculations mentally. Repeat for all five start numbers.

Challenge 1

Start numbers:

a 320   b 350   c 480   d 410   e 440

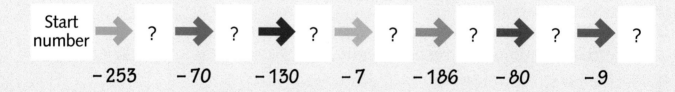

Start number → ? → ? → ? → ? → ? → ? → ?
        −30   −7   −100   −50   −3   −62   −48

Challenge 2

Start numbers:

a 740   b 770   c 810   d 850   e 920

Start number → ? → ? → ? → ? → ? → ? → ?
        −253   −70   −130   −7   −186   −80   −9

Challenge 3

Start numbers:

a 1050   b 1140   c 1200   d 1250   e 1300

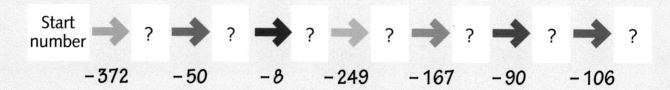

Start number → ? → ? → ? → ? → ? → ? → ?
        −372   −50   −8   −249   −167   −90   −106

Written subtraction (1)

- Subtract numbers with up to 4 digits using the formal written method of columnar subtraction
- Estimate and use inverse operations to check answers to a calculation

a 574 – 251	b 675 – 432	c 682 – 356	d 574 – 248
e 636 – 318	f 754 – 329	g 766 – 548	h 827 – 419

1 Write an estimate for these calculations before you work them out.

a 763 – 381	b 873 – 458	c 839 – 273	d 775 – 448
e 853 – 476	f 865 – 479	g 872 – 695	h 841 – 764

2 Choose four of your calculations and check your answers using the inverse operation.

1 Write an estimate for these calculations before you work them out.

a 953 – 488	b 926 – 549	c 910 – 642	d 1267 – 1159
e 1358 – 1126	f 1326 – 1153	g 1462 – 1274	h 1514 – 1236

2 Choose four of your calculations and check your answers using the inverse operation.

Written subtraction (2)

- Subtract numbers with up to 4 digits using the formal written method of columnar subtraction
- Estimate and use inverse operations to check answers to a calculation

Challenge
1

a   548 – 267   b   635 – 218   c   672 – 359   d   741 – 328

e   692 – 355   f   717 – 432   g   783 – 257   h   725 – 468

Challenge
2

1   Write an estimate for these calculations before you work them out.

a   1273 – 1165   b   1149 – 1064   c   2176 – 1352   d   2268 – 1441

e   2281 – 1536   f   2435 – 1672   g   3283 – 2616   h   2753 – 2578

2   Choose four of your calculations and check your answers using the inverse operation.

3   Using the cards, make eight subtraction calculations and work them out.

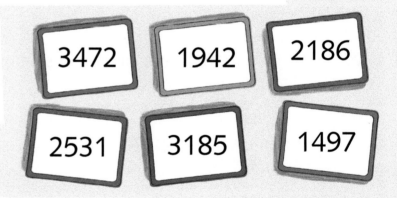

3472   1942   2186

2531   3185   1497

Challenge
3

1   Write an estimate for these calculations before you work them out.

a   3271 – 2448   b   3356 – 2781   c   3417 – 2632   d   3792 – 1876

e   4053 – 2318   f   4147 – 1519   g   4326 – 2715   h   4516 – 2738

2   Choose four of your calculations and check your answers using the inverse operation.

Trip problems

Solve 2-step problems in contexts,
deciding which operations to use and why

Challenge 1

1 On the day of the school trip, 150 Year 7 children turn up
late and 240 turn up on time. How many Year 7s are there altogether?

2 A teacher asks how many Year 7 children have remembered to bring
a drink. Out of 290 children, 130 put up their hand. How many
children have forgotten their drink?

3 A teacher has a museum ticket for 378 children. 264 children have
entered so far. How many more children can enter on the ticket?

Challenge 2

1 A teacher is counting children as they arrive at school. 254 Year 7s, 162 Year 8s
and 307 Year 9s have arrived so far. How many children are in school?

2 The museum is expecting 746 children to go to a lecture. 258 arrive early and
367 arrive on time. How many children are late?

3 364 children bring juice to drink, 275 bring water to drink and 378 bring squash.
How many brought drinks?

Challenge 3

1 Travelling by train there are 47 teachers, 235 Year 7s and 365 Year 8s.
How many people in total travel by train?

2 By 9 o'clock, 487 Year 7 children have arrived, 535 Year 8s and some Year 9s.
1347 children are there in total. How many Year 9 children have arrived?

3 On the way back from the museum, 682 children say they have lost their
coats and 529 children say they have lost their bags. The next day 425 items
have been found. How many children still have missing coats and bags?

4 1263 children are asked if the trip was useful for their learning. 876 say it
was really useful, 255 say it was mostly useful and the rest were not sure.
How many were not sure about the trip?

Acute and obtuse angles

Identify acute and obtuse angles

You will need:
• right-angle tester

1 Use your right-angle tester to find the acute and obtuse angles.

> **Hint**
>
> An acute angle is less than a right angle. An obtuse angle is greater than a right angle.

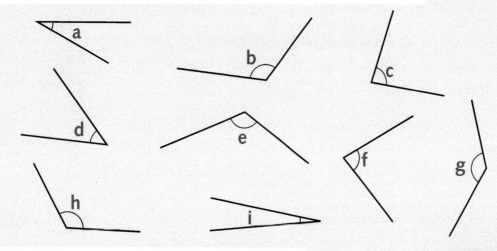

2 Copy and complete the table.

Acute angle	Obtuse angle
a,	

1 List the acute and obtuse angles in the circle.

2 a Using Resource 32: 12-dot circles, investigate drawing a continuous line in a 12-dot circle which makes at least two acute and two obtuse angles.

b Colour the acute angles red and the obtuse angles blue.

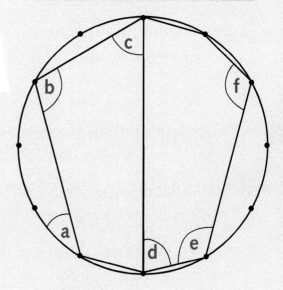

You will need:
• Resource 32: 12-dot circles
• red and blue pencils

Acute and obtuse angles in 2-D shapes

Identify acute and obtuse angles in 2-D shapes

Challenge 1

Name the marked angle in each shape as acute or obtuse.

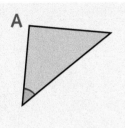 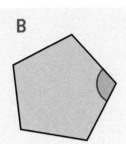 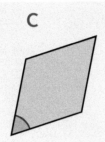 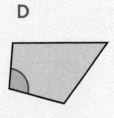 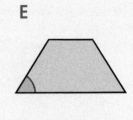

A   B   C   D   E

Challenge 2

Name the marked angle in each shape as acute or obtuse.

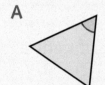 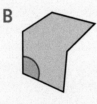 

A   B   C   D

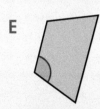 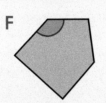 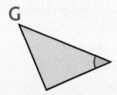 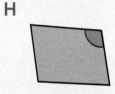

E   F   G   H

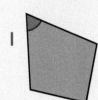 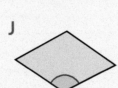 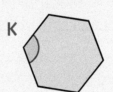 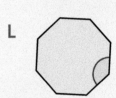

I   J   K   L

Challenge 3

Write the letters of the shapes in Challenge 2 that have:

a   at least two acute angles   b   at least two obtuse angles

c   two pairs of acute angles and two pairs of obtuse angles

13

Ordering angles by size

Compare and order angles up to two right angles by size

Use your right-angle tester. Write which fans show:

You will need:
• right-angle tester

a an acute angle   **b** an obtuse angle

   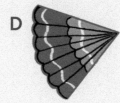

1 Using the right-angle tester, write all the angles that are acute in the angles below.

2 Using the right-angle tester, write all the angles that are obtuse in the angles below.

3 Using both testers, order the angles that are acute.

4 Using both testers, order the angles that are obtuse.

You will need:
• right-angle tester
• half right-angle tester

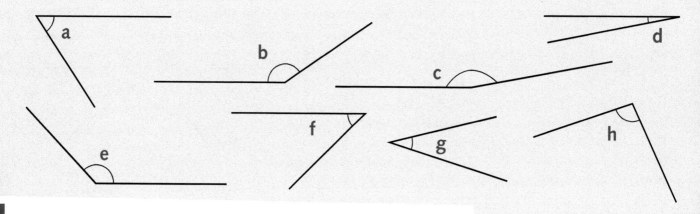

Write the letter of the angle in Challenge 2 which is:

a about half a right angle   **b** about half a right angle plus a right angle

c the smallest obtuse angle   **d** the greatest acute angle

Regular polygons

Decide if a polygon is regular or irregular by comparing lengths and angles

A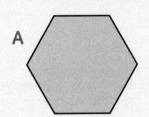

B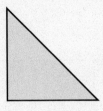

C

D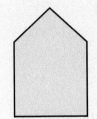

E

F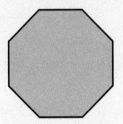

G

H

I

Challenges 1,2

1 Use your ruler to measure the sides of each 2-D shape. Write the letters of the shapes which have:

You will need:
• ruler

   a all sides equal   b all angles equal

2 Copy and complete the table for shapes A to I.

Regular	Irregular
A,	

Challenge 3

Look for lines of symmetry in shapes A to I and complete the table.

Property	Regular	Irregular
One line of symmetry	A,	
More than one line of symmetry		

15

Multiples of 25, 100 and 1000

Count in multiples of 25, 100 and 1000

Challenge 1

Write the missing numbers.

a	1000	2000								10 000
b	6100			6400					6900	
c	25		75		125					

Challenge 2

Find the multiples of 1000, 100 and 25.

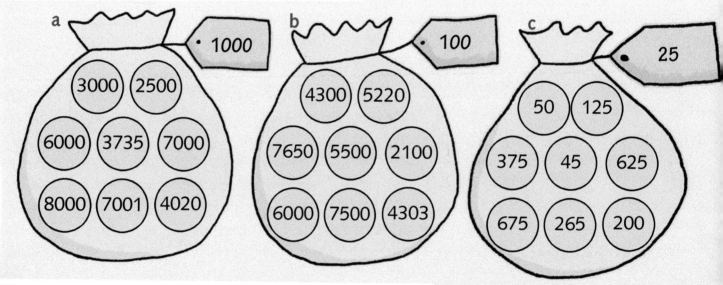

Challenge 3

1 Write a multiple of 25 that matches each clue.

a 10 times larger than 25

b the same as 6 groups of 25

c 75 less than 225

d 25 less than 1000

e 25 more than 750

f 10 times smaller than 500

g 75 more than 325

h the same as 50 add 25 add 75

2 Make up your own multiple of 25 clue to share with a partner.

Multiplication using the formal written method

Use the formal written method to calculate TO × O

Challenge 1

Find the missing number in each calculation.

a $3 \times 9 = \bigcirc$ b $\square \times 6 = 36$ c $8 \times 8 = \blacktriangle$ d $9 \times \bigcirc = 63$

e $4 \times \blacksquare = 28$ f $7 \times \triangle = 35$ g $6 \times \bullet = 48$ h $\square \times 8 = 88$

Challenge 2

Choose a number from box A and a number from box B. Multiply them together and write the answer. Make eight calculations. Choose different numbers each time.

Challenge 3

1   Estimate the answer to each calculation.

a	b	c	d	e	f	g	h
75 × 4	63 × 8	46 × 7	84 × 4	87 × 9	59 × 5	49 × 6	76 × 8

2   Work out the answer to each of the calculations above using the formal written method of multiplication. Check your answer is close to your estimated answer.

Example

$68 \times 6 \rightarrow 70 \times 6 = 420$

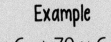

H	T	O
	6	8
×	4	6
4	0	8

Multiplication using the most efficient method

Use the most efficient method to calculate TO × O

Write the answers to these multiplication facts.

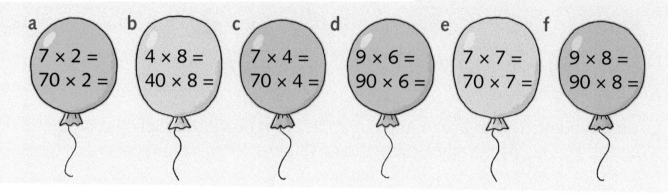

a
7 × 2 =
70 × 2 =

b
4 × 8 =
40 × 8 =

c
7 × 4 =
70 × 4 =

d
9 × 6 =
90 × 6 =

e
7 × 7 =
70 × 7 =

f
9 × 8 =
90 × 8 =

Challenge 2

Sort these calculations into two groups: those you would work out mentally and those where you would use a written method. Then work out the answer to each calculation using the most efficient method.

33 × 3   42 × 3   55 × 4   62 × 3   76 × 8   89 × 7

67 × 8   34 × 2   53 × 3   75 × 2   79 × 9   86 × 7

Challenge 3

Play this game with a partner. Each player chooses a number from the number cards. Take turns to:
- roll the 1–9 dice
- multiply the number on the dice by your chosen number
- choose the most appropriate method to calculate the answer, mental or written.

If you choose a written method, write the estimated answer first and then show your working out. Compare your answers each time. The player with the largest answer scores one point. The first player to score 5 points is the winner.

You will need:
• 1–9 dice

56   87

24   68   49   75

93   27   38   66

Solving word problems (1)

Solve problems and reason mathematically

 Answer each calculation then write the inverse multiplication or division fact.

a $24 \div 3 =$ ⬚ b $6 \times 7 =$ ⬚ c $8 \times 6 =$ ⬚ d $54 \div 9 =$ ⬚

e $7 \times 9 =$ ⬚ f $7 \times 4 =$ ⬚ g $32 \div 4 =$ ⬚ h $56 \div 7 =$ ⬚

Using the information in the pictures, write a calculation to find the total number of items in each order.

 89 74  86  63 37  95

Order a   3 boxes of calculators

Order b   2 boxes of rulers and 1 box of paintbrushes

Order c   2 boxes of coloured pencils

Order d   1 box of rulers and 1 box of calculators

Order e   2 boxes of paintbrushes

Order f   1 box of coloured pencils and 1 box of crayons

 Use the information in the pictures above to answer the questions below.

a Glue sticks are sold in packs of 3. How many packs of glue sticks in one box?

b The school buys 8 boxes of paintbrushes. Each box costs €10. What is the total cost?

c What is the difference in the number of coloured pencils and the number of crayons in a box?

d The school needs 50 calculators but only has 1 box. How many more calculators do they need?

e Boxes of crayons come in 5 colours. How many of each colour?

f The Year 4 children need 100 glue sticks but only have 1 box. How many extra sticks do they need?

Fractions and number lines

Use the number line to connect fractions and numbers

Challenge 1

Write the fractions that are missing from the number lines.

a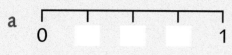

b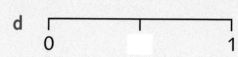

c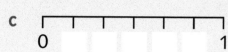

d

Challenge 2

Write the fractions that are missing from the number lines.

a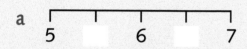

b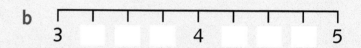

c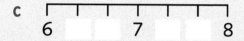

d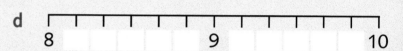

e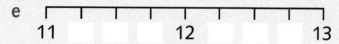

f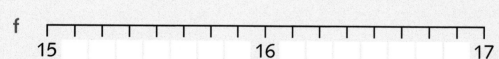

Challenge 3

1 Write the fractions that are missing from the number lines. Use two different denominators in your fractions.

a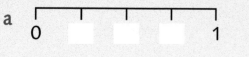

b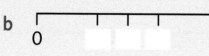

c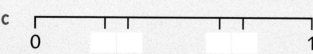

2 Draw a number line 12 cm long. Mark the half and the quarter intervals on your number line.

Hundredths and tenths

- Count up and down in hundredths
- Recognise that hundredths arise when dividing by 100 and dividing tenths by 10

Write the missing hundredths.

a $\frac{13}{100}$, $\frac{14}{100}$, ____, $\frac{16}{100}$, ____, ____, $\frac{19}{100}$, ____, $\frac{21}{100}$, ____

b $\frac{27}{100}$, ____, $\frac{29}{100}$, ____, ____, $\frac{32}{100}$, ____, ____, $\frac{35}{100}$, ____

c $\frac{62}{100}$, ____, ____, ____, $\frac{66}{100}$, ____, ____, ____, $\frac{70}{100}$, ____

d ____, $\frac{50}{100}$, ____, ____, ____, $\frac{54}{100}$, ____, ____, ____, $\frac{58}{100}$

1 Count on in hundredths 10 times from these fractions.

a $\frac{25}{100}$ b $\frac{38}{100}$ c $\frac{50}{100}$ d $\frac{67}{100}$ e $\frac{80}{100}$ f $\frac{86}{100}$ g $\frac{90}{100}$

2 Count back in hundredths 10 times from these fractions.

a $\frac{60}{100}$ b $\frac{81}{100}$ c $\frac{32}{100}$ d $\frac{99}{100}$ e $\frac{55}{100}$ f $\frac{73}{100}$ g $\frac{62}{100}$

3 For each 100 grid, write the fraction that is shaded blue.

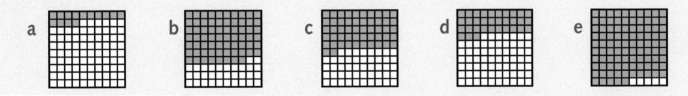

a   b   c   d   e

Write a tenth and a hundredth describing what fraction of each 100 grid is shaded blue.

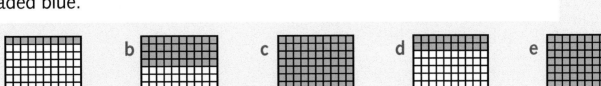

a   b   c   d   e

Finding tenths and hundredths

Use multiplication and division to find non-unit tenths and hundredths

Challenge 1

1 Work out these tenths.

a $\frac{1}{10}$ of 30 b $\frac{1}{10}$ of 50 c $\frac{1}{10}$ of 60 d $\frac{1}{10}$ of 90

e $\frac{1}{10}$ of 70 f $\frac{1}{10}$ of 80 g $\frac{1}{10}$ of 100 h $\frac{1}{10}$ of 120

2 Work out these hundredths.

a $\frac{1}{100}$ of 500 b $\frac{1}{100}$ of 700 c $\frac{1}{100}$ of 400 d $\frac{1}{100}$ of 800

Challenge 2

1 Work out these tenths.

a $\frac{5}{10}$ of 30 b $\frac{7}{10}$ of 90 c $\frac{4}{10}$ of 50 d $\frac{9}{10}$ of 70

e $\frac{3}{10}$ of 140 f $\frac{6}{10}$ of 150 g $\frac{2}{10}$ of 180 h $\frac{3}{10}$ of 240

2 Work out these hundredths.

a $\frac{3}{100}$ of 400 b $\frac{6}{100}$ of 500 c $\frac{35}{100}$ of 300 d $\frac{41}{100}$ of 700

Challenge 3

1 Work out these tenths.

a $\frac{7}{10}$ of 610 b $\frac{3}{10}$ of 770 c $\frac{8}{10}$ of 560 d $\frac{5}{10}$ of 700

e $\frac{3}{10}$ of 940 f $\frac{2}{10}$ of 1320 g $\frac{4}{10}$ of 1250 h $\frac{6}{10}$ of 1430

2 Work out these hundredths.

a $\frac{6}{100}$ of 2500 b $\frac{8}{100}$ of 3400 c $\frac{7}{100}$ of 4000 d $\frac{5}{100}$ of 6700

Fraction problems

Solve fraction problems to calculate quantities including non-unit fractions

1

1 Harvey orders a small milkshake. It holds 300 ml. He drinks a $\frac{1}{3}$ of it but then his brother drinks the rest. How much did Harvey drink?

2 For lunch, the cook is making 200 pizzas. Unfortunately, she burns $\frac{1}{5}$ of them. How many will she be able to serve up?

3 Harvey needs to spend 40 minutes doing his homework. He has spent $\frac{1}{8}$ of the time working out what he needs to do. How much time does he have left?

2

1 Mr Smith is 160 cm tall. His brother is $\frac{7}{8}$ as tall as him. How tall is his brother?

2 Skateboards cost €81 in one shop. In another shop they are only $\frac{7}{9}$ of the price. How much do they cost there?

3 Harvey collects 256 conkers. He loses $\frac{3}{8}$ of them on his way home. How many does he have left?

4 A café sells milkshakes in two sizes, small and large. The small milkshake is 360 ml. The large milkshake is $\frac{2}{3}$ more. What is the size of the large milkshake?

3

1 In the café, Harvey and his friend buy a small and a large milkshake. Harvey has drunk $\frac{3}{4}$ of his 360 ml shake and his friend has drunk $\frac{2}{3}$ of his 480 ml shake. Who has drunk the most?

2 Mr Smith is growing an enormous pumpkin. He weighs it every week. Last week it weighed 112 kg. This week it is $\frac{4}{7}$ heavier. What does it weigh this week?

3 When the local football team last played at home, the stadium was full. It can hold 4000 fans. $\frac{7}{10}$ of the spectators were the home fans and the rest were away fans. How many fans came to support the home team?

Kilometres and metres

Convert between kilometres and metres and record lengths using decimals

Challenge 1

Copy and complete the table. The first one has been done for you.

1·0 km	0·5 km	0·1 km	⬚ km	0·3 km	⬚ km	0·9 km
1000 m	⬚ m	⬚ m	800 m	⬚ m	⬚ m	⬚ m
1 km	$\frac{1}{2}$ km	$\frac{1}{10}$ km	$\frac{8}{10}$ km	⬚ km	$\frac{4}{10}$ km	⬚ km

Challenge 2

1 Write these distances in metres.

> **Example**
> 2·7 km = 2000 m + 700 m
> = 2700 m

   a 3·6 km   **b** 5·5 km   **c** 8·9 km   **d** 10·2 km   **e** 12·8 km   **f** 15·4 km

2 Write these distances in kilometres.

> **Example**
> 6400 m = 6 km 400 m
> = 6·4 km

   a 4800 m   **b** 7200 m   **c** 5600 m   **d** 9100 m   **e** 8300 m   **f** 11 200 m

3 Write these distances in order, starting with the shortest.

   1690 m   1·7 km   1 km 960 m   1·9 km   1906 m   1·6 km

4 The table shows how far each hiker walked in 1 hour.

   a Who walked the furthest distance in 1 hour?

   b How many metres was Joe ahead of Len?

   c How many metres was Mike behind Harry?

Hiker	Distance
Harry	5·8 km
Joe	5 km 750 m
Len	$5\frac{1}{2}$ km
Mike	5400 m

Challenge 3

The length of each rectangular caravan park is double its width.
Find the length and perimeter of each caravan park if they have widths of:

   a 70 m   **b** 0·2 km   **c** 160 m   **d** $\frac{1}{4}$ km

DIY measurements

Convert from larger to smaller units and record lengths using decimals

1 Copy and complete.

> **Example**
>
> 9 cm = 90 mm

a ⬤ m = 500 cm   b 5 cm = ⬤ mm   c ⬤ m = 5000 mm

d 8 m = ⬤ cm   e 8 cm = ⬤ mm   f 8 m = ⬤ mm

g 0·5 m = ⬤ cm   h 0·5 cm = ⬤ mm   i ⬤ m = 500 mm

2

1 Write these lengths as metres using decimals.

a   40 cm   b   60 cm   c   90 cm   d   250 cm

e   380 cm   f   500 mm   g   800 mm   h   900 mm

2 Draw a triangle relationship for these lengths.

> **Example**
>
>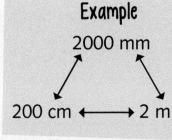
> 2000 mm
>
> 200 cm ⟷ 2 m

a   300 mm b   60 cm   c   0·5 m

d   700 mm e   80 cm   f   2·4 m

3 Write these lengths of wood in centimetres.

> **Example**
>
> 7·3 m = 730 cm

a   4·2 m   b   8·1 m   c   5·7 m   d   3·9 m

4 Write these widths of tiles in millimetres.

> **Example**
>
> 1·1 m = 1100 mm

a   0·6 m   b   1·3 m   c   2·8 m   d   3·5 m

3
A window has 6 panes of glass each measuring 600 mm by 300 mm.
What is the height and width of the window in metres?

Fixing the fence in metres

Estimate and compare length and round numbers using measuring tapes

Write the length shown by each nail:

a   in millimetres

b   to the nearest centimetre

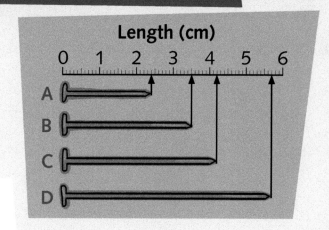

Length (cm)

1   Round the length shown by each arrow:

a   to the nearest centimetre   b   to the nearest 10 centimetres

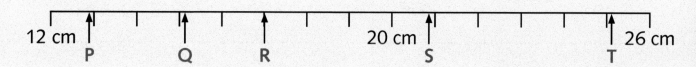

12 cm   P   Q   R   20 cm   S   T   26 cm

2   Estimate then work out in metres the distance between:

a   posts A and C   b   posts B and D   c   posts A and D

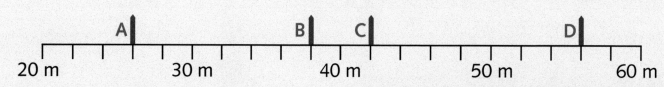

20 m   30 m   40 m   50 m   60 m

3   The table shows the length of one roll of Farmer Fraser's wire mesh. Copy and complete the table for his rolls of wire mesh with these lengths:

Length of roll of wire mesh	Rounded to nearest:	
	10 cm	metre
A 472 cm	470 cm	5 m
B		

B   274 cm   C   742 cm   D   427 cm   E   724 cm   F   247 cm

Farmer Fraser needs exactly 12 m of wire mesh to complete his fence. He wants to finish the job without wasting too much of his stock of wire mesh. Which three rolls from his stock of wire mesh should he use? Give a reason for your answer.

On the map measures

Calculate different measures of length using decimals to one place

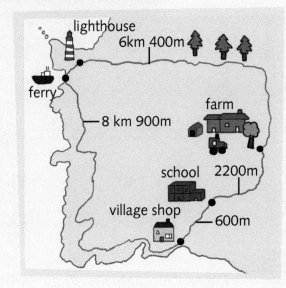

Challenge 1

Look at the map then write the shortest distance between these places using decimals.

a village shop to ferry

b ferry to school

c school to farm

d farm to lighthouse

e lighthouse to village shop

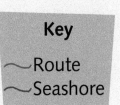

Key

~ Route
~ Seashore

Challenge 2

1 The lighthouse is 60·9 metres tall. The height of the school building is 20 m 30 cm.

a What is the difference in height between the two buildings?

b How many times taller is the lighthouse than the school building?

2 Fiona lives on the farm. How far, in kilometres, does she cycle to and from school:

a in one day?   b in one school week?

3 What is the total distance from the ferry, past the village shop and school to the farm?

Challenge 3

Copy the number line below and mark the distance each cyclist is from the lighthouse.

Sam	400 m behind Pat
Nico	$\frac{1}{2}$ km ahead of Sam
Jo	$\frac{3}{10}$ km behind Nico
Pat	0·3 km from the lighthouse

Pat

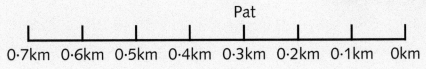

0·7km 0·6km 0·5km 0·4km 0·3km 0·2km 0·1km 0km

27

Adding mentally

Use mental methods for addition

1 a 534 + 50   b 568 + 9   c 527 + 400   d 672 + 40

   e 695 + 7   f 742 + 80   g 382 + 600   h 861 + 90

2 In these calculations, first add the 100s and then the 10s.

   a 528 + 130   b 562 + 150   c 591 + 210   d 645 + 260

   e 673 + 220   f 621 + 290   g 704 + 340   h 815 + 360

1 These calculations all cross the 1000 boundary.

   a 972 + 80   b 953 + 90   c 997 + 8   d 626 + 500

   e 966 + 50   f 512 + 700   g 948 + 70   h 999 + 40

2 In these calculations, first add the 100s and then the 10s.

   a 975 + 130   b 843 + 250   c 961 + 270   d 982 + 320

   e 1005 + 340   f 1073 + 490   g 1178 + 420   h 1259 + 480

1 Choose your strategy to work out these calculations.

   a 1276 + 370   b 1298 + 340   c 1382 + 360   d 1404 + 420

   e 1439 + 450   f 1591 + 370   g 2235 + 410   h 2638 + 530

2 In these calculations, first add the 100s, then the 10s and then the 1s.

   a 1150 + 365   b 1270 + 424   c 1320 + 487   d 1390 + 538

   e 1450 + 527   f 1610 + 634   g 1860 + 682   h 2180 + 728

Subtracting mentally

Use mental methods for subtraction

1 a 567 – 40   **b** 581 – 7   **c** 624 – 60   **d** 649 – 500

   e 662 – 70   **f** 735 – 8   **g** 853 – 400   **h** 722 – 50

2 In these calculations, first subtract the 100s and then the 10s.

   a 643 – 120   **b** 657 – 180   **c** 682 – 230   **d** 716 – 140

   e 745 – 220   **f** 757 – 270   **g** 872 – 250   **h** 838 – 340

1 a 1286 – 50   **b** 1239 – 60   **c** 1373 – 8   **d** 1351 – 200

   e 1426 – 60   **f** 1479 – 300   **g** 1532 – 80   **h** 1683 – 600

2 In these calculations, first subtract the 100s and then the 10s.

   a 1352 – 140   **b** 1225 – 170   **c** 1443 – 190   **d** 1462 – 240

   e 1526 – 310   **f** 1588 – 340   **g** 1537 – 420   **h** 1683 – 490

1 Choose your strategy to work out these calculations.

   a 1684 – 560   **b** 1762 – 420   **c** 1873 – 360   **d** 1627 – 470

   e 1712 – 390   **f** 1805 – 430   **g** 2067 – 240   **h** 2251 – 270

2 In these calculations, first subtract the 100s, then the 10s and then the 1s.

   a 1480 – 261   **b** 1590 – 342   **c** 1630 – 475   **d** 1680 – 543

   e 1470 – 582   **f** 1860 – 634   **g** 2080 – 312   **h** 2150 – 238

Writing 2-step problems

Write 2-step problems in contexts, deciding which operations and methods to use and why

Challenge 1

1 Write a 1-step word problem for each of these calculations and work it out.

    a 237 + 80   **b** 548 + 240   **c** 752 − 70   **d** 871 − 400

2 Ask your partner to work out the answers to two of your problems. Check if they got them right.

Challenge 2

1 Write a 2-step word problem for each of these calculations and work it out.

    a 428 + 260 + 345   **b** 862 − 300 − 360   **c** 1220 − 530 + 375

2 Ask your partner to work out the answers to two of your problems. Check if they got them right.

3 Now make up four calculations of your own and write a two-step word problem for each. Remember to use numbers that can be calculated mentally.

    a ☐ + ☐ + ☐ =   **b** ☐ − ☐ − ☐ =

    c ☐ + ☐ − ☐ =   **d** ☐ + ☐ + ☐ =

Challenge 3

1 Make up four calculations of your own and write a two-step word problem for each. Remember to use numbers that can be calculated mentally.

    a ☐ × ☐ + ☐ =   **b** ☐ ÷ ☐ − ☐ =

    c ☐ × ☐ − ☐ =   **d** ☐ + ☐ ÷ ☐ =

2 Ask your partner to work out the answers to your problems. Check if they got them right.

Written addition (3)

- Add numbers with up to 4 digits using the formal written method of columnar addition
- Estimate and use inverse operations to check answers to a calculation

Challenge 1

Estimate the answer to these calculations and then work them out.

a 573 + 154	b 438 + 357	c 641 + 329	d 684 + 253
e 564 + 461	f 748 + 235	g 752 + 624	h 834 + 741
i 576 + 722	j 825 + 642	k 538 + 465	l 472 + 485

Challenge 2

1 Estimate the answer to these calculations and then work out them out.

a 1273 + 1349	b 1625 + 1535	c 2718 + 1627	d 2285 + 2476
e 3629 + 2446	f 3277 + 2188	g 4831 + 2543	h 4065 + 1367
i 3802 + 2458	j 4444 + 2739	k 5382 + 4598	l 6052 + 2983

2 Choose four of the calculations and check your answers using the inverse operation.

Challenge 3

1 Estimate the answer to these calculations and then work them out.

a 2571 + 1619	b 2287 + 2943	c 3695 + 1536	d 3483 + 2748
e 4726 + 3787	f 4473 + 4689	g 5784 + 3857	h 4962 + 4659
i 7699 + 1877	j 6837 + 2855	k 7367 + 2908	l 5826 + 6391

2 Choose four of the calculations and check your answers using the inverse operation.

Written addition (4)

- Add numbers with up to 4 digits using the formal written method of columnar addition
- Estimate and use inverse operations to check answers to a calculation

 Challenge 1

1 Estimate the answers to these calculations, then work them out.

    a 562 + 243   **b** 627 + 281   **c** 593 + 342   **d** 426 + 447

2 These calculations add up to more than 1000.

    a 649 + 624   **b** 753 + 552   **c** 617 + 748   **d** 863 + 692

 Challenge 2

1 Estimate the answers to these calculations, then work them out.

    a 2641 + 2419   **b** 3627 + 1782   **c** 2836 + 2085   **d** 3525 + 2647

    e 2371 + 3159   **f** 3628 + 2753   **g** 4183 + 2907   **h** 5351 + 3829

2 Now estimate the answers to these calculations, then work them out.

    a 4763 + 2578   **b** 3384 + 4839   **c** 3962 + 2159   **d** 4295 + 3827

 Challenge 3

1 Estimate the answers to these calculations, then work them out.

    a 6276 + 2845   **b** 5395 + 3716   **c** 4876 + 2978   **d** 5075 + 3935

2 Check your calculations using the inverse operation.

3 Can you think of a more efficient way than the written method for working out the answer to this calculation: 2999 + 2999?

Written subtraction (3)

- Subtract numbers with up to 4 digits using the formal written method of columnar subtraction
- Estimate and use inverse operations to check answers to a calculation

Challenge 1

a 628 – 354	b 781 – 426	c 677 – 283	d 706 – 324
e 643 – 281	f 866 – 292	g 870 – 354	h 892 – 565
i 967 – 683	j 992 – 755	k 849 – 372	l 851 – 537

Challenge 2

1 Write an estimate for these calculations before you work them out.

a 3673 – 1835	b 3827 – 2448	c 4346 – 1571	d 4386 – 2197
e 5184 – 2358	f 6396 – 4759	g 7826 – 4188	h 7069 – 2371
i 7176 – 5338	j 7275 – 4444	k 8627 – 4708	l 8642 – 3266

2 Choose four of your calculations and check your answers using the inverse operation.

Challenge 3

1 Write an estimate for these calculations before you work them out.

a 7738 – 3819	b 7628 – 5189	c 7364 – 6715	d 8672 – 3781
e 8267 – 4598	f 8461 – 2783	g 9363 – 2495	h 9532 – 4955

2 Choose four of your calculations and check your answers using the inverse operation.

3 Can you think of a more efficient way than the written method for working out the answer to this calculation: 3999 – 1001?

Written subtraction (4)

- Subtract numbers with up to 4 digits using the formal written method of columnar subtraction
- Estimate and use inverse operations to check answers to a calculation

Challenge 1

a	2372 – 1541	b	2635 – 1853	c	3462 – 1358	d	4276 – 2628
e	4037 – 1564	f	4183 – 2605	g	4286 – 1493	h	4436 – 2177
i	5862 – 2924	j	5387 – 2839	k	5063 – 2235	l	5275 – 3428

Challenge 2

1 Write an estimate for these calculations before you work them out.

a	5287 – 2498	b	5295 – 2497	c	5826 – 1958	d	6328 – 3269
e	6284 – 2596	f	6752 – 4873	g	7431 – 3658	h	7532 – 2765
i	7444 – 3777	j	7115 – 4227	k	8396 – 4598	l	8175 – 6486

2 Choose four of your calculations and check your answers using the inverse operation.

Challenge 3

1 Write an estimate for these calculations before you work them out.

a	7749 – 3830	b	7639 – 5200	c	7375 – 6726	d	8683 – 3792
e	8278 – 4609	f	8472 – 2794	g	9374 – 2506	h	9543 – 4966
i	9736 – 1857	j	9236 – 5877	k	8664 – 4788	l	8267 – 3690

2 Choose four of your calculations and check your answers using the inverse operation.

3 Can you think of a more efficient way than the written method for working out the answer to this calculation: 5000 – 1999?

4 What other 3- or 4-digit calculations might be done more efficiently a different way?

34

Football problems

Solve 2-step problems in contexts, deciding
which operations and methods to use and why

1 At the football match, 463 fans are buying a cup of tea and 254 fans are
buying coffee. How many people are buying a hot drink?

2 637 fans have arrived so far. 451 of these are supporting the home
team. How many are supporting the away team?

3 382 fans are in one part of the football ground and then
another 140 arrive. How many fans are there now?

4 €275 is spent on hot dogs and €443 is spent on burgers.
How much money was spent altogether?

1 1748 fans are sitting in one part of the football ground, 1325 in another part
and 1583 in another. How many altogether?

2 The snack stall takes €3450. €890 was spent on drinks, €1650 was spent on
cooked food and the rest was spent on cold food. How much was spent on
cold food?

3 Out of 4820 fans, 1884 are men, 1798 are women and the rest are children.
How many children were at the match?

4 3896 fans have arrived so far, then 2010 more arrive and then a further
2600. How many altogether?

1 The fans like to wear hats and scarves to support their team.
Out of 5400 fans, 2150 are wearing hats only, 1890 are wearing
scarves only and the rest are wearing both. How many fans are
wearing a hat and a scarf?

2 The Snack Stall starts the day with 5870 hot dogs to sell. After
an hour, it has 3276 left and after 2 hours, it has 1085 left. How
many hot dogs were sold?

3 3874 fans are sitting down, 4759 are standing and 1673 are away
from their seats getting food. How many fans altogether?

Sports bar charts

Interpret and present discrete data using scaled bar charts

You will need:
- squared paper
- ruler

Challenge 1

1 Year 4 voted for their favourite after school clubs. The tally chart shows the results.

Copy and complete the frequency table using the data in the tally chart.

Club	Number of votes
Art	IIII II
Chess	IIII
Drama	IIII I
Football	IIII IIII
ICT	IIII IIII II

Club	Frequency
Art	
Chess	
Drama	
Football	
ICT	

2 Copy and complete the bar chart using the data in the table.

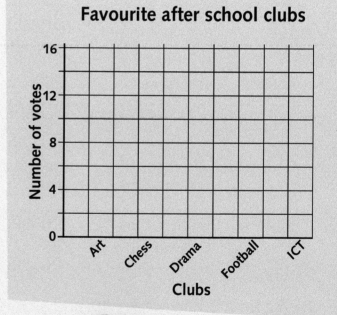

Favourite after school clubs

3 Which club is:

a the most popular?

b the least popular?

4 How many more children voted for ICT than:

a Art?   b Drama?

5 How many votes were there altogether?

The local sports centre made this pictogram to show the number of people taking part in these activities on one evening.

You will need:
• squared paper
• ruler

Numbers of people taking part in sports activities

Bowls 5-a-side Judo Badminton Swimming

Key 10 people

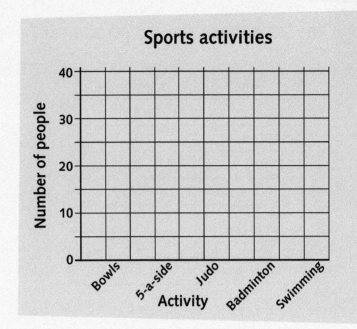

Sports activities

1 Copy and complete the bar chart using the data in the pictogram.

2 Which activity is:

  a the most popular?   b the least popular?

3 How many more people played bowls than:

  a 5-a-side?   b Badminton?

4 How many fewer people took the Judo class than went to the swimming pool?

Jessica is training for a race.

  a Describe her training schedule for weeks one to six.

  b Can you think of a reason why there was a fall in the number of kilometres she ran in week seven?

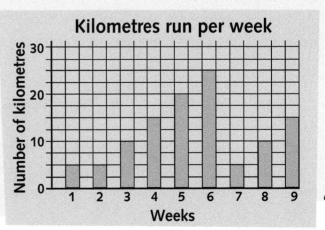

Kilometres run per week

School time graphs

Interpret and present continuous data in simple time graphs

Challenge 1

The table shows the temperature in Tim's classroom on one day.

You will need:
- squared paper
- ruler

Time	Temperature (°C)
9:00 a.m.	16
10:00 a.m.	18
11:00 a.m.	20
12:00 noon	20
1:00 p.m.	22
2:00 p.m.	21
3:00 p.m.	19

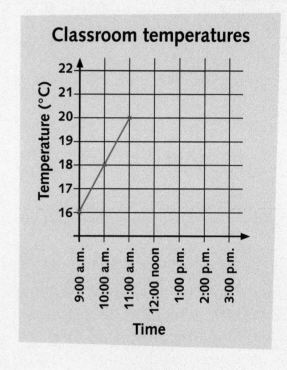

1 Copy and complete the time graph.

   a Mark each point on the graph using a cross.

   b Join the crosses using straight lines to make your time graph.

2 At what time was the room temperature:

   a at its warmest?

   b at its coolest?

3 Write two times when the temperature was the same.

4 After what time did the temperature in the room begin to fall?

1 The table shows the temperature outside on one day.
Use the information in the table to complete the time graph.

Time	Temperature
9:00 a.m.	6°C
10:00 a.m.	8°C
11:00 a.m.	10°C
12:00 noon	13°C
1:00 p.m.	15°C
2:00 p.m.	14°C
3:00 p.m.	11°C

2 Write the time when it was:

   a coldest outside   b warmest outside

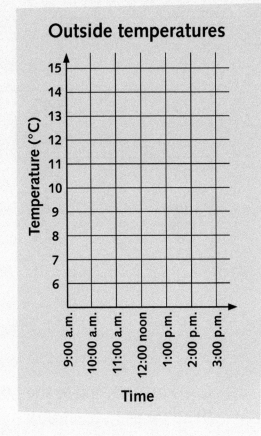

Outside temperatures

3 Between which two hours did the temperature:

   a rise the most?   b fall the most?

4 Between which times was the temperature
10°C or warmer?

1 The table shows the temperature in the school's kitchen.

Time	10:30 a.m.	11:00 a.m.	11:30 a.m.	12:00 noon	12:30 p.m.	1:00 p.m.
Temp. in °C	16	18	23	25	20	17

   a Describe how the temperature in the kitchen changed between 10:30 a.m. and 1:00 p.m.

   b What was the approximate temperature in the kitchen at 11:45 a.m.?

Football pictograms and bar charts

Solve problems using data presented in scaled pictograms, bar charts and tables

Challenge 1

The pictogram shows the distance the players in the school's football team could kick the ball during football practice.

Distances kicked by school's football team

Distances kicked in practice	Number of players
20 m	⚽ ⚽ ◖
25 m	⚽ ⚽ ⚽ ⚽ ⚽
30 m	⚽ ⚽ ⚽ ⚽ ⚽ ⚽ ⚽ ◖
35 m	⚽ ⚽ ⚽ ⚽ ⚽ ⚽
40 m	⚽ ⚽ ⚽ ⚽

Number of players

Key ⚽ 2 players ◖ 1 player

1 Copy and complete the table below using the data in the pictogram.

2 What was the maximum distance most players could kick the football?

3 a How many players could not kick the football as far as 30 m?

 b How many players could kick the football further than 30 m?

4 How many players attended the school's football practice?

Distance	Number of players
20 m	
25 m	
30 m	
35 m	
40 m	

40

The bar chart shows the number of goals scored by the school's top five players during the season.

1 Using the data in the bar chart, copy and complete the table.

2 a Who was the top scorer for the football season?

b How many more goals did Ashrif score than Angela?

c How many goals did Jackie and Jordan score between them?

d How many fewer goals did Simon score than Jordan?

e Jordan scored 14 penalty goals. How many of his goals were not penalty goals?

f What was the total number of goals scored by all 5 players?

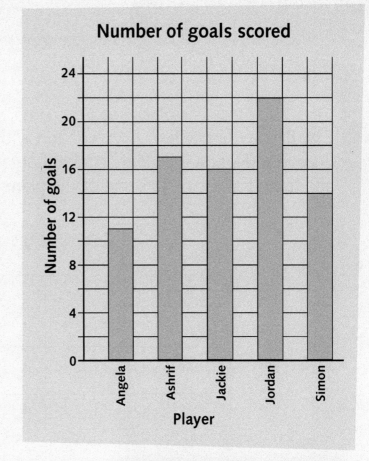

Number of goals scored

Player	Number of goals
Angela	
Ashrif	
Jackie	
Jordan	
Simon	

Challenge 3

Work with a partner.

- Take 20 turns each to spin the spinner and make a tally mark for each goal scored.

- Count the tally marks and complete the frequency column in the table.

- Draw a bar chart using the data from the frequency table.

- Write three questions about the bar chart for your partner to answer.

You will need:
- Resource 46: Football spinner
- paper clip and pencil – for the spinner
- squared paper

41

Holiday in Orlando

Solve problems using data presented in simple time graphs

Challenge
1
The Barclay family flew from London and landed at Tampa Airport in Florida. The flight took 8 hours. The graph shows the temperature in the cabin of the plane during their flight.

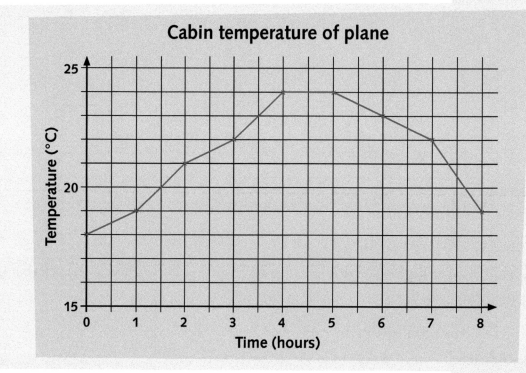

1 What was the temperature in the cabin of the plane when:

   a it took off from London?   b it landed at Tampa?

2 What was the temperature in the cabin:

   a at 2 hours into the flight?   b at 7 hours into the flight?

3 Between which 2 hours was the temperature in the cabin at its warmest?

4 By how many degrees Celsius did the temperature in the cabin drop between the 7th and the 8th hour of the flight?

5 What was the approximate temperature in the cabin at $3\frac{1}{2}$ hours into the flight?

At Tampa Airport, Mrs Barclay collected their hire car. The petrol gauge showed it had a full tank at 60 litres. The graph shows how much petrol was used on the 2-hour journey by car from Tampa to Orlando.

1 Copy and complete the table.

2 How many litres did the petrol gauge show:

a at the end of 1 hour?

b at the end of 2 hours?

Time (minutes)	Petrol (litres)
0	60
20	
40	
60	
80	
100	
120	

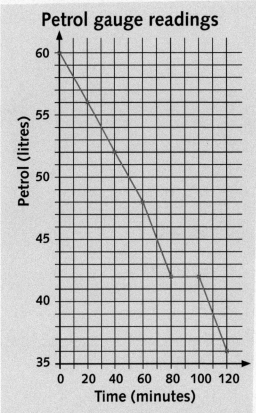

Petrol gauge readings

3 How many litres of petrol were used for the journey?

4 How many minutes into the journey did the Barclays make a short stop for refreshments?

1 The graph shows the temperature in Orlando for each day of their holiday. Between which two days did the temperature:

a rise by 2°C?   b fall by 2°C?

2 Describe how the temperature changed between Thursday and Saturday.

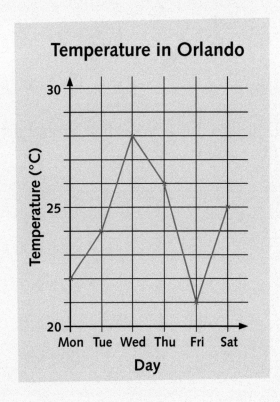

Temperature in Orlando

Multiplication HTO × O using partitioning

Use partitioning to calculate HTO × O

Challenge 1

1 a 7 × 2 =

   b 70 × 2 =

   c 700 × 2 =

2 a 4 × 8 =

   b 40 × 8 =

   c 400 × 8 =

3 a 7 × 4 =

   b 70 × 4 =

   c 700 × 4 =

4 a 9 × 6 =

   b 90 × 6 =

   c 900 × 6 =

5 a 7 × 7 =

   b 70 × 7 =

   c 700 × 7 =

6 a 9 × 8 =

   b 90 × 8 =

   c 900 × 8 =

Challenge 2

Write the answer to each of these calculations. Work the answer out mentally, using partitioning.

a 333 × 3
b 243 × 2
c 322 × 4
d 344 × 2
e 414 × 2
f 622 × 3

Challenge 3

Estimate the answer first, then partition each of these calculations to work out the answer.

a 467 × 4   b 468 × 6

c 738 × 4   d 383 × 3

e 267 × 9   f 691 × 7

g 684 × 5   h 794 × 8

i 815 × 9   j 609 × 8

Example

463 × 5 ⟶ 500 × 5 = 2500
= (400 × 5) + (60 × 5) + (3 × 5)
= 2000 + 300   +   15
= 2315

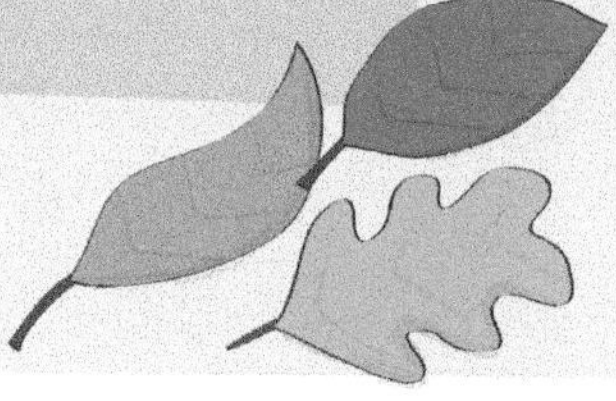

Multiplication HTO × O using partitioning and the grid method

Use the grid method to calculate HTO × O

Challenge 1

Write the multiples of 100 that each of these numbers is between. Circle the multiple of 100 it is closest to.

Example

300 ← 386 → (400)

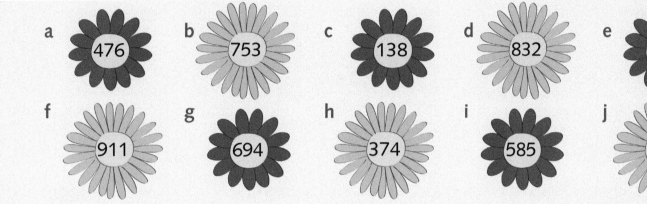

a 476 b 753 c 138 d 832 e 216

f 911 g 694 h 374 i 585 j 647

Challenge 2

Choose a flower pot and a flower and multiply the numbers together. Estimate your answer first, then use the grid method to work out the answer. Make six calculations. Choose different numbers each time.

Example

625 × 8 → 600 × 8 = 4800

×	600	20	5	
8	4800	160	40	= 5000

453 675 486 759

637 598 477 368

7 5 6 8

4 9 3 2

Challenge 3

One of these calculations is different to the others. Can you find out why?

 468 × 4

 624 × 3

 234 × 8

 732 × 2

Multiplication HTO × O using the expanded written method

Use the expanded written method to calculate HTO × O

Count in multiples of the first number in each row.
Copy and complete each sequence.

a 25, ____, 75, ____, ____, ____, ____, 200, ____, ____, ____, 300

b 40, 80, ____, ____, ____, ____, 280, ____, ____, ____, ____, ____

c 60, 120, ____, ____, ____, ____, ____, ____, ____, ____, 720

d 80, 160, ____, ____, ____, ____, ____, ____, 800, ____,

e 90, ____, 270, ____, ____, ____, 720, ____, ____, ____, 1080

1 Estimate the answer to each calculation.

a 346 × 3   b 673 × 4   c 732 × 9   d 986 × 6

e 548 × 5   f 888 × 8   g 647 × 8   h 747 × 5

2 For each of the calculations in Question 1,
use the expanded written method to work
out the answer.

One of the answers in Challenge 2 is the odd
one out. Can you find it? Explain how it is
different from the other answers.

Example

Th	H	T	O	
	4	6	3	
×			8	
		2	4	(3 × 8)
	4	8	0	(60 × 8)
3	2	0	0	(400 × 8)
3	7	0	4	
	1			

Solving word problems (2)

Solve problems and reason mathematically

Challenge 1

Copy the calculations and fill in the missing signs.

a $4 \bigcirc 8 = 32$ b $60 = 12 \ \square \ 5$ c $72 = 9 \ \square \ 8$ d $15 \ \bullet \ 3 = 12$

e $64 \ \blacksquare \ 8 = 8$ f $7 \ \triangle \ 8 = 15$ g $32 \ \blacktriangle \ 8 = 24$ h $96 \ \bigcirc \ 12 = 8$

Challenge 2

Choose a sports item from the pictures. Roll the 0–9 dice to find out how many of that item you will buy. If you roll 0 or 1, roll the dice again. Write a multiplication calculation. Estimate the answer and then work it out. Make six calculations. Choose a different sports item each time.

You will need:
• 0–9 dice

Challenge 3

Answer these questions about the sports equipment above.

a Tennis balls are sold in packs of 3. How much do 90 tennis balls cost?

b What is the difference in cost between a rugby ball and a cricket ball?

c The tennis club buys 8 tennis nets, 8 tennis racquets and 8 sets of tennis balls. What is the total cost?

d There are 30 children in Year 4. Each child buys a pair of rugby boots. How much money is spent?

e If I buy 1 cricket bat, 2 sets of cricket stumps and 3 cricket balls, how much do I spend?

f The sports store has sold out of hockey sticks. They cost 4 times more than a set of tennis balls. What is the cost of a hockey stick?

Decimal hundredths

Understand the place value of hundredths

Challenge 1

1 Count the hundredths that are shaded blue and record them as a fraction and a decimal fraction.

a   b   c   d

Example

$$\frac{17}{100} = 0.17$$

2 Copy the number line and write the fractions and decimal fractions.

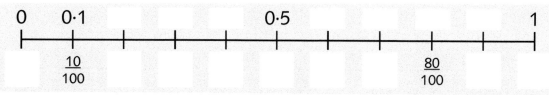

Challenge 2

1 Write the decimal fraction that is of equal value to these fractions.

a $\frac{7}{100}$ b $\frac{18}{100}$ c $\frac{22}{100}$ d $\frac{48}{100}$ e $\frac{56}{100}$ f $\frac{63}{100}$ g $\frac{76}{100}$ h $\frac{81}{100}$

2 Write these amounts as a decimal fraction.

a 26c b 37c c 44c d 57c e 65c f 77c g 84c h 99c

Challenge 3

1 What is the decimal fraction that is of equal value to these mixed numbers?

a $1\frac{34}{100}$ b $2\frac{48}{100}$ c $2\frac{81}{100}$ d $3\frac{75}{100}$ e $4\frac{3}{100}$ f $4\frac{95}{100}$ g $5\frac{72}{100}$ h $5\frac{83}{100}$

2 Write the approximate values as decimal hundredths for the arrows marked on the number line.

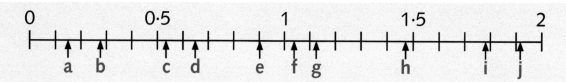

Comparing decimals (2)

Compare numbers with two decimal places

0·25, 0·26, 0·27, 0·28 and 0·29.

lenge 1

Count on in hundredths for five numbers from these decimals.

a 0·13	b 0·46	c 1·25	d 2·76	e 3·88
f 3·59	g 4·01	h 4·38	i 4·72	j 5·09

lenge 2

1 Write these decimal numbers in order, smallest to largest.

a 1·35, 1·63, 1·82, 1·15, 1·27   b 2·82, 2·16, 2·44, 2·19, 2·95

c 3·84, 3·27, 3·38, 3·15, 3·29   d 3·38, 3·32, 3·11, 3·89, 3·71

2 Write the decimal numbers that are one hundredth smaller and one hundredth larger than these numbers.

a 2·13   b 2·69   c 2·81   d 3·04   e 3·72

llenge 3

1 Write a decimal number in each of the spaces, keeping each set of decimals in order.

a 5·98, ___, 6·10, ___, ___, 6·50, ___, ___, ___, ___, ___, 7·25

b ___, 7·16, ___, 7·28, ___, ___, ___, 8, ___, ___, ___, 9·34

c ___, ___, 8·01, ___, ___, 8·43, ___, ___, ___, ___, ___, 10·06

d ___, 9·21, ___, ___, ___, 9·99, ___, ___, ___, ___, ___, 12·68

2 Write the greater than > or less < than sign between these numbers.

a 2·65 ___ 2·78   b 2·12 ___ 2·02   c 2·10 ___ 2·16   d 3·41 ___ 3·14

e 4·83 ___ 4·38   f 5·27 ___ 5·29   g 7·62 ___ 7·25   h 9·99 ___ 9·89

49

Dividing by 10

Divide 1- and 2-digit numbers by 10

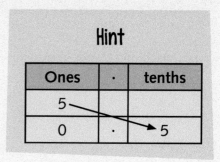

Challenge 1

1 Divide these numbers by 10.

a	4	b	3	c	9	d	6
e	1	f	7	g	2	h	8

Hint

Ones	·	tenths
5		
0	·	5

2 Complete this sentence: When a 1-digit number is divided by 10 …

Challenge 2

1 Divide these numbers by 10.

a	26	b	18	c	42	d	59
e	37	f	81	g	55	h	87

Hint

Tens	Ones	·	tenths
2	8		
	2	·	8

2 Complete this sentence: When a 2-digit number is divided by 10 …

Challenge 3

1 Work out these calculations.

a	63 ÷ 10	b	98 ÷ 10	c	5 ÷ 10	d	62 ÷ 10
e	59 ÷ 10	f	77 ÷ 10	g	46 ÷ 10	h	15 ÷ 10

2 Apply the rule for dividing by 10 to these 3-digit numbers.

a	145	b	186
c	256	d	374
e	598	f	601

Hint

Hundreds	Tens	Ones	·	tenths
2	6	3		
	2	6	·	3

3 Complete this sentence: When a 3-digit number is divided by 10 …

Dividing by 100

Divide 1- and 2-digit numbers by 100

1 Divide these numbers by 100.

a	4	b	3	c	9	d	6
e	1	f	7	g	2	h	8

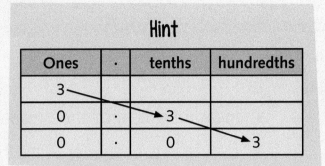

Hint

Ones	·	tenths	hundredths
3			
0	·	3	
0	·	0	3

2 Complete this sentence: When a 1-digit number is divided by 100 …

1 Divide these numbers by 100.

a	43	b	27	c	35	d	57
e	81	f	74	g	62	h	94

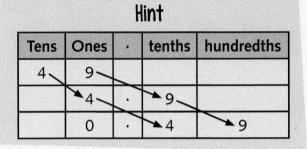

Hint

Tens	Ones	·	tenths	hundredths
4	9			
	4	·	9	
	0	·	4	9

2 Complete this sentence: When a 2-digit number is divided by 100 …

1 Work out these calculations.

a	39 ÷ 100	b	7 ÷ 100	c	28 ÷ 100	d	99 ÷ 100
e	84 ÷ 100	f	71 ÷ 100	g	65 ÷ 100	h	53 ÷ 100

2 Apply the rule for dividing by 100 to these 3-digit numbers.

a	172	b	385		
c	391	d	574		
e	658	f	701		

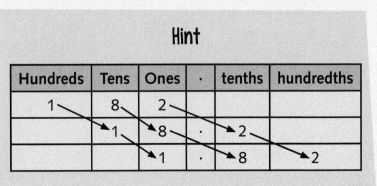

Hint

Hundreds	Tens	Ones	·	tenths	hundredths
1	8	2			
	1	8	·	2	
		1	·	8	2

Perimeter of rectangles

Measure and calculate the perimeter of rectangles using the rule P = 2(a + b)

Challenge 1

Copy each diagram on to 1 cm squared paper then:

- measure its length and breadth

- calculate its perimeter using the rule
  perimeter = twice (length plus breadth)

You will need:
- ruler
- 1 cm squared paper

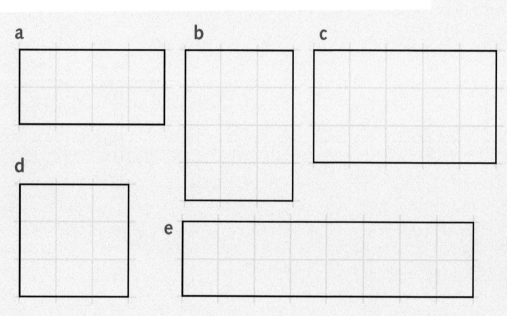

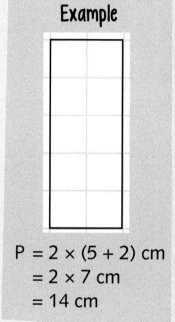

Example

P = 2 × (5 + 2) cm
  = 2 × 7 cm
  = 14 cm

Challenge 2

Use the rule from Challenge 1 to find the perimeter of these rectangular fields.

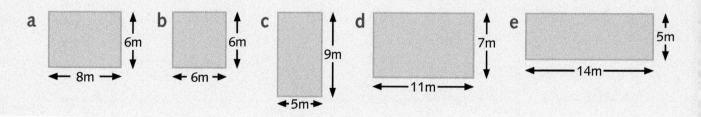

a 6m, 8m   b 6m, 6m   c 9m, 5m   d 7m, 11m   e 5m, 14m

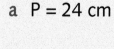 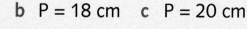

Challenge 3

Copy and complete these rectangles on 1 cm squared paper so they have the perimeters given.

a P = 24 cm   b P = 18 cm   c P = 20 cm

Counting squares for area

Find the area of rectangles by counting squares

You will need:
• centicubes

llenge 1

Write the number of centicubes you need to cover each rectangle.

 a 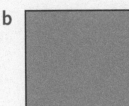 b 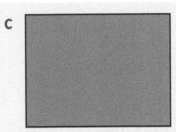 c 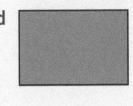 d

llenge 2

1 Find the area of each rectangle by counting the number of squares.

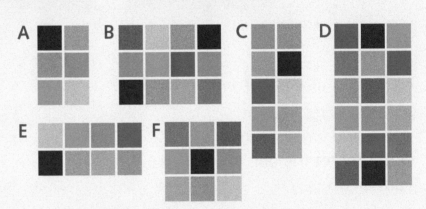

2 Which rectangle has:

a the smallest area?

b the greatest area?

c half the area of rectangle D?

d an area 2 squares less than rectangle E?

llenge 3

1 Use interlocking squares to make the four shapes below.

2 Fit the shapes together to make a rectangle 5 units by 4 units.

3 Copy the rectangle on to 1 cm squared paper.

4 Use coloured pencils to show how the four shapes fit together.

5 Record the area and perimeter of your rectangle.

You will need:
• interlocking squares
• 1 cm squared paper
• coloured pencils

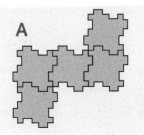 A 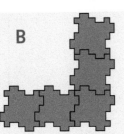 B 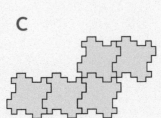 C 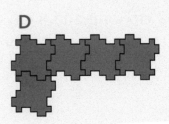 D

Finding area

Find the area of rectangles and other shapes by counting squares

Challenge 1

Find the area of each shape on the pinboard by counting the number of squares.

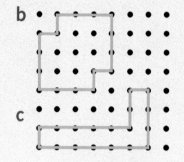

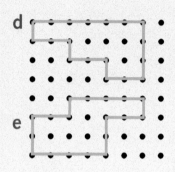

Challenge 2

Count the number of green squares in each shape and write its area. Don't forget the unit in your answers.

Challenge 3

Draw these rectangles on 1 cm squared paper. Below each one, write its area.

a   6 cm long and 2 cm wide

b   7 cm long and 4 cm wide

c   9 cm long and 5 cm wide

You will need:
• 1 cm squared paper
• ruler

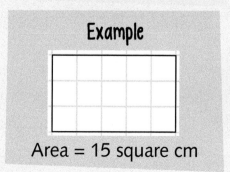

Example

Area = 15 square cm

54

Calculating area

Use multiplication to calculate the area of rectangles

Challenge 1

Each small square is 1 square cm.
Calculate the area of these rectangles.

a   b   c

Example

2 rows of 2 squares
Area = 2 × 2 square cm
= 4 square cm

Challenge 2

Each small square is 1 square cm.
Calculate the area of these rectangles.

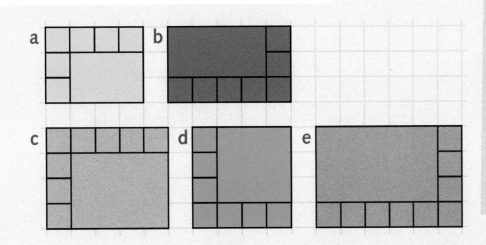

Example

3 rows of 3 squares
Area = 3 × 3 square cm
= 9 square cm

Challenge 3

Draw squares A to D on 1cm square dot paper.

a Find the area of each square.

b Draw the next two squares in the pattern.
Label them E and F.

c Find the area of squares E and F.

d Predict the areas of squares G and H.

e Check your predictions by drawing the squares.

You will need:
• 1 cm square dot paper
• ruler

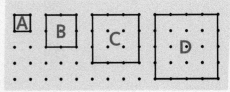

Maths facts

Problem solving

The seven steps to solving word problems

1 Read the problem carefully.   2 What do you have to find?   3 What facts are given?
4 Which of the facts do you need?   5 Make a plan.
6 Carry out your plan to obtain your answer.   7 Check your answer.

Number and place value

1000	2000	3000	4000	5000	6000	7000	8000	9000
100	200	300	400	500	600	700	800	900
10	20	30	40	50	60	70	80	90
1	2	3	4	5	6	7	8	9
0.1	0.2	0.3	0.4	0.5	0.6	0.7	0.8	0.9
0.01	0.02	0.03	0.04	0.05	0.06	0.07	0.08	0.09

Positive and negative numbers

-10 -9 -8 -7 -6 -5 -4 -3 -2 -1 0 1 2 3 4 5 6 7 8 9 10

Addition and subtraction

Number facts

+	0	1	2	3	4	5	6	7	8	9	10
0	0	1	2	3	4	5	6	7	8	9	10
1	1	2	3	4	5	6	7	8	9	10	11
2	2	3	4	5	6	7	8	9	10	11	12
3	3	4	5	6	7	8	9	10	11	12	13
4	4	5	6	7	8	9	10	11	12	13	14
5	5	6	7	8	9	10	11	12	13	14	15
6	6	7	8	9	10	11	12	13	14	15	16
7	7	8	9	10	11	12	13	14	15	16	17
8	8	9	10	11	12	13	14	15	16	17	18
9	9	10	11	12	13	14	15	16	17	18	19
10	10	11	12	13	14	15	16	17	18	19	20

+	11	12	13	14	15	16	17	18	19	20
0	11	12	13	14	15	16	17	18	19	20
1	12	13	14	15	16	17	18	19	20	
2	13	14	15	16	17	18	19	20		
3	14	15	16	17	18	19	20			
4	15	16	17	18	19	20				
5	16	17	18	19	20					
6	17	18	19	20						
7	18	19	20							
8	19	20								
9	20									

+	0	10	20	30	40	50	60	70	80	90	100
0	0	10	20	30	40	50	60	70	80	90	100
10	10	20	30	40	50	60	70	80	90	100	110
20	20	30	40	50	60	70	80	90	100	110	120
30	30	40	50	60	70	80	90	100	110	120	130
40	40	50	60	70	80	90	100	110	120	130	140
50	50	60	70	80	90	100	110	120	130	140	150
60	60	70	80	90	100	110	120	130	140	150	160
70	70	80	90	100	110	120	130	140	150	160	170
80	80	90	100	110	120	130	140	150	160	170	180
90	90	100	110	120	130	140	150	160	170	180	190
100	100	110	120	130	140	150	160	170	180	190	200

+	110	120	130	140	150	160	170	180	190	200
0	110	120	130	140	150	160	170	180	190	200
10	120	130	140	150	160	170	180	190	200	210
20	130	140	150	160	170	180	190	200	210	220
30	140	150	160	170	180	190	200	210	220	230
40	150	160	170	180	190	200	210	220	230	240
50	160	170	180	190	200	210	220	230	240	250
60	170	180	190	200	210	220	230	240	250	260
70	180	190	200	210	220	230	240	250	260	270
80	190	200	210	220	230	240	250	260	270	280
90	200	210	220	230	240	250	260	270	280	290
100	210	220	230	240	250	260	270	280	290	300

Written methods – addition

Example: 2456 + 5378

```
    2 4 5 6
  + 5 3 7 8
  ─────────
    7 8 3 4
      1 1
```

Written methods – subtraction

Example: 6418 – 2546

```
    5 13 11
    6 4 1̸ 8
  − 2 5 4 6
  ─────────
    3 8 7 2
```

Multiplication and division

Number facts

×	2	3	4	5	6	7	8	9	10	11	12
1	2	3	4	5	6	7	8	9	10	11	12
2	4	6	8	10	12	14	16	18	20	22	24
3	6	9	12	15	18	21	24	27	30	33	36
4	8	12	16	20	24	28	32	36	40	44	48
5	10	15	20	25	30	35	40	45	50	55	60
6	12	18	24	30	36	42	48	54	60	66	72
7	14	21	28	35	42	49	56	63	70	77	84
8	16	24	32	40	48	56	64	72	80	88	96
9	18	27	36	45	54	63	72	81	90	99	108
10	20	30	40	50	60	70	80	90	100	110	120
11	22	33	44	55	66	77	88	99	110	121	132
12	24	36	48	60	72	84	96	108	120	132	144

Written methods – multiplication

Example: 356 × 7

Partitioning

356 × 7 = (300 × 7) + (50 × 7) + (6 × 7)
     = 2100 + 350 + 42
     = 2492

Grid method

×	300	50	6	
7	2100	350	42	= 2492

Expanded written method

```
    3 5 6
  ×     7
  ─────────
      4 2  ( 6 × 7)
    3 5 0  ( 50 × 7)
  2 1 0 0  ( 300 × 7)
  ─────────
  2 4 9 2
```

Formal written method

```
    3 5 6
  × ₃₄7
  ─────────
  2 4 9 2
```

Written methods – division

Example: 486 ÷ 9

Partitioning

486 ÷ 9 = (450 ÷ 9) + (36 ÷ 9)
     = 50 + 4
     = 54

Formal written method

```
      5 4
  9) 4 8³6
```

Expanded written method

```
        5 4
  9) 4 8 6
     4 5 0  | 50 × 9
     ───────
       3 6
       3 6  | 4 × 9
     ───────
         0  |
```

57

Fractions and decimals

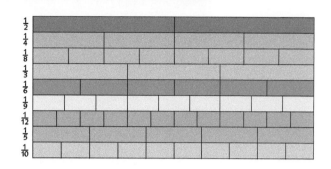

$$\frac{1}{100} = 0{\cdot}01$$

$$\frac{2}{100} = \frac{1}{50} = 0{\cdot}02$$

$$\frac{5}{100} = \frac{1}{20} = 0{\cdot}05$$

$$\frac{10}{100} = \frac{1}{10} = 0{\cdot}1$$

$$\frac{20}{100} = \frac{1}{5} = 0{\cdot}2$$

$$\frac{25}{100} = \frac{1}{4} = 0{\cdot}25$$

$$\frac{50}{100} = \frac{1}{2} = 0{\cdot}5$$

$$\frac{75}{100} = \frac{3}{4} = 0{\cdot}75$$

$$\frac{100}{100} = 1$$

Measurement

Length

1 kilometre (km) = 1000 metres (m)

0·1 km = 100 m

1 m = 100 centimetres (cm) = 1000 millimetres (mm)

0·1 m = 10 cm = 100 mm

1 cm = 10 mm

0·1 cm = 1 mm

Mass

1 kilogram (kg) = 1000 grams (g)

0·1 kg = 100 g

0·01 kg = 10 g

Capacity

1 litre (*l*) = 1000 millilitres (ml)

0·1 *l* = 100 ml

0·01 *l* = 10 ml

Time

1 year = 12 months

= 365 days

= 366 days (leap year)

1 week = 7 days

1 day = 24 hours

1 hour = 60 minutes

1 minute = 60 seconds

30 days has September,
April, June and November.
All the rest have 31, except
February alone which has
28 days clear and 29 in
each leap year.

12-hour clock **24-hour clock**

Properties of shape

2-D shapes

 circle

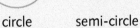 semi-circle

 right-angled triangle

 equilateral triangle

 isosceles triangle

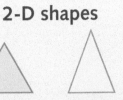 scalene triangle

 square

 rectangle

 rhombus

 kite

 parallelogram

 trapezium

 pentagon

 hexagon

 heptagon

 octagon

3-D shapes

 cube

 cuboid

 cone

 cylinder

 sphere

 hemisphere

 triangular prism

triangular-based pyramid (tetrahedron)

square-based pyramid

Angles

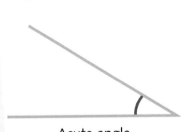

Acute angle

Right angle

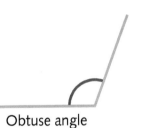

Obtuse angle

Position and direction

Coordinates

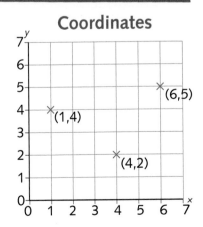

Translation

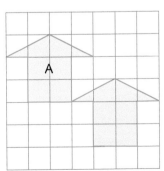

Shape A has been translated 3 squares to the right and 2 squares down.

Reflection

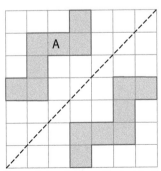

Shape A has been reflected in the diagonal line of symmetry.

William Collins' dream of knowledge for all began with the publication of his first book in 1819. A self-educated mill worker, he not only enriched millions of lives, but also founded a flourishing publishing house. Today, staying true to this spirit, Collins books are packed with inspiration, innovation and practical expertise. They place you at the centre of a world of possibility and give you exactly what you need to explore it.

Collins. Freedom to teach.

Published by Collins
An imprint of HarperCollins*Publishers*
The News Building
1 London Bridge Street
London
SE1 9GF

HarperCollins *Publishers*
1st Floor
Watermarque Building
Ringsend Road
Dublin 4
Ireland

Browse the complete Collins catalogue at
www.collins.co.uk

© HarperCollins*Publishers* Limited 2015

10 9 8 7 6 5 4

ISBN 978-0-00-815747-0

British Library Cataloguing in Publication Data
A Catalogue record for this publication is available from the British Library

Edited by Catherine Dakin, Donna Cole and Jean Rustean
Cover design and artwork by Amparo Barrera
Internal design concept by Amparo Barrera
Designed by Niki Merrett
Illustrations by Louise Forshaw, Steven Woods, Gwyneth Williamson and Eva Sassin
European edition edited by: Ros and Chris Davies

Printed and bound in the UK using 100% Renewable
Electricity at CPI Group (UK) Ltd

SUPERCUTE SEWING

20 Easy Sewing Patterns for Soft Toys and Accessories

Melanie McNeice

DAVID & CHARLES

www.davidandcharles.com

CONTENTS

INTRODUCTION

Sewing a gift for a child can be as exciting and fun for us as the finished toy is for the lucky recipient, and that is certainly true of the toys I designed in this book. Each creature, character and creation bursts with personality and is, of course, oh so very cute! Perfectly proportioned for little hands and big hugs, there is the perfect softie for every child.

Elephants, seals and monkeys quickly capture their imagination; robots, aliens and UFOs have so much potential for storytelling. Is there a child who doesn't wish they could meet a rainbow unicorn or friendly dragon? Maybe they want to transform themselves into a high-spirited princess or flying superhero. Even the sweet floral quilt and adorable ladybug bag will catch their eye and melt your heart.

Each of the twenty patterns have step-by-step instructions, illustrated with beautiful colour photographs and detailed diagrams. I have provided actual-size templates to get you started straight away. Read through the pattern before you begin to decide whether it will be a quick-and-easy make (great for gifting with short notice!) or one to help you build your toy making skills. In special sections, I give guidance on the tools and materials used, plus techniques including stitching and stuffing. However, should you need a little more help, please visit my website and look through the fabulous tutorials section where there is even more advice to help you on your toy-making journey.

I hope you enjoy your time planning and making these supercute design. The resulting toys will bring the mini marvels in your life many hours of imagination-filled play, memorable moments and comforting cuddles.

MELLY

www.mellyandme.com

Safety note

If making these toys for a small child, omit the buttons for the eyes and joints as they are a potential choking hazard; alternatives are provided in the steps.

MATERIALS & EQUIPMENT

Listed here is the essential equipment you will need for making the toys featured in this book.

TRACING PAPER OR TEMPLATE PLASTIC

These are ideal for copying and tracing the templates onto your fabrics. You can see your fabrics through them and therefore it is easier to ensure correct placement. The template markings can also be easily transferred onto your paper or plastic with a pencil or permanent marker.

FABRIC MARKERS

There are many different methods and products for marking your fabric. However, vanishing markers or tailor's chalk are the best options to avoid leaving permanent marks on your toys. A light grey lead pencil is a handy substitute. A pink pencil can be used for marking rosy cheeks on the faces of some of the completed toys.

ROTARY CUTTER, MAT AND RULER

These tools are designed to make the cutting of strips and squares a simple and accurate procedure. Although highly recommended, they are not essential items and you can use a tape measure, ruler and scissors instead.

SEWING SCISSORS

These are frequently used in any fabric project and I recommend that you invest in good-quality scissors to make your sewing experience more pleasurable and accurate. If you have both a large and a small pair of scissors you will be able to do everything, from cutting out your fabrics to snipping seams and threads.

SEWING THREAD

It is essential when making toys to use a good-quality polyester thread suitable for machine sewing. Strong, durable seams are required when stuffing toys –cotton thread will result in split seams. To achieve near-invisible seams, match your thread to the colour of the fabrics.

SEWING MACHINE

For strong, durable toys that withstand stuffing and boisterous play, use a sewing machine. A basic model with a straight and zigzag stitch – is all you need, but blanket stitch will come in very useful for machine appliqué.

HAND-SEWING NEEDLES

There is usually some hand sewing involved in making toys and therefore it is necessary to have some good-quality hand-sewing needles. I recommend a size 10 embroidery needle for all hand sewing, and a selection of dollmaker's needles of different lengths are essential for button jointing or attach items such as button eyes.

FABRIC AND FELT

I have used 100% cotton quilting fabrics and 100% pure wool-felt. Use these same materials to complete your toys if you want to achieve results like mine. Other fabrics may have more or less stretch and can create a very different result.

FUSIBLE FLEECE

Some of the patterns require lightweight fusible fleece, a white, lofty interfacing often used in bag construction, and helps to give a thicker structure while retaining the softness that you will want for a toy. The one I buy is approx. 100cm (40in) wide.

FUSIBLE WEBBING

This widely available iron-on material is used to adhere all appliqué pieces and facial features for example. Be sure to check the manufacturer's instructions for your specific product before using.

Note: All measurements in this book are given as height x width throughout.

TOY FILLING

Choose a good-quality polyester toy filling for stuffing. Some fillings can create lumps inside your toys, giving them an uneven finish. To check a filling for quality, take a small handful and roll it gently into a ball between your palms. If the filling remains in a tight ball, it will create lumps; if it springs back, it's ideal

TURNING AND STUFFING TOOLS

A pair of tweezers makes turning through small limbs so simple. A wooden skewer is useful when turning and stuffing very small pieces), but only use the blunt end – the point is liable to break your seams. A round-ended wooden paintbrush makes a great double-sided turning/stuffing tool. The smooth handle is perfect for turning your soft toy pieces and smoothing seams; the bristle end becomes the ideal stuffing tool with just a little modification, as explained in Stuffing Techniques.

EMBROIDERY THREAD (FLOSS)

Use good-quality six-strand embroidery thread (floss) for embroidering facial features and for hand appliqué.

BUTTONS

Round buttons in a variety of sizes make excellent toy eyes, and are required when button jointing toy limbs. However, if you are making these toys for a baby or small child, omit the buttons as they are a potential choking hazard: alternatives are provided in the steps.

DRESSMAKER'S PINS

Good-quality, sharp pins are useful for keeping your fabric pieces together prior to stitching.

IRON AND IRONING BOARD

Iron your fabric to get rid of creases before transferring the templates. You will also need to press seams, especially when joining fabric panels, and when using fusible fleece and webbing.

STUFFING TECHNIQUES

It is essential to stuff your toys very firmly – you will be surprised at how much filling they will need.

As you will have sewn the seams using small stitches and polyester thread, they will be robust enough to withstand a lot of stuffing. So when you think that your toy is fully stuffed, keep on stuffing. Don't be scared to use large wads of filling as this will give your finished toy more structure.

Using your paintbrush tool: To transform a found paintbrush into a stuffing tool, trim the bristles to 6mm–13mm (¼in–½in) long. Rub the remaining bristles against a hard surface until you have thoroughly messed them up. Shaggy bristles will grip onto your filling firmly, allowing you to easily manoeuvre it into your toy. This will also enable you to position the filling where you want it and to keep stuffing right to the end of the pieces until they are super-firm.

PETAL THE PONY

When I was a little girl, my favourite part of any visit to the fair was always the pony rides. In my imaginary world, I had my very own pony. We were the best of friends and rode together all day long, with the wind in our hair! These memories inspired me to create this little carousel horse with her candy-coloured mane and tail for your children to enjoy.

YOU WILL NEED

Note: *Buttons should be omitted if making this toy for a very small child. Use 100% cotton patchwork fabric with a width of 106cm–114cm (42in–44in).*

- ★ 25cm (10in) x full fabric width of main fabric (body, legs)

- ★ 15cm (6in) x full fabric width of contrasting fabric (hooves, ears)

- ★ 5cm x 10cm (2in x 4in) lightweight fusible fleece

- ★ Two skeins of perle 5 rainbow or variegated thread (mane and tail)

- ★ Four 2.5cm (1in) buttons for button jointing

- ★ Six-strand embroidery thread (floss): colour to match button-jointing buttons

- ★ Two small black buttons for eyes (or circles of felt), and matching thread

- ★ Dollmaker's needle: 12.5cm (5in) or longer

- ★ Good-quality polyester thread (if cotton thread is used, your seams could break during stuffing)

- ★ Good-quality polyester toy filling

FINISHED SIZE: 25cm (10in) tall x 23cm (9in) long

CUTTING YOUR FABRICS

Note: *Trace the Petal the Pony templates (see Templates) onto tracing paper or template plastic, transferring all of the markings, and cut them out around the traced lines. When using these templates to trace the pattern pieces onto your fabric, do ensure that the marked grain line on the template matches the fabric grain line (the direction of the fabric parallel with the selvedge).*

FROM YOUR MAIN FABRIC:

Cut one piece 25cm x 46cm (10in x 18in) for the legs.

Fold remaining fabric in half with right sides together. Trace the body template once onto the wrong side of the folded fabric, transferring all markings. ***Do not*** cut out.

FROM YOUR CONTRASTING FABRIC:

Cut two strips 7cm (2¾in) high x 46cm (18in) wide for the hooves.

Cut one piece 10cm x 10cm (4in x 4in) for the ears.

Trace the hoof template four times onto the remaining fabric and cut out along the traced lines.

PREPARING TO SEW

1 Interface one half of the 10cm (4in) contrasting fabric square with the fusible fleece.

2 Tail and mane: Take the perle 5 thread and cut into 30 lengths, each measuring approx. 1m (40in) long, placing them together in a neat, even bundle. Measuring 12.5cm (5in) from the end, wrap a very small piece of adhesive tape around the bundle to enclose the threads. Measure another 12.5cm (5in) along the length and, again, tape the threads together. Continue in this way to the end of the thread bundle to divide it into eight equal sections, ending each one with a piece of tape. Cut through the threads after each piece of tape to give you eight thread bundles – one for the tail and seven for the mane (see **Fig. 1**).

3 Set your sewing machine to a small stitch length of approx. 1.5 for stitching the toy and use a good-quality polyester thread for strong seams.

MAKING THE PONY

Note: A 6mm (¼in) seam allowance is included in all pattern pieces unless advised otherwise. Read through all instructions before beginning to avoid any surprises.

1 Take the main fabric piece with the pony body traced onto it, and machine stitch around the traced line leaving three gaps open as indicated by the broken lines on the template.

2 Cut out the pony body 6mm (¼in) outside the sewn/traced lines. **Do not** turn right side out.

3 Take one of the thread bundles and guide the taped end through the tummy gap in the pony body, to push it up through the tail gap so that the taped end is poking out;. Now stitch along the tail gap to secure the tail thread bundle in place (**Fig. 2**), and cut off the taped end.

4 Take your remaining seven thread bundles, ready to sew these into position along the gap on the top of the head to make the mane. Starting at the front (fringe region), position the thread bundles evenly along the gap so that the taped sections are poking out and·the loose threads are sitting neatly inside the body. Clip or tack (baste) the thread bundles in place, then sew the gap closed along the traced line to secure the mane evenly in your stitching (**Fig. 3**). Cut off the taped ends.

5 Turn the body right side out through the turning gap in the tummy, and stuff firmly with toy filling. Ladder stitch the opening closed (see Stitching Techniques), adding a little more filling as you go to avoid a dimple.

FiG. 1

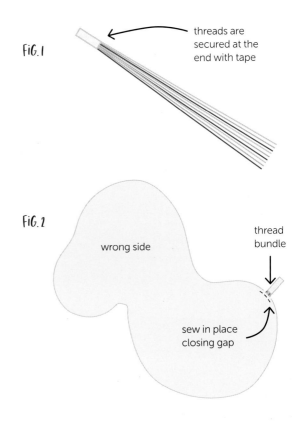

threads are secured at the end with tape

FiG. 2

wrong side

thread bundle

sew in place closing gap

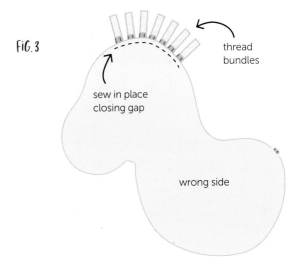

FiG. 3

sew in place closing gap

thread bundles

wrong side

Handy Tip

It may be easier to clip the hair bundles in place rather than pinning or tacking (basting) them. If you don't have any sewing clips, simple metal hair clips will work, too.

6 Take the remaining main fabric (leg) piece and the two strips of contrasting (hoof) fabric each measuring 46cm (18in) long. Sew one of the contrasting (hoof) strips to each 46cm (18in) edge of the main fabric (**Fig. 4**). Press the seams well to the hoof fabric side.

7 Fold the joined panel in half, right sides together, so that the two hoof fabric strips sit neatly and evenly on top of each other. Take the leg template and trace around it four times onto the panel, making sure to align the straight (broken line) edge with the raw edge of the hoof fabric, leaving a 1.3cm (½in) space between each traced leg to allow for cutting out after stitching (see step 8).

8 Machine stitch the legs together along the traced lines, leaving the straight (broken line) edge unstitched. Cut out each leg approx. 6mm (¼in) outside the sewn lines. **Do not** turn right side out.

9 Take one of the hoof base pieces and ease this into place, right sides facing, along the bottom raw edge of one of the legs. Tack (baste) well, then machine stitch in place. To ensure there is no puckering, it will help after each small section is sewn to stop stitching with the needle down, and to rotate and smooth the leg fabric underneath before continuing. Complete all four legs.

10 To turn the legs right side out, cut the small turning slit as marked on the template on **one side only** of each leg (single fabric thickness). Stuff each leg firmly with toy filling, then ladder stitch the opening closed (see Stitching Techniques: Attaching Parts). Because the turning gaps will be hidden against the body of the pony, there is no need to worry about perfect stitching.

11 Now button joint the front legs to the front of the pony's body, referring to **Fig. 5**. Thread the dollmaker's needle with a long length of six-strand embroidery thread (floss). Tie a double knot in the end of your length of thread and trim close to the knot. Start by threading the needle through one side of the pony's body at the desired leg location (refer to photograph as a positioning guide), taking it right through the body and out the other side at exactly the same level. Thread the needle through one of the legs, then through one of the buttons, then go back through all of the layers again (button, leg, body) to come back out close to your start point. Here, thread the needle carefully through the remaining leg and button (shown in **Fig. 5**) and return again through the body to the other side. Continue in the same way, taking the needle through all the layers a few times, pulling the threads taut after each pass through. Tie off your thread and sink the knot into the leg (see Stitching Techniques).

FIG. 4

leg piece

FIG. 5

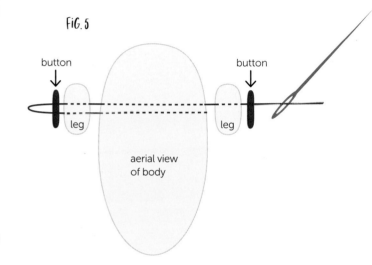

button

button

leg

leg

aerial view
of body

12 Repeat the button joining process to attach the back legs to the back of the body. Attach the back legs slightly higher than the front legs.

13 Take your ear fabric square and fold it in half with right sides together, so that one side is interfaced and one side is not. Trace around the ear template twice onto the interfaced side. Machine stitch along the traced lines, leaving the turning gap open as indicated by the broken line on the template. Snip the corners, turn through to the right side and press.

14 Using a strong polyester thread, ladder stitch the base of the ears onto the pony's head working first along the front edge, then along the back edge for added strength.

15 Using black thread, sew the button eyes into place on the pony's face, referring to the finished photograph for positioning. Sew into place following the same method as for button jointing the legs (see step 11), pulling the thread to indent the eyes ever so slightly if desired.

16 To finish, trim the mane as you prefer: I cut the front section a little shorter to make a fringe, then trimmed the remainder until I was pleased with the overall effect.

Handy Tip

If you are making this toy for a small child, join the legs as in step 11 but without the buttons. For the eyes, use small circles of black wool-felt or create with satin stitch (see stitching techniques).

ELEPHANT FAMILY

One grey elephant balancing,
Step by step on a piece of string,
He thought it was such a wonderful stunt,
That he called for another elephant.

I fondly remember my children singing this tune when they were little and I will admit that I found myself singing it constantly as I created this cute elephant family for you to make for yours.

YOU WILL NEED

Note: Buttons should be omitted if making this toy for a very small child. Use 100% cotton patchwork fabric with a width of 106cm–114cm (42in–44in).

(FOR ONE ELEPHANT)

★ 21cm (8in) x full fabric width of main body fabric (body, inner legs)

★ 20cm x 25cm (8in x 10in) contrasting fabric (ears)

★ 20cm x 12.5cm (8in x 5in) lightweight fusible fleece

★ 10cm (4in) matching cord for tail

★ 100% wool-felt: white 5cm x 7.5cm (2in x 3in) and blue 2.5cm x 5cm (1in x 2in) for eyes

★ 7.5cm x 7.5cm (3in x 3in) fusible web

★ Two small black buttons for pupils, and matching thread

★ Good-quality polyester thread (if cotton thread is used, your seams could break during stuffing)

★ Good-quality polyester toy filling

FINISHED SIZES: Mummy/daddy 15cm (6in) tall x 20cm (8in) long;baby 12.5cm (5in) tall x 16.5cm (6½in) long

CUTTING YOUR FABRICS

Note: Trace the Elephant Family templates (see Templates) on to tracing paper or template plastic, transferring all of the markings, and cut them out around the traced lines. When using these templates to trace the pattern pieces onto your fabric, do ensure that the marked grain line on the template matches the fabric grain line (the direction of the fabric parallel with the selvedge).

FROM YOUR MAIN FABRIC:

Fold the fabric in half with right sides together. Trace the body and inner leg templates once onto the wrong side of the folded fabric, transferring all markings. Cut out along the traced lines to give you two mirror-image pieces of each.

FROM YOUR CONTRASTING FABRIC:

Fold the fabric in half with right sides together and trace the ear template twice onto the wrong side of the folded fabric. Cut out along the traced lines to give you four ear pieces.

FROM YOUR FUSIBLE FLEECE:

Trace the ear template twice onto the fleece, flipping the template for your second trace. Cut out along the traced lines to give you two ear pieces.

PREPARING TO SEW

1 Interface two of the fabric ear pieces with the matching fusible fleece pieces.

2 Trace the inner and outer eyes twice each on to the paper side of the fusible web and roughly cut out. Fuse the inner eyes to the blue felt and the outer eyes to the white felt, and cut out along the traced lines.

3 Set your sewing machine to a small stitch length of approx. 1.5 for stitching the toy and use a good-quality polyester thread for strong seams.

MAKING THE ELEPHANT

Note: A 6mm (¼in) seam allowance is included in all pattern pieces unless advised otherwise. Read through all instructions before beginning to avoid surprises.

1 First attach the eyes to the body pieces. Peel off the backing paper from the white outer eye pieces and fuse in place on the body pieces as marked on the template. Machine appliqué into position using white thread. Repeat to fix the blue inner eye pieces in position, making sure to change to a matching thread colour. Hand sew a small black button in place for the pupil (see photograph for positioning guide).

2 Take one of the body pieces and your length of matching cord. Secure the cord ends with a little adhesive tape to avoid fraying. Position the cord on to the body piece, right sides together, so that one raw end meets the tail position marked on the template (**Fig. 1**). Machine tack (baste) the cord tail into place.

3 Pair up the ear pieces, one with fleece and one without fleece, and place together with right sides facing. Pin, then machine sew each pair together, leaving the inner edges open for turning as indicated by the broken line on the template. Snip along the curved edges, turn through to the right side and press well.

4 Take one body piece and one ear, and place the ear on top of the body piece, right sides together, so that the raw edge of the ear meets the front raw edge of the dart, aligning with the bottom of the dart. Carefully easing the curve of the ear to match the curve of the dart edge, machine sew the ear into place (**Fig. 2**).

5 Now fold the body piece to position the two raw edges of the dart on top of each other, right sides together, so that the ear is between the two layers. Sew the dart into place, leaving a 5cm (2in) gap for turning in the centre of the ear section and easing your stitching to the folded edge as shown in **Fig. 3**.

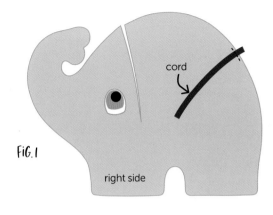

FIG. 1

cord

right side

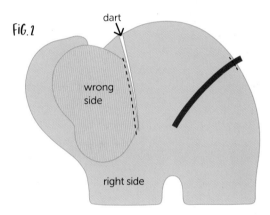

FIG. 2

dart

wrong side

right side

Handy Tip:

If you are making this toy for a small child, omit the button and make the pupil of the elephant's eye by working a triple wrap French knot (see Stitching Techniques) using all six strands of six-strand embroidery thread (floss).

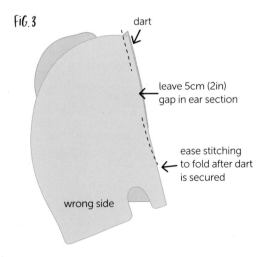

FIG. 3

dart

leave 5cm (2in) gap in ear section

ease stitching to fold after dart is secured

wrong side

6 Repeat steps 4 and 5 to join the remaining ear to the remaining body piece. However, this time **do not** leave a turning gap.

7 Take one body piece and one inner leg piece, and place the inner leg piece on top of the body piece, right sides together. Referring to **Fig. 4**, machine sew the inner leg to the body ensuring that you start stitching right at the raw edge of the fabric and gradually turn into a 6mm (¼in) seam before tapering to the raw edge again at the other end. Repeat to join the remaining body and inner leg pieces.

8 Now sew the dart on the inner leg sections of the joined body/inner leg pieces. Fold each inner leg section in half, right sides together, so that the fold goes down the centre of the dart marking. Sew each dart into place in the inner leg only, following the marked dart line. Trim any excess fabric away from your darts.

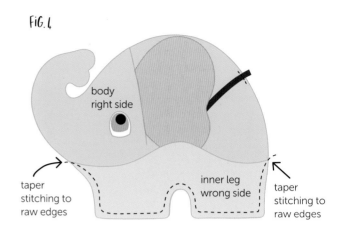

FIG. 4

body right side

inner leg wrong side

taper stitching to raw edges

taper stitching to raw edges

Handy Tip

Sew the inner leg darts into place **after** sewing the inner legs to the body to ensure that all of the leg edges match flat and even when sewing them together.

9 Place the body pieces on top of each other, right sides facing (with the inner legs in between) and tack (baste) together. When you reach the inner leg section you need to ensure you are tacking (basting) the **top** edges of the inner legs together, right sides facing. It may be easier to do this by folding the legs up against either side of the body as shown in **Fig. 5**, but do check that the ears are clear of your tacking (basting) stitches.

10 Machine sew the body/inner leg pieces together, making sure that the ears are clear of your stitching.

11 Turn the elephant right side out through the turning gap (behind one of the ears); press the ears if required. Stuff your elephant firmly with toy filling (stuff the trunk first), then ladder stitch (see Stitching Techniques) the opening closed, adding a little more filling as you go to avoid a dimple.

12 To finish the elephant, tie a knot into the tail at the desired length and then trim off the excess.

FiG. 5

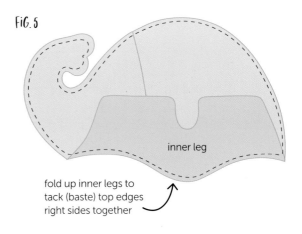

inner leg

fold up inner legs to tack (baste) top edges right sides together

Handy Tip

To stuff the trunk, use a stuffing tool, such as the blunt end of a wooden skewer, to manoeuvre small pieces of filling to the very end of the trunk and then stuff firmly from there.

LEWIN THE LION

Lions are my favourite animal of all. If you are a 'cat person', you can't help but be in awe of these majestic creatures. They look so cuddly yet command our respect. If, like me, you have always wanted one as a pet, then make this fun fellow from bright cotton fabric. His sweet, smiley face is framed by an eye-catching mane made from jumbo ric-rac.

YOU WILL NEED

Note: Buttons should be omitted if making this toy for a very small child. Use 100% cotton patchwork fabric with a width of 106cm–114cm (42in–44in).

★ 21cm (8in) x full fabric width of main fabric (body, inner legs, head top)

★ 12.5cm x 50cm (5in x 20in) contrasting fabric (head bottom, ears, tail)

★ 7.5cm (3in) matching cord for tail

★ 50cm (20in) matching jumbo ric-rac for mane

★ 100% wool-felt: brown 5cm x 6cm (2in x 2½in) for nose

★ Six-strand embroidery thread (floss): brown to match wool-felt

★ 5cm x 6cm (2in x 2½in) fusible web

★ Two small black buttons for eyes, and matching thread

★ Good-quality polyester thread (if cotton thread is used, your seams could break during stuffing)

★ Good-quality polyester toy filling

FINISHED SIZE: 18cm (7in) tall x 22.5cm (8½in) long

CUTTING YOUR FABRICS

Note: Trace the Lewin the Lion templates (see Templates) onto tracing paper or template plastic, transferring all of the markings, and cut them out around the traced lines. When using these templates to trace the pattern pieces onto your fabric, do ensure that the marked grain line on the template matches the fabric grain line (the direction of the fabric parallel with the selvedge).

FROM YOUR MAIN FABRIC:

Fold the fabric in half with right sides together. Trace the body, inner leg and head top templates once onto the wrong side of the folded fabric, transferring all markings. Cut out along the traced lines to give you two mirror-image pieces of each.

FROM YOUR CONTRASTING FABRIC:

Fold the fabric in half with right sides together and trace the head bottom template once onto the wrong side of the folded fabric. Cut out along the traced lines to give you two pieces. (You will use the remaining fabric for the tail and ears a little later, so set aside for now.)

PREPARING TO SEW

1 Trace the nose onto the paper side of the fusible web and roughly cut out. Fuse this to the brown wool-felt and cut out along the traced line.

2 Set your sewing machine to a small stitch length of approx. 1.5 for stitching the toy and use a good-quality polyester thread for strong seams.

MAKING THE LION

Note: A 6mm (¼in) seam allowance is included in all pattern pieces unless advised otherwise. Read through all instructions before beginning to avoid surprises.

1 Take the remaining piece of contrasting fabric and, still working with it folded, right sides together, trace the ear template twice and the tail template once onto the wrong side of the folded fabric, ensuring that you leave at least 1.3cm (½in) between each tracing. Machine sew along the traced lines of the ears and the tail, leaving the straight edges unstitched as indicated by the broken line on the template. Cut out the ears and the tail approx. 3mm (⅛in) outside the sewn line, snip corners and turn right side out.

Handy Tip

To turn out small pieces, such as the lion's tail, insert a pair of tweezers into the open end of the piece to be turned, pinch the sewn end and pull it through.

2 Setting aside the ears for now, finish making the tail. Turn the raw edges in by approx. 6mm (¼in) and finger press. Lightly stuff the tail with a little toy filling. Take the length of cord and tape one end to prevent it from fraying.

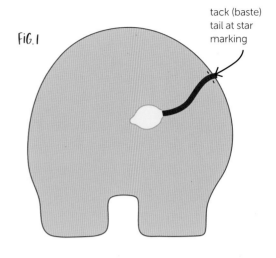

tack (baste) tail at star marking

FiG. 1

Insert the taped end into the tail until the tape is enclosed within. Take small hand running stitches around the folded-in edge of the tail, then gather up the stitches so that the tail fits snugly over the cord. Finish by taking a few stitches through the cord itself to secure it. Trim the loose end of the cord to the desired tail length.

3 Position the completed tail onto the right side of one of the body pieces (see tail placement position indicated on the template), so that it is lying at an angle (see **Fig. 1**). Machine tack (baste) the tail into place close to the edge.

4 Take an inner leg piece and place on top of the body piece with tail attached, right sides together. Referring to **Fig. 2**, machine sew the inner leg to the body ensuring that you start stitching right at the raw edge of the fabric and gradually turn into a 6mm (¼in) seam before tapering to the raw edge again at the other end. Repeat to join the remaining body and inner leg pieces.

5 Now sew the dart on the inner leg sections of the joined body/inner leg pieces. Fold each inner leg section in half, right sides together, so that the fold goes down the centre of the dart marking. Sew each dart into place in the inner leg only, following the marked dart line. Trim any excess fabric away from your darts.

Handy Tip

Sew the inner leg darts into place **after** sewing the inner legs to the body to ensure that all of the leg edges match flat and even when sewing them together.

FiG. 2

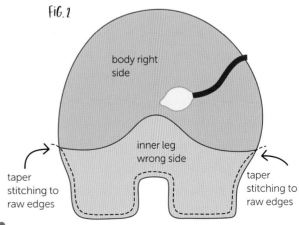

body right side

inner leg wrong side

taper stitching to raw edges

taper stitching to raw edges

6 Place the body pieces on top of each other, right sides facing (with the inner legs in between) and tack (baste) together. When you reach the inner leg section you need to ensure you are tacking (basting) the **top** edges of the inner legs together, right sides facing. It may be easier to do this by folding the legs up against either side of the body as shown in **Fig. 3**.

7 Machine sew the body together starting and ending at either end of the turning gap, indicated by a broken line on the template. Snip into the curves and angles of the inner leg before turning the lion's body right side out through the turning gap.

8 Stuff the lion's body very firmly with toy filling and ladder stitch the opening closed (see Stitching Techniques): as the stitching will be covered by the head, there is no need to worry about perfect stitching. Put the body aside for now.

9 Sew the dart into place on the bottom of the head pieces. Fold each piece in half, right sides together, so that the raw dart edges are on top of each other and machine sew using a 6mm (¼in) seam (see **Fig. 4**).

10 Take one head top and one head bottom piece and place together with right sides facing and straight edges aligning. Pin, then machine stitch together. Open out and press. Repeat to join the remaining head top and bottom pieces, but this time leave a 5cm (2in) turning gap in the centre of the seam.

11 Position the ears onto the front of the head (without turning gap), right sides together, as shown in **Fig. 5**. Machine tack (baste) the ears in place.

12 Now arrange the jumbo ric-rac mane into place all the way around the edge of the front of the head, bearing in mind the 6mm (¼in) seam allowance. When you are happy with this, machine tack (baste) into place, close to the edge, carefully easing the ends of the ric-rac to the outside of the head to create a neat starting and ending point (see **Fig. 6**).

13 Place the head pieces together, right sides facing, ensuring that the lower face seams meet evenly at the sides; pin or tack (baste) in position. Machine sew all the way around the edge. Trim away the excess ric-rac, then turn the head right side out through the gap in the back of the head. Stuff the lion's head firmly with toy filling, then ladder stitch the opening closed (see Stitching Techniques).

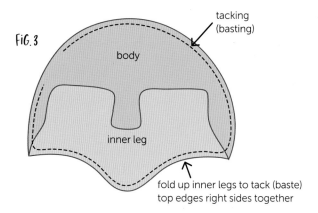

FiG. 3

tacking (basting)

body

inner leg

fold up inner legs to tack (baste) top edges right sides together

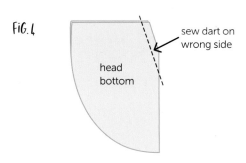

FiG. 4

sew dart on wrong side

head bottom

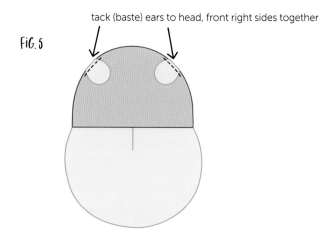

FiG. 5

tack (baste) ears to head, front right sides together

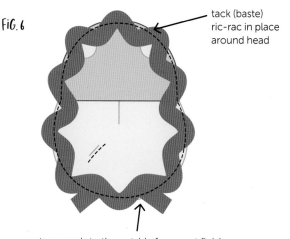

FiG. 6

tack (baste) ric-rac in place around head

taper ends to the outside for a neat finish

14 Using black thread, sew the button eyes into place on the lion's face referring to the photograph for positioning. Take the brown felt nose, peel off the backing paper, and fuse it into place on the lion's head. Blanket stitch the nose to secure using two strands of brown embroidery thread (floss). Mark the mouth, whiskers and nose line onto the lion's face with a fabric marker, and backstitch over the lines using four strands of brown embroidery thread (floss), sinking your knot to finish (see Stitching Techniques).

Handy Tip

If you are making this toy for a small child, substitute a small piece of black wool-felt for the buttons, or create the eyes with satin stitch (see Stitching Techniques).

15 Place the lion's head onto the front of the body so that it is lying on top of the turning gap, adjusting it until you are pleased with its position. Hand tack (baste) in place – I like to put the head on at a slight angle to give the toy a little extra personality.

Handy Tip

When you are happy with where the head is sitting, do make sure that it is hiding both turning gaps before tacking (basting) it into place.

16 Ladder stitch (see Stitching Techniques) the head onto the body using a double length of strong polyester thread. Essentially you will be stitching them together in an oval shape, where head meets body, surrounding (and so hiding) the turning gaps. Go around your stitching twice for added strength and keep your thread tension tight as you work to create a close, strong join.

SEAL WITH A KISS

Seals are such clever, curious creatures and they put on quite a show as they duck and dive while feeding. With their sweet puppy-dog eyes and sleek, gliding bodies, who could resist them? They are so easy to love and this delightful pair of seal pups would agree that nothing could possibly be better than a wet, fishy kiss!

YOU WILL NEED

NOTE: *Buttons should be omitted if making this toy for a very small child. Use 100% cotton patchwork fabric with a width of 106cm–114cm (42in–44in).*

(FOR ONE SEAL)

★ 32cm (12½in) x full fabric width of main fabric (body, head gusset, tail, flippers)

★ 12.5cm x 30cm (5in x 12in) contrasting fabric (tummy gusset)

★ 100% wool-felt: black scrap for nose

★ 20cm x 30cm (8in x 12in) lightweight fusible fleece

★ Small scrap of fusible web

★ Six-strand embroidery thread (floss): black and colour to match your main fabric for whiskers

★ Dollmaker's needle

★ Two small black buttons for eyes, and matching thread

★ Good-quality polyester thread (if cotton thread is used, your seams could break during stuffing)

★ Good-quality polyester toy filling

FINISHED SIZE: 25cm (10in) tall x 32cm (12½in) long

CUTTING YOUR FABRICS

Note: Trace the Seal with a Kiss templates (see Templates) onto tracing paper or template plastic, transferring all of the markings, and cut them out around the traced lines. To make the full template join Body 1 and Body 2 templates along the dashed lines. When using these templates to trace the pattern pieces onto your fabric, do ensure that the marked grain line on the template matches the fabric grain line (the direction of the fabric parallel with the selvedge).

FROM YOUR MAIN FABRIC:

Fold the fabric in half with right sides together, then trace the body and tail templates once onto the wrong side of the folded fabric, transferring all markings. Cut out along the traced lines to give you two mirror-image pieces of each.

Opening out the remaining fabric to a single layer, trace the head gusset template once only and cut out along the traced line.

Also from single layer fabric, cut one piece 20cm x 30cm (8in x 12in) for making the flippers.

FROM YOUR CONTRASTING FABRIC:

Trace the tummy gusset template once onto the fabric. Cut out along traced line.

PREPARING TO SEW

1 Trace the nose onto the paper side of the fusible web and roughly cut out. Fuse this to the black wool-felt and cut out along the traced line.

2 Interface the 20cm x 30cm (8in x 12in) panel of main fabric with the matching piece of fusible fleece.

3 Set your sewing machine to a small stitch length of approx. 1.5 for stitching the toy and use a good-quality polyester thread for strong seams.

MAKING THE SEAL

Note: A 6mm (¼in) seam allowance is included in all pattern pieces unless advised otherwise. Read through all instructions before beginning to avoid surprises.

1 Take one of the body pieces and the head gusset piece and place together, right sides facing, matching up the star markings so that one side of the head gusset aligns with the head part of the seal's body from nose to neck. Pin or tack (baste) in place then, referring to **Fig. 1**, machine sew the head gusset into position ensuring that you start stitching right at the raw edge of the fabric and gradually turn into a 6mm (¼in) seam before tapering to the raw edge again at the end of your stitching.

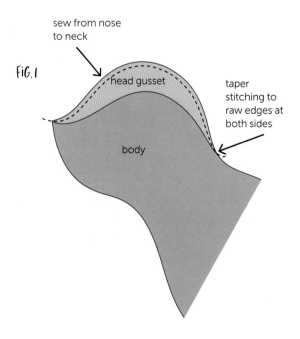

sew from nose to neck

FiG. 1

head gusset

taper stitching to raw edges at both sides

body

2 Take the remaining body piece and place this on top of the remaining raw edge of the head gusset piece, right sides together. Pin or tack (baste) the body piece along the head gusset, ensuring it is evenly matched up with the first body piece. When you reach the end of the head gusset, continue pinning or tacking (basting) the back of the main body pieces together until you reach the corner of the tail section. Check the fit, then machine sew together from nose to tail.

3 Place the two tail pieces right sides together and machine sew along the curved edges, leaving the straight edge open as indicated by the broken line on the template. Snip into the curved edges and inner angle, then turn right side out. Snip the bottom layer only along the snip line marked on the template.

4 Take the seal's body, open up at the tail end and lay this flat on your work surface, right side up. Take the tail and open out from the slit to lay the full straight edge right sides together with the tail section of the body. Tack (baste) in place and machine sew together (see **Fig. 2**).

5 Take the interfaced piece of main fabric and fold in half, right sides together. Trace the flipper template twice onto the wrong side of the folded panel, ensuring that there is at least 1.3cm (½in) between each tracing. Machine sew along the traced lines, leaving the straight edges open for turning as indicated by the broken line on the template. Cut out the flippers approx. 3mm (⅛in) outside of the sewn line and snip along the curved edges. Turn right side out, press well and then topstitch close to the sewn edges. Mark the definition lines onto your flipper from the template and topstitch these lines into place stitching over the markings.

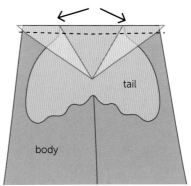

open out tail from slit and sew to opened up tail end of body

FIG. 2

tail

body

Snipping into curves and angles on your seam allowances will help to ensure a good shape is achieved when stuffing. Using the tip of your scissors, make small cuts and be very careful not to snip into your stitches.

6 Take one of the flippers and place it right sides together on top of one side of the seal's body, matching up the dot (see **Fig. 3**). Machine tack (baste) into place close to the edge. Repeat to join the second flipper to the other side of the body.

7 Take the tummy gusset piece and place one side of it along one side of the seal's body, matching up the square markings as your starting point. Ease and tack (baste) the pieces together making sure that you do not pull or stretch either piece; when you have finished there should be approx. 5.5cm (2¼in) of the body piece remaining before the tail. Machine sew the tummy gusset into place, ensuring that you start stitching right at the raw edge of the fabric, gradually turn into a 6mm (¼in) seam and then taper to the raw edge again at the end of your stitching (see step 1). When sewing the section after the flipper, do make sure that you do not catch the free sides of the flipper in your stitching.

8 Repeat step 7 to join the remaining side of the tummy gusset to the remaining side of the body, but this time also tack (baste) the section from the nose to the tummy gusset and from the tummy gusset to the end of the tail slit. Machine sew all the way from the nose to the end of the tail slit, leaving the gap (after tummy gusset) open for turning as indicated by the broken line on the body template.

9 Snip the corner at the nose and then turn the seal's body right side out. Stuff firmly with toy filling, ensuring that you firmly stuff the head before continuing on to stuff the remainder of the body. Before stitching the opening closed, check that your seal stands properly with the flippers giving some support. Add more toy filling as necessary to ensure the seal can sit up straight. Once you are happy, ladder stitch (see Stitching Techniques) the opening closed.

10 Take the black felt nose, peel off the backing paper and position it over the nose point on the seal's face. Fuse the nose in place, then blanket stitch (see Stitching Techniques) to fix using two strands of black embroidery thread (floss). Backstitch (see Stitching Techniques) a smile approx. 1.3cm (½in) below the nose.

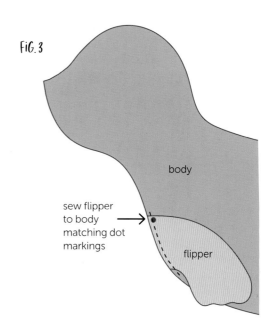

FiG. 3

body

sew flipper
to body
matching dot
markings

flipper

Handy Tip

If the seal's nose is not stuffed firmly enough, it may be necessary to use fabric glue to tack (baste) the black felt nose in place prior to stitching (see stitching techniques).

11 Using black thread, sew the button eyes into place referring to the photograph for positioning.

12 Thread the doll-maker's needle with a long length of four strands of matching embroidery thread (floss) and tie a knot approx. 2.5cm (1in) from the end. Decide where you want your whiskers to be, then take your needle through from one side of the nose to the other, pulling through until the knot catches. Now tie a knot right up against the fabric on this side and trim the thread approx. 2.5cm (1in) from the knot. Repeat this process twice more.

Handy Tip

If you are making this toy for a small child, substitute a small piece of black wool-felt for the buttons, or create the eyes with satin stitch.

MONKEY MISCHIEF

I could watch monkeys for hours, either on their own, or playing with the rest of their troop – they are fascinating. Cheeky and mischievous, yet so incredibly loving, they have inspired me to create a pair of monkeys just for you. They are made from bright cotton fabric and pure wool-felt for strength and washability. Make the sweet little bow as a hair accessory or fun bow-tie!

YOU WILL NEED

Note: Buttons should be omitted if making this toy for a very small child. Use 100% cotton patchwork fabric with a width of 106cm–114cm (42in–44in).

(FOR ONE MONKEY)

★ 25cm (10in) x full fabric width of main fabric (body, head top, arms, legs, inner ears, nose back)

★ 18cm x 38cm (7in x 15in) contrasting fabric (shorts, bow/bow tie)

★ 100% wool-felt: 25cm x 25cm (10in x 10in) in colour to match main fabric (nose front, outer ears, chest patch, eye patch)

★ 10cm x 15cm (4in x 6in) fusible web

★ Six-strand embroidery thread (floss): black

★ Two small black buttons for eyes, and matching thread

★ Good-quality polyester thread (if cotton thread is used, your seams could break during stuffing)

★ Good-quality polyester toy filling

FINISHED SIZE: 37cm (14½in) tall

CUTTING YOUR FABRICS

Note: *Trace the Monkey Mischief templates (see Templates) onto tracing paper or template plastic. Transfer all of the markings, and cut them out around the traced lines. When using these templates to trace the pattern pieces onto your fabric, ensure that the marked grain line on the template matches the fabric grain line (the direction of the fabric parallel with the selvedge).*

FROM YOUR MAIN FABRIC:

Fold the fabric in half with right sides together, then trace the body and head top templates once onto the wrong side of the folded fabric, transferring all markings. Cut out along the traced lines to give you two mirror-image pieces of each.

Opening out the remaining fabric to a single layer, trace the nose back once only and cut out along the traced line.

Also, from single layer fabric, cut one piece 7.5cm x 12.5cm (3in x 5in) for the ear fronts.

Refold the remaining fabric and trace the leg and arm templates twice each on the wrong side of the fabric. **Do not** cut out.

FROM YOUR CONTRASTING FABRIC:

For the bow/bow tie, cut two strips 5cm x 14cm (2in x 5½in) for the bow and one strip 4.5cm x 7.5cm (1¾in x 3in) for the cincher (middle bit).

Trace the shorts template twice onto the remaining fabric and cut out along the traced lines.

FROM THE WOOL-FELT:

Trace the nose front twice and cut out along the traced lines.

Cut one piece 7.5cm x 12.5cm (3in x 5in) for the ears backs.

PREPARING TO SEW

1 Trace the eye patch and the chest patch shapes onto the paper side of the fusible web and roughly cut out. Fuse to your remaining wool-felt and cut the shapes out along the traced lines.

2 Set your sewing machine to a small stitch length of approx. 1.5 for stitching the toy and use a good-quality polyester thread for strong seams.

MAKING THE MONKEY

Note: *A 6mm (¼in) seam allowance is included in all pattern pieces unless advised otherwise. Read through all instructions before beginning to avoid surprises.*

1 Take one head top and one body piece and fuse the eye patch and chest patch felt shapes onto these fabric pieces as marked on the templates. Using a matching thread colour, machine appliqué the eye patch and chest patch in place.

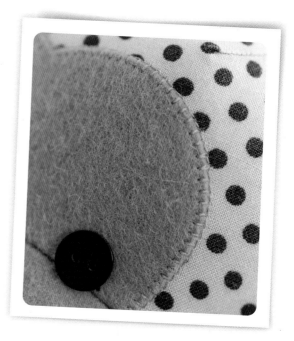

Handy Tip

I used a small blanket stitch to attach my pieces. If your machine doesn't have blanket stitch, use a machine zigzag stitch or hand blanket stitch your pieces into place (see stitching techniques).

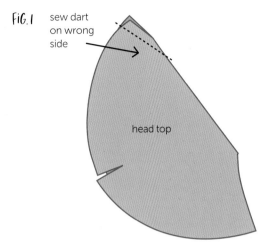

FIG. 1 sew dart on wrong side

head top

2 Sew the darts into place on the head top pieces. Fold each piece in half, right sides together, so that the raw dart edges are on top of each other and machine sew using a 6mm (¼in) seam (see **Fig. 1**).

3 Place the two felt nose front pieces on top of each other and pin, then sew along the curved edge only, tapering the stitching to and from the 6mm (¼in) seam allowance at either end (see **Fig. 2**). Turn through.

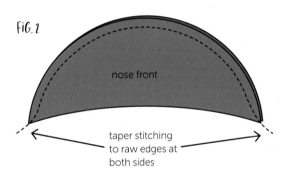

FIG. 2

nose front

taper stitching to raw edges at both sides

4 Take the joined nose front and the head top front (with eye patch) and place on top of each other, right sides together, ensuring that the head top front is centred within the raw edge of one side of the nose front. Machine sew together, carefully easing the curve of the nose into the curve of the head top as you go. Once complete, the head front should look like **Fig. 3** from the right side. Then, join the nose back and the head top back in the same way.

5 Take the completed head front and place the bottom (raw) edge of the nose front on the neckline of the body front (with chest patch), right sides together. Centre the body within the nose and then machine sew together, easing the curve of the body into the curve of the nose as you go. Join the completed head back to the body back in the same way.

6 Place the joined head/body front and joined head/body back together, right sides facing, and pin or tack (baste) evenly all the way around the edge, ensuring that all seams meet neatly. Machine sew from one side to the other, leaving the bottom edge of the body open as indicated by the broken line on the template.

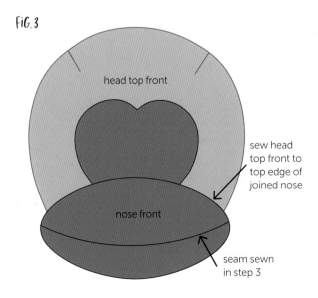

FIG. 3

head top front

nose front

sew head top front to top edge of joined nose

seam sewn in step 3

7 Remove the pins or tacking (basting) and turn the monkey right side out. Fold the bottom raw edge of the body in by approx. 6mm (¼in) and press in place.

8 Take the main fabric piece with the arms and legs traced onto it, and stitch the arms and legs together by machine sewing along the traced lines, leaving the straight ends unstitched as indicated by the broken line on the templates. Cut out each limb approx. 6mm (¼in) outside your sewn lines and then turn all pieces right side out.

Handy Tip

To turn a limb, open and rearrange the foot/hand end a little so that you can push a long, thin stick (chopstick or wooden skewer) against the sewn end, through the inside of the limb and out of the open end.

FiG. 4

topstitch legs in place between the folded in edges

9 Stuff the legs up to the indicated fill line (see template) and then machine sew across the fill line to secure. Tack (baste) the open ends together to hold them in place.

10 Insert the legs between the folded edges at the base of the monkey's body, ensuring that the big toes are facing inwards and positioning each leg against the body seams to leave a gap in between (see **Fig. 4**). Tack (baste) in place, then machine topstitch through all layers, leaving the stuffing gap between the legs open.

11 Now stuff the monkey's head and body firmly with toy filling, then ladder stitch the neat folded-in opening between the legs closed (see Stitching Techniques).

12 Stuff the arms firmly, leaving the top 2.5cm (1in) only lightly stuffed to ensure that the jointing of the monkey's arm is floppy and relaxed for a realistic finished look. Turn the raw edges in by approx. 6mm (¼in) and hand gather the folded edge. Working with two strands of strong polyester thread in your needle, take small running stitches all the way around the folded edges, then

pull up the threads and secure the gathers with a knot. Ladder stitch (see Stitching Techniques : Attaching Parts) the arms in place at the sides of the body, referring to the photo of the finished monkey as a guide to positioning (the thumbs should be facing inwards). I recommend that you go around the ladder stitching two or three times.

13 Using black thread, sew the button eyes into place on the monkey's face referring to the photograph for positioning. Use a pencil to mark on the monkey's mouth (see template) and nostrils, and stitch in place with four strands of black embroidery thread (floss) using backstitch for the mouth and French knots for the nostrils (see Stitching Techniques).

Handy Tip

If you are making this toy for a small child, substitute a small piece of black wool-felt for the buttons, or create the eyes with satin stitch (see stitching techniques).

14 Now make the ears. Take the main fabric and wool-felt squares each measuring 7.5cm x 12.5cm (3in x 5in) and place together, right sides facing. Trace the ear template onto the felt side, then machine sew along the traced lines, leaving the straight edges open. Cut out the ears approx. 3mm–6mm (⅛in–¼in) outside the sewn lines. Snip around the curved edges before turning the ears right side out, then press the raw edges in neatly.

15 Using a strong polyester thread and referring to the photo of the finished monkey as a guide to positioning, ladder stitch the ears onto the monkey's face working first along the front edge, then along the back edge for added strength (see Stitching Techniques : Attaching Parts).

MAKING THE CLOTHES

Note: *A 6mm (¼in) seam allowance is included in all pattern pieces unless advised otherwise. Read through all instructions before beginning to avoid surprises.*

1 Place the contrasting fabric shorts pieces together, right sides facing, and machine sew along both the crotch lines (as shown in **Fig. 5**).

2 Open out the shorts and re-align them so that the front and back crotch seams you have just sewn are sitting on top of each other, right sides together. Now machine sew the shorts along the inner legs (**Fig. 6**).

3 Snip along all seams before turning the shorts right side out; press. To hem the legs of the shorts, fold under the edges by approx. 6mm (¼in) and press; fold under again by another 6mm (¼in) and press once more; topstitch the double-fold hems into place. Now hem the waist: fold the edge under by 6mm (¼in), press, then topstitch in place.

4 Fit the shorts onto your monkey. If they are a little too loose, it just means that you have stuffed your monkey a little less than I did mine. Simply take a few ladder stitches in the shorts and the body side seams to secure the shorts in place (see Stitching Techniques).

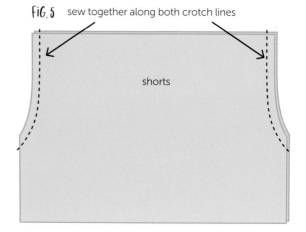

FIG. 5 sew together along both crotch lines

shorts

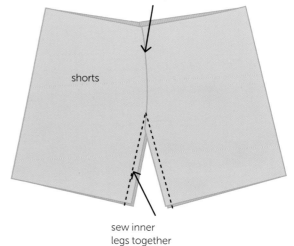

FIG. 6 crotch lines sit on top of each other

shorts

sew inner legs together

Handy Tip

If your monkey's shorts are still too loose, you can hand gather the top edge a little before securing in place.

FiG. 7

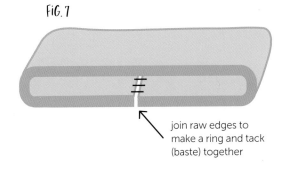

join raw edges to
make a ring and tack
(baste) together

5 Now to make the hair bow or bow tie. Take the two pieces of contrasting fabric measuring 5cm x 14cm (2in x 5½in), place together, with right sides facing, and machine sew each long edge. Turn to the right side and press well. Join the raw edges of the strip together to make a ring and hand tack (baste) to secure. Press the ring flat so that the join is at the centre bottom (as shown in **Fig. 7**). This is your bow piece.

6 Take the remaining piece of contrasting fabric for the cincher and fold this in half, right sides facing out, to create a folded strip measuring 7.5cm x 2.25cm (3in x ⅞in); press. Turn the raw edges in to the fold and press again. Topstitch along the long edges of the strip. Use the completed cincher strip to wrap around and gather the centre of your bow piece, covering the join at the back of your bow in the process. Sew the ends of the cincher strip together with small hand stitches to the desired tightness and trim away any excess.

7 Attach the bow to your monkey's head or neck by ladder stitching along the top and bottom of the cincher (see Stitching Techniques: Attaching Parts), to hide the seam against the toy.

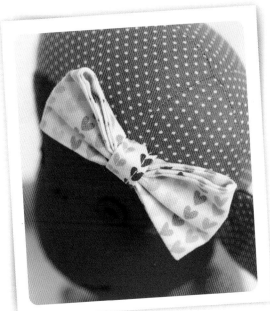

ARCHIE THE ALIEN

Ready to meet your very first alien? Don't be nervous – this little green extraterrestrial being truly does come in peace. Topped off with an antenna transmitter used to contact his friends back home in a galaxy far, far away, he has huge round eyes to take in the wonders of our world. Having travelled all across the universe, Archie the Alien has decided that Earth is his favourite holiday destination!

CUTTING YOUR FABRICS

Note: Trace the Archie the Alien templates (see Templates) onto tracing paper or template plastic, transferring all of the markings, and cut them out along the traced lines. When using these templates to trace the pattern pieces onto your fabric, do ensure that the marked grain line on the template matches the fabric grain line (the direction of the fabric parallel with the selvedge).

FROM YOUR GREEN SPOT-PRINT FABRIC:

Cut one strip 16.5cm x 30.5cm (6½in x 12in).

Cut one strip 7.5cm x 30.5cm (3in x 12in).

Fold the remaining fabric in half with right sides together; trace the arm template twice onto the folded fabric, but **do not** cut out (these will be sewn on the traced line).

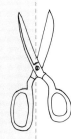

PREPARING TO SEW

1 Trace the eye circle twice onto the paper side of the fusible web and roughly cut out; fuse the eyes to the white wool-felt and cut out along the traced lines.

2 Set your sewing machine to a small stitch length of approx. 1.5 for stitching the toy and use a good-quality polyester thread for strong seams.

MAKING THE ALIEN

Note: A 6mm (¼in) seam allowance is included in all pattern pieces unless advised otherwise. Read through all instructions before beginning to avoid surprises.

1 Take the strip of green spot-print fabric measuring 16.5cm x 30.5cm (6½in x 12in) and your red star-print fabric strip. Place fabrics together with right sides together, aligning along one long edge and stitch to create a panel (see **Fig. 1**). Press seam open.

2 Fold your fabric panel in half widthways with right sides together so that the short edges meet and fabric seams meet evenly. Place the head template onto the folded fabric panel making sure that the marked antenna line matches up with the fabric seam. Trace around the template and cut the head out along the traced line to give you two head pieces.

3 Take your second strip of green spot-print fabric and join it to the blue space-print fabric to make a second fabric panel (see **Fig. 2**). Press seam open.

4 Take this fabric panel and fold in half widthways, so that the short edges meet and right sides are together, and making sure that the fabrics and seam line are perfectly aligned. Place the body template onto the folded fabric panel making sure that the leg line matches up with the seam in the fabric. Trace around the template and then cut the body out along the traced line to give you two body pieces.

5 Take the remaining piece of folded green spot-print fabric that has the arms traced onto it and, keeping the fabric folded, sew along the traced lines of the arms, leaving the straight ends unstitched as indicated by the broken line on the template. Cut out each arm approx. 3–6mm (⅛– ¼in) outside your sewn lines, lightly snip the seam between the fingers. To turn the arms effortlessly, insert a pair of tweezers into the arm and pinch the sewn end, hold tight and pull through to the right side.

6 Firmly stuff the arms to the very ends with toy filling, leaving the last 2cm (¾in) unstuffed. Tack (baste) the open ends closed.

7 Take one of the body pieces and place it right side up on your work surface. Place the arms on top of the body aligning the raw edge of the arms with the raw edge of the neckline and positioning the arms approx. 1.3cm (½in) in from the sides. Machine tack (baste) in position close to the raw edge (see **Fig. 3**).

8 Take one head piece and the body piece with arms and place on top of each other with right sides together so that they are aligned at the neckline. Pin in place, and then sew along the neckline. This is the joined front piece.

9 Take your remaining body and head pieces and place on top of each other with right sides together so that they are aligned at the neckline. Pin in place, and then sew along the neckline, leaving the middle section open for turning and stuffing as indicated by the broken line on the body template. This is the joined back piece.

10 Take your joined front and your joined back piece and place on top of each other, right sides together, and pin in place all the way around the outside edge making sure that the neckline seams meet evenly. Sew the body pieces together all the way around the pinned edge.

11 Turn the body right-side out through the neckline gap. Stuff firmly with toy filling. Ladder stitch the opening closed (see Stitching Techniques), stuffing in a little more as you go to avoid a dimple.

12 Take the white eye circles and fuse them in place on the face. Using two strands of white embroidery thread (floss), blanket stitch the eyes in place, sinking the knots to start and finish (see Stitching Techniques).

13 Mark the mouth onto the face (see template for position) and backstitch over the marked line using two strands of black embroidery thread (floss). Finally, sew on the two small black button eyes. If you are making this toy for a small child, substitute a small piece of black wool-felt for the buttons, or create the eyes with satin stitch (see Stitching Techniques).

FiG. 1

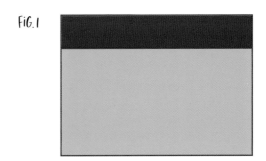

FiG. 2

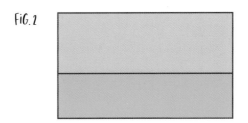

FiG. 3

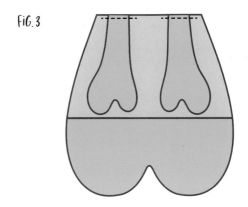

OTiS THE FUN UFO

Look who's just landed – it's Otis, our very friendly flying saucer. This is his first mission to Earth, where he is hoping to bump into Archie the Alien to find out all about his adventures on his voyage of intergalactic discovery. With bright flashing lights on his colourful saucer and a very winning smile, Otis brightens up the night sky, so you can't fail to spot him as he flies by.

YOU WILL NEED

Note: Use 100% cotton patchwork fabric.

★ 25cm x 20cm (10in x 8in) green spot-print fabric (dome)

★ 20cm x 20cm (8in x 8in) each of four contrasting print fabrics (saucer sides and base)

★ 20cm (8in) x full width lightweight fusible fleece

★ 100% wool-felt: lime 7.5cm x 15cm (3in x 6in) for saucer lights

★ 100% wool-felt: white 5cm x 10cm (2in x 4in) and black 2.5cm x 2.5cm (1in x 1in) for eyes

★ 60cm (24in) medium-lime cotton ric-rac

★ 15cm x 15cm (6in x 6in) fusible web

★ Six-strand embroidery thread (floss): black, white

★ Good-quality polyester thread (if cotton thread is used, your seams could break during stuffing)

★ Good-quality toy filling

FINISHED SIZE: 15cm (6in) tall

CUTTING YOUR FABRICS

Note: *Trace the Otis the Fun UFO templates (see Templates) onto tracing paper or template plastic, transferring all of the markings, and cut them out along the traced lines. When using these templates to trace the pattern pieces onto your fabric, do ensure that the marked grain line on the template matches the fabric grain line (the direction of the fabric parallel with the selvedge).*

FROM YOUR GREEN SPOT-PRINT FABRIC:

Trace the dome template twice onto folded fabric and cut out along the traced lines to give you four dome pieces.

FROM YOUR FOUR CONTRASTING PRINT FABRICS:

Interface each piece with fusible fleece.

Trace the base template once and the saucer template twice onto the fleece side of each of your contrasting print fabric pieces and cut out along the traced lines.

PREPARING TO SEW

1 Working on the paper side of the fusible web, trace the light circle eight times, the larger eye circle twice, and the smaller pupil circle twice, and roughly cut out all the circles. Putting the larger eye circles aside for now, fuse the light circles to the lime wool-felt and the pupils to the black wool-felt, and cut out along the traced lines.

2 Set your sewing machine to a small stitch length of approx. 1.5 for stitching the toy and use a good-quality polyester thread for strong seams.

MAKING THE UFO

Note: *A 6mm (¼in) seam allowance is included in all pattern pieces unless advised otherwise. Read through all instructions before beginning to avoid surprises.*

1 Take the eight fleece-backed saucer pieces and fuse a green light circle in the centre of each (see saucer template). Machine appliqué each circle in place by topstitching close to the edge.

2 Take two contrasting saucer pieces and place on top of each other with right sides together. Sew sew along one side edge to create your first quarter section (see **Fig. 1**). Press the seams open.

3 Repeat step 2 with the remaining saucer pieces to complete the quarter sections that make up the sides of the saucer (see **Fig. 2**).

4 Take one of the quarter side sections and one of the green spot-print dome pieces and place on top of each other with right sides together so that the bottom edge of the dome piece aligns with the top edge of the quarter side section. Pin along the edge so that the dome piece is neatly centred on the quarter side section, and then sew along this seam (see **Fig. 3**). Repeat to join the remaining three-quarter side sections to the remaining three dome pieces. You now have four joined dome/side sections.

FiG. 1

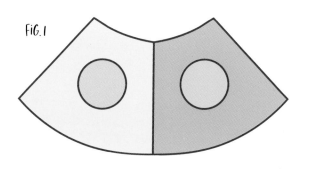

Handy tip

Snipping into the seams of the interfaced fabric, especially at the dome/saucer junctions, will allow more flexibility for turning and ensures a better shape.

FiG. 2

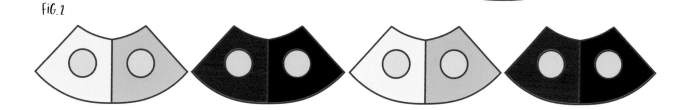

5 Take two of your dome/side sections, making sure they are different colours, and place on top of each other with right sides together. Sew the two sections together along one side edge from the top point of the dome to the bottom corner of the side section. Snip into the seam. Repeat to join the remaining two dome/side sections so that the side colours run in the same order.

6 Take the two halves of your flying saucer (dome/sides) and place on top of each other with right sides together. Sew the two halves together at each side to complete the flying saucer top, remembering to snip into the seams.

7 Now to make the flying saucer base. Being mindful of the final colour placement, take two of the fleece-backed base pieces, and place on top of each other with right sides together. Sew together along one straight edge only and press seams open to give you a half circle. Repeat with the remaining two base pieces to give you a second half circle.

8 Take the two half circles and place on top of each other with right sides together. Sew together along the straight edge leaving a 7cm (2¾in) gap in the middle for turning. Press seams open.

FiG. 3

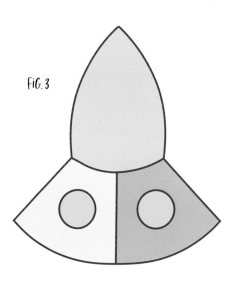

9 Take your length of ric-rac and referring to **Fig. 4**, position this neatly around the outer edge of your base circle, right sides together. Machine tack (baste) into place, curving the raw ends of the ric-rac to the outside of your circle where they meet.

10 Take the flying saucer top and base and place them on top of each other with right sides together. Matching up the seams at the quarter points, pin and then sew together all the way around the outer edges of the circle. Trim all the layers of this seam allowance to approx. 3mm (⅛in) to allow more flexibility, and then turn the flying saucer to the right side through the gap in the base.

11 Stuff the UFO very firmly with toy filling: stuff the dome section well first before continuing to stuff the saucer, making sure to fill out all of the curves and edges neatly – using the paintbrush tool will help (see Stuffing Techniques). Once fully stuffed, ladder stitch the opening closed (see Stitching Techniques), stuffing in a little more as you go to avoid a dimple.

FIG. 4

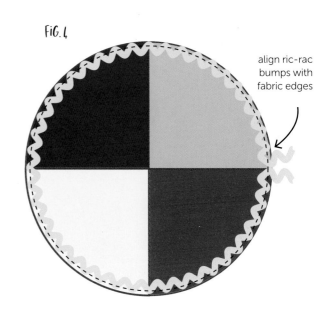

align ric-rac bumps with fabric edges

12 Now to make the eyes. Fuse the small circles of black wool-felt (pupils) onto your piece of white wool-felt, ensuring there is enough room between to allow you to cut out the eye shapes. Machine appliqué the pupils in place by topstitching close to the edge.

13 Take your pieces of set-aside fusible web with the eye circles traced on and fuse them to the reverse of your white felt, using the stitching line of the pupils as a guide to positioning.

14 Cut the eyes out along the traced lines. Fuse the eyes in place on the dome referring to the photograph. Using two strands of white embroidery thread (floss), blanket stitch the eyes in place, sinking the knots to start and finish (see Stitching Techniques).

15 Mark the position of the mouth onto the toy and chain stitch along the marked line using two strands of black embroidery thread (floss) (see Stitching Techniques).

MiLi AND MiLO

Meet Mili and Milo, a pair of monster twins who are always ready to play. They love to hide under the bed or behind open wardrobe doors, ready to jump out at you. When they do, they are sure to bring a squeal of laughter rather than a yelp of alarm, as they are all about fun. With their big eyes and cuddle-ready arms, this adorable duo will capture your heart.

(FOR EACH MONSTER)

Note: Use 100% cotton patchwork fabric.

- ★ 25cm x 46cm (10in x 18in) patterned fabric (body)
- ★ 15cm x 15cm (6in x 6in) spot-print fabric (arms)
- ★ 20cm (8in) matching jumbo ric-rac
- ★ 100% wool-felt: colour to match 10cm x 12.5cm (4in x 5in) for face
- ★ 100% wool-felt: black 10cm x 10cm (4in x 4in) for eyes
- ★ 100% wool-felt: white 7.5cm x 7.5cm (3in x 3in) for face details
- ★ 100% wool-felt: pink 5cm x 5cm (2in x 2in) for Mili's cheeks
- ★ 12.5cm x 20cm (5in x 8in) fusible web
- ★ Six-strand embroidery thread (floss): black
- ★ Good-quality polyester thread (if cotton thread is used, your seams could break during stuffing)
- ★ Good-quality toy filling

FINISHED SIZE: 19cm (7½in) tall

CUTTING YOUR FABRICS

Note: Trace the Mili and Milo templates (see Templates) onto tracing paper or template plastic. Transfer all of the markings, and cut them out around the traced lines.

FROM YOUR SPOT-PRINT FABRIC:

Fold the fabric in half with right sides together. Trace the arm template twice onto the folded fabric but **do not** cut out.

FROM YOUR FUSIBLE WEB AND FELT:

Trace the face, eyes and face details for your chosen monster onto the paper side of the fusible web and roughly cut out. Fuse the cut out shapes to your relevant wool-felt pieces, and then cut out along the traced lines.

PREPARING TO SEW

1 Set your sewing machine to a small stitch length of approx. 1.5 for stitching the toy and use a good-quality polyester thread for strong seams.

MAKING THE MONSTER

Note: A 6mm (¼in) seam allowance is included in all pattern pieces unless advised otherwise. Read through all instructions before beginning to avoid surprises.

1 Take your piece of patterned (body) fabric and fold in half widthways with right sides together (now measures 25cm x 23cm/10in x 9in). Press to create a crease at the halfway mark. Unfold and lay it on your work surface with right side facing up. Fuse the felt face shape in the centre of the right-hand side (see **Fig. 1**). Machine appliqué the face in place with straight stitch very close to the edge.

Handy tip

Change your sewing thread to black when stitching the black eye circles in place for a neater look.

FIG. 1

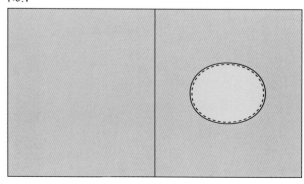

2 Take your remaining felt face shapes and refer to the templates and the detail photographs of each monster's face for where to position and the order in which to place, fuse and sew in place.

3 Referring to the templates, mark any stitching lines (mouth, eyelashes, eyebrows, cheek spots) onto your chosen monster's face. Stitch along the marked lines using four strands of black embroidery thread (floss) and backstitch, with the exception of Milo's cheeks, which are worked with running stitch (see Stitching Techniques).

4 Refold the fabric panel with right sides together, so that the side with the back of the face appliqué stitching is facing you. Take the body template and place it on the fabric so that the marked face shape lines up with the face appliqué stitching. Trace around the template making sure to mark both the turning gap and the ric-rac gap (the broken lines on the template). ***Do not*** cut out.

Handy tip

When fusing the monsters' facial details work from the bottom layers up, using the detail photographs of Mili and Milo as your guide.

Handy tip

The turning gap and the ric-rac gap can be flipped from one side to the other depending on your preference.

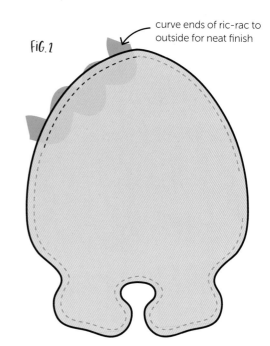

FiG. 2

curve ends of ric-rac to outside for neat finish

5 Sew the body together on the traced line, leaving the marked turning and ric-rac gaps open. Cut out the body approx. 6mm (¼in) outside your sewn and traced lines.

6 Take your length of jumbo ric-rac and position it neatly at the ric-rac gap along one side of the head. You want to fit three bumps of the ric-rac into the gap, curving the raw ends to the outside of your body shape (see **Fig. 2**). Sew the ric-rac in place by stitching the gap closed along the traced line. Trim any excess ric-rac.

7 Before turning your monster right side out, snip into the angled seam allowance between its legs. Turn the body through the turning gap in the side, and then stuff very firmly with toy filling. Ladder stitch the opening closed (see Stitching Techniques) adding a little more stuffing as you go to avoid a dimple.

8 Take your folded piece of spot-print fabric with the arms traced onto it and, keeping the fabric folded, sew along the traced lines of the arms, leaving the straight ends unstitched as indicated by the broken line on the template. Cut out each arm approx. 3–6mm (⅛– ¼in) outside your sewn lines, lightly snip the seam between the fingers, and turn the arms right side out.

9 Fold the raw ends of the turning gaps in on each arm by approx. 6mm (¼in) and finger press in place. Stuff the arms firmly right to the folded ends.

10 Position an arm onto one side of your monster, referring to the photo as a guide to positioning. Hold the arm in place by pinning through the arm and into the body, much like a pin cushion. Using strong polyester thread, ladder stitch the arm in place (see Stitching Techniques: Attaching Parts): work the ladder stitch in a circle and go around at least twice to ensure a firm attachment. Repeat to sew on the second arm.

Handy tip

To add a finishing touch to Mili, why not ladder stitch a small flower embellishment to her head? Small felt or crochet flowers can be bought, or you could make your own.

MIA THE MERMAID

Meet Mia the Mermaid, but you'll have to be quick as she will soon be off with a swish of her tail, seeking another adventure in her underwater world. Her favourite pastime is to scour the ocean floor, seeking the very brightest of starfish to decorate her hair. She is particularly proud of her latest find as it is the perfect shade of purple to match her lovely hair bunches.

YOU WILL NEED

Note: Use 100% cotton patchwork fabric.

★ 25cm x 30.5cm (10in x 12in) plain (skin-coloured) fabric (head front, body, arms)

★ 28cm x 28cm (11in x 11in) green print fabric (tail, flippers)

★ 100% wool-felt: aqua 30cm x 15cm (12in x 6in) for head back, hair

★ 100% wool-felt: purple 5cm x 12.5cm (2in x 5in) for stars

★ 7.5cm x 28cm (3in x 11in) lightweight fusible fleece

★ 15cm x 20cm (6in x 8in) fusible web

★ Six-strand embroidery thread (floss): black, red

★ 120cm (47in) purple mini ric-rac for hair bunches

★ 50cm (20in) narrow ribbon in colour to match

★ Pink pencil

★ Good-quality polyester thread (if cotton thread is used, your seams could break during stuffing)

★ Good-quality toy filling

FINISHED SIZE: 28cm (11in) tall

CUTTING YOUR FABRICS

Note: *Trace the Mia theMermaid templates (see Templates) onto tracing paper or template plastic, transferring all the markings, and cut them out along the traced lines. When using these templates to trace the pattern pieces onto your fabric, do ensure that the marked grain line on the template matches the fabric grain line (the direction of the fabric parallel with the selvedge).*

FROM YOUR PLAIN (SKIN-COLOURED) FABRIC:

Cut one piece 10cm x 20cm (4in x 8in) for the arms.

Trace the head template once and the body template twice onto the remaining fabric and cut out along the traced lines.

FROM YOUR GREEN PRINT FABRIC:

Cut one piece 7.5cm x 28cm (3in x 11in) for the flippers.

Fold the remaining fabric in half with right sides together. Trace the tail template once onto the folded fabric and cut out along the traced line to give you two tail pieces.

FROM YOUR AQUA WOOL-FELT:

Trace the head template once onto one half of your felt and cut out along the traced line: this is the head back.

PREPARING TO SEW

1 Interface the green print flippers fabric strip with the fusible fleece.

2 Trace the hair template once and the star template three times onto the paper side of the fusible web and roughly cut out. Fuse the hair shape to your remaining aqua wool-felt and the three stars to the purple wool-felt, and cut out all the pieces along the traced lines.

3 Set your sewing machine to a small stitch length of approx. 1.5 for stitching the toy and use a good-quality polyester thread for strong seams.

MAKING THE MERMAID

Note: *A 6mm (¼in) seam allowance is included in all pattern pieces unless advised otherwise. Read through all instructions before beginning to avoid surprises.*

1 Take the plain (skin-coloured) fabric head piece and the aqua felt hair piece. Fuse the hair piece onto the right side of the head piece, making sure the pieces are neatly and evenly aligned. Referring to the photo, machine appliqué the hair piece into place along the face edge only using straight stitch worked very close to the edge of the felt.

2 Take one of the purple felt stars and fuse it onto the hair in your desired position. Machine appliqué into place.

3 Trace the eye and mouth markings onto Mia's face. Using two strands of black embroidery thread (floss), stitch the eyes with satin stitch then backstitch the eyelashes (see Stitching Techniques). Using two strands of red embroidery thread (floss), backstitch the mouth.

4 Take one of the plain (skin-coloured) fabric body pieces and the two remaining purple felt stars. Fuse the stars onto the body piece, positioning them 6mm (¼in) apart and 1.3cm (½in) down from the neckline, and machine appliqué into place (see **Fig. 1**). This is the body front.

5 Take your folded piece of plain (skin-coloured) fabric with the arms traced onto it and, keeping the fabric folded, sew along the traced lines of the arms, leaving the straight ends unstitched as indicated by the broken line on the template. Cut out each arm approx. 3–6mm (⅛–¼in) outside your sewn lines, and then turn right side out. Firmly stuff the arms with toy filling, leaving the last 2cm (¾in) unstuffed. Tack (baste) the open ends closed.

6 Take the body front (with stars) and place it right side up on your work surface. Place the arms on top of the body aligning the raw edge of the arms with the raw edge of the neckline and positioning the arms approx. 1.3cm (½in) in from the sides. Machine tack (baste) in position close to the raw edge (see **Fig. 2**).

FiG. 1

FiG. 2

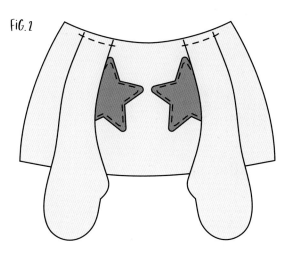

7 Take the head front and the body front and place these on top of each other with right sides together, making sure that they are aligned so that the centre of the body front neckline meets the centre of the bottom of the head; pin in place. Sew together along the neckline.

8 Take the joined front body/head piece and one of the green print tail pieces and place on top of each other, right sides together, so they are centrally aligned at the waistline; pin in place and sew together.

9 Take the remaining plain (skin-coloured) fabric body piece and the aqua felt head piece, and place them on top of each other with right sides together, aligning them at the neckline. Pin in place and then sew together along the neckline, leaving the middle section open for turning and stuffing as indicated by the broken line on the body template. This is the joined back body/head.

10 Take the remaining tail piece and joined back body/ head and place them on top of each other with right sides together, so that they are aligned at the waistline. Pin in place, then sew together.

11 To make Mia's hair bunches, start by taking your length of ric-rac and cut it into 12 pieces measuring approx. 10cm (4in) each. Take six of the ric-rac pieces and fold in half; secure the raw ends together tightly with a small piece of tape to make a hair bunch (see **Fig. 3**). Make a second bunch with the remaining six lengths of ric-rac.

12 Place Mia front right side up on your work surface. Position the ric-rac hair bunches on top, so that the taped ends of the bunches sit beyond the sides of the head front with the bunches pointing inwards towards the face (see **Fig. 4** for positioning). Machine tack (baste) into place.

FiG. 3   sticky tape

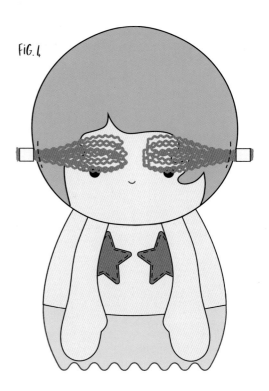

FiG. 4

13 Place the mermaid front and the mermaid back on top of each other with right sides together and pin in place. Sew all the way around the body, leaving the flipper gaps at the bottom of the tail unstitched as indicated by the broken lines on the tail template. **Do not** turn the body through just yet as the flippers must be added first.

14 Take the fleece-backed green print fabric strip and fold in half, right sides together. Trace the flipper template twice onto one side of the folded strip, flipping the template for the second tracing. Sew along the traced lines, leaving the straight ends unstitched as indicated by the broken line on the template. Cut out approx. 3mm (⅛in) outside the sewn lines, turn right side out and press.

15 Take the mermaid body and insert one of the flippers, raw edges first, through the turning gap on the back of the neckline, guiding the raw edge into one of the flipper gaps along the bottom edge of the tail. Making sure that the raw edge of the flipper aligns with the raw edge of the gap, and following the traced line of the body, sew the flipper in place. (Note: the flipper is inside the body.) Repeat for the second flipper in the remaining gap.

16 Turn the mermaid right side out through the gap in the neckline, and then stuff firmly with toy filling. Ladder stitch the opening closed (see Stitching Techniques), stuffing in a little more as you go to avoid a dimple.

17 Using the pink pencil, draw and colour in the cheek circles on Mia's face. Take your narrow ribbon and cut in half, and use each length to tie a bow around the base of Mia's bunches.

Handy Tip

For a more permanent fixing, secure the bow knots with a spot of fabric glue.

RUFUS THE ROBOT

Rufus the Robot is ready for action at the flick of a switch – he is programmed to be a child's best friend, helping with chores like cleaning up a messy bedroom or rustling up a midnight snack. If only that were so, who wouldn't want a Rufus of their own! When switched off, he will spend his time sitting on a bedroom shelf, legs dangling, patiently awaiting activation.

YOU WILL NEED

Note: Buttons should be omitted if making this toy for a very small child. Use 100% cotton patchwork fabric.

- ★ 12.5cm x 81cm (5in x 32in) cream patterned fabric (head)
- ★ 12.5cm x 63.5cm (5in x 25in) blue space-print fabric (body)
- ★ 15cm x 66cm (6in x 26in) red star-print fabric (headlights, hands, feet)
- ★ 36cm (14in) lightweight fusible fleece
- ★ 25cm (10in) of 2cm- (¾in-) wide twill tape (arms, legs)
- ★ Six-strand embroidery thread (floss): black
- ★ Two medium black buttons for eyes
- ★ Two medium red buttons for front of body
- ★ Good-quality polyester thread (if cotton thread is used, your seams could break during stuffing)
- ★ Good-quality toy filling

FINISHED SIZE: 25cm (10in) tall

CUTTING YOUR FABRICS

Note: Trace the Rufus the Robot templates (see Templates) onto tracing paper or template plastic, transferring all of the markings; cut them out along the traced lines.

FROM YOUR CREAM PATTERNED FABRIC:

First interface the fabric piece with fusible fleece, then cut the following pieces from the interfaced fabric:

Cut two pieces 11cm x 15cm (4¼in x 6in).

Cut two pieces 7.5cm x 15cm (3in x 6in).

Cut two pieces 11cm x 7.5cm (4¼in x 3in).

FROM YOUR BLUE SPACE-PRINT FABRIC:

First interface the fabric piece with fusible fleece, then cut the following pieces from the interfaced fabric.

Cut two pieces 11cm x 11.5cm (4¼in x 4½in).

Cut two pieces 7.5cm x 11.5cm (3in x 4½in).

Cut two pieces 11cm x 7.5cm (4¼in x 3in).

FROM YOUR RED STAR-PRINT FABRIC:

Trace the headlights template twice onto the fabric and cut out along the traced line.

Cut one piece 7.5cm x 15cm (3in x 6in) for the hands.

Interface the remaining fabric with the fusible fleece, then cut the following pieces from the interfaced fabric.

Cut one piece 7.5cm x 15cm (3in x 6in) for the hands.

Cut twelve squares 4.5cm x 4.5cm (1¾in x 1¾in) for the feet.

PREPARING TO SEW

1 Take the fleece-backed red star-print fabric measuring 7.5cm x 15cm (3in x 6in) and trace the hand template twice onto the wrong (fleece-backed) side, allowing at least 1cm (⅜in) between each tracing.

2 Cut the twill tape into four lengths each measuring 5cm–5.5cm (2in–2¼in).

3 Set your sewing machine to a small stitch length of approx. 1.5 for stitching the toy and use a good-quality polyester thread for strong seams.

MAKING THE ROBOT

Note: A 6mm (¼in) seam allowance is included in all pattern pieces unless advised otherwise. Read through all instructions before beginning to avoid surprises.

1 To make the robot's face, take one of the cream patterned fabric pieces measuring 11cm x 15cm (4¼in x 6in) and working about 3.25cm (1¼in) up from the bottom edge, mark the mouth (see template) centring it on the fabric width. Using all six strands of black embroidery thread (floss), backstitch along the marked line. Sew on a black button eye to either side of the mouth (see **Fig. 1**). If you are making this toy for a small child, substitute a small piece of black wool-felt for the buttons. Alternatively, create the eyes with satin stitch (see Stitching Techniques).

2 Take one cream patterned fabric piece measuring 11cm x 7.5cm (4¼in x 3in) and another piece measuring 7.5cm x 15cm (3in x 6in), place one on top of the other with right sides together aligning along the short edges. Sew together starting and ending your stitches 6mm (¼in) from each corner (see **Fig. 2a**), and continue in the same way to join another 11cm x 7.5cm (4¼in x 3in) piece and the final 7.5cm x 15cm (3 x 6in) piece to create a panel as in **Fig. 2b**.

3 Sew together the short ends of this panel to create a ring, starting and ending your stitching 6mm (¼in) from each corner. This is the head gusset ring.

FiG. 1

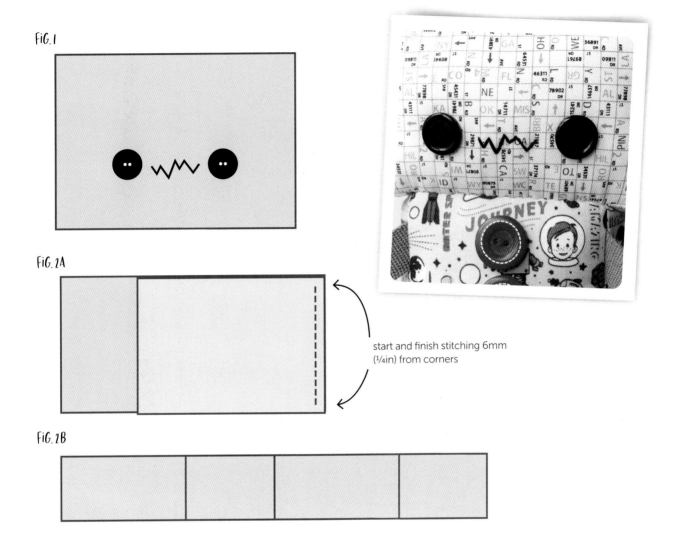

FiG. 2A

start and finish stitching 6mm
(¼in) from corners

FiG. 2B

4 Taking your head gusset ring and the face piece,
match up one of the longer edges of the head gusset
ring with the top edge of the face, right sides together.
Sew together, starting and ending 6mm (¼in) from the
corners (these start and end points should correlate with
the stitching start points on the gusset seams to create a
corner). Now match up the other long edge of the head
gusset ring with the bottom edge of the face, again right
sides together, and sew together as before. Now continue
to sew the shorter edges of the head gusset ring to the
side edges of the face in the same way.

5 Now join the final 11cm x 15cm (4¼in x 6in) piece of
the cream patterned fabric to the head gusset ring to
complete the back of the robot's head. Join the back of
the head to the head gusset ring as described in step 4,
always starting and ending your stitching 6mm (¼in) from
the corners. **Do not** leave a turning gap.

6 To turn the completed head through to the right side, make a slit in the centre of the base gusset panel approx. 5cm (2in) long. This slit will be hidden against the robot's body when the head is sewn in place. Turn the head through the slit and stuff it with toy filling. Whip stitch the gap closed (remember this will be hidden so there is no need to be super neat). Put the head aside for now.

Handy Tip

One of the easiest way to create a slit with added control is to use a seam ripper (quick unpick).

7 To make one of the robot's legs, take six of the red star-print squares and one of your lengths of twill tape. Place two squares on top of each other with right sides together and lay the twill tape in between so that the raw edge of the tape is centred and aligned with one of the edges of the fabric squares as shown in **Fig. 3**. Sew the layers together along this edge, starting and ending your stitching 6mm (¼in) from the corners (see **Fig. 3**).

8 Join two more red star-print squares to make a panel of four joined squares, then join the short ends into a ring, as you did for the head gusset ring. Always remember to start and end your stitching 6mm (¼in) from each corner and take care not to catch the twill tape as you sew.

9 Sew the remaining two red star-print squares to each side of the ring to create a cube (in the same way as you did when making the head), but this time when sewing one of the edges, leave a 2cm (¾in) turning gap in the centre of the stitching line. Turn the foot right side out.

10 Repeat steps 7–9 to make a second leg for your robot. (Note: the feet will be stuffed later in the making process.)

FiG. 3

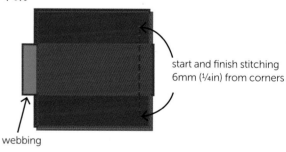

start and finish stitching 6mm (¼in) from corners

webbing

Handy Tip

Strapping or webbing can be used in place of twill tape, just as long as it's tough enough to endure play!

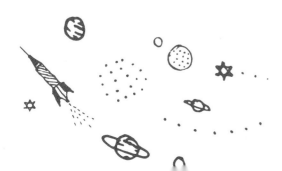

11 To make the robot's arms, start by taking the two pieces of red star-print fabric measuring 7.5cm x 15cm (3in x 6in) and place them on top of each other with right sides together. Working fleece-side up, sew along the traced lines of the hands, leaving the straight ends unstitched as indicated by the broken line on the tem plate. Cut out each hand approx. 3mm (⅛in) outside your sewn lines, and then turn the hands right side out. Fold the raw edges in by approx. 6mm (¼in) and press folds in place.

12 Lightly stuff the hands with toy filling. Take the remaining twill tape pieces and insert one end of each into the open ends of the hand, pushing them in by approx. 6mm (¼in). Topstitch along the folded in edges to catch the twill tape lengths in place to complete the arms.

13 Take one of your blue space-print fabric pieces measuring 11cm x 11.5cm (4¼in x 4½in) and sew on two red buttons in the centre approx 1.5cm (⅝in) down from the top edge (see **Fig. 4**) If you are making this toy for a small child, substitute two small pieces of red wool-felt for the buttons, or create the buttons with satin stitch, and add two black French knots as button holes (see Stitching Techniques). This is the front of the robot's body.

14 Now place your arms and legs in position onto the body front as in **Fig. 5**, so that the arms are approx. 2cm (¾in) down from the top corners and placed at an angle and the legs are approx. 2.5cm (1in) apart from the centre of the bottom edge. Machine tack (baste) the limbs in place close to the edge.

FiG. 4

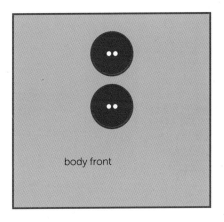

body front

FiG. 5

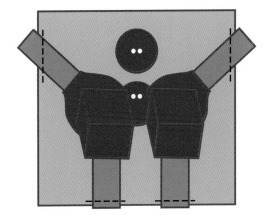

15 Take the blue space-print fabric pieces measuring 7.5cm x 11.5cm (3in x 4½in) and 11cm x 7.5cm (4¼in x 3in) and sew together alternately along the 7.5cm (3in) edges to create a panel, then join the short ends of the panel to make the body gusset ring, in the same way as you did to make the head gusset ring (see steps 2 and 3), starting and ending your stitches 6mm (¼in) from each corner.

16 Take your body gusset ring and the body front. Match up one of the longer edges of the body gusset ring to the top edge of the body front, right sides together. Sew together, starting and ending 6mm (¼in) from the corners (these start and end points correlate with the stitching start points on the gusset seams to create a corner).

17 Now match up the other long edge of the body gusset ring with the bottom edge of the body front, again right sides together, and sew together as before. Now

continue to sew the shorter edges of the body gusset ring to the sides of the body front in the same way, making sure to catch the arms in the seams as you sew.

18 Now join the final 11cm x 11.5cm (4¼in x 4½in) piece of the blue space-print fabric to the body gusset ring to complete the back of the robot's body in the same way, always stopping and starting 6mm (¼in) from the corners. **Do not** leave a turning gap.

19 To turn the completed body through to the right side, make a slit in the centre of the top gusset approx. 6.5cm (2½in) long. This slit will be hidden against the robot's head when the body and head are sewn together. Turn the body through the slit and stuff it with toy filling. Whip stitch the gap closed (remember this will be hidden so there is no need to be super neat). To complete the stuffing, fill the feet firmly with toy filling, and ladder stitch the turning gap closed (see Stitching Techniques).

20 To join the body and the head, place the head so it sits neatly centred on the body. Using two strands of strong polyester thread, ladder stitch the body to the head (see Stitching Techniques : Attaching Parts) stitching together just outside the seam along all edges to give a neat join. Go around your stitching twice, pulling tightly as you go to form a firm strong attachment.

21 To make the first headlight, take one of your red star-print fabric circles and, securing the end of your thread with a knot, make small hand running stitches all the way around the raw edge. When you reach your start point, pull the thread to gather the circle, and when it is half gathered, place a little stuffing into the centre, then gather it up all the way, securing the gathers with a knot. Make a second headlight with the remaining star-print circle.

22 Ladder stitch a headlight to each side of the robot's head (refer to the close up photo as a positioning guide). (see Stitching Techniques: Attaching Parts). Work the ladder stitch in a circle and go around at least twice to ensure the headlights are firmly attached.

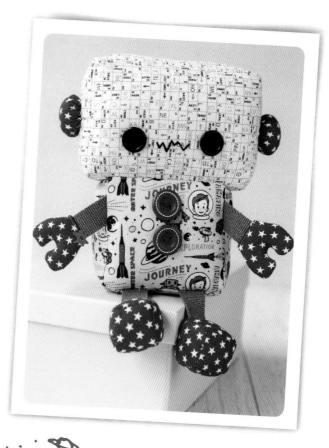

YUMI THE UNICORN

As the sun shines through the rain clouds and a rainbow arches across the sky, look closely and you may just catch a glimpse of Yumi the Unicorn. This eye-catching character loves to frolic in the fantasy land at the end of the rainbow. It's her favourite place to play, although with brightly coloured ric-rac mane and patterned horn, she can be very difficult to spot.

YOU WILL NEED

Note: Buttons should be omitted if making this toy for a very small child. Use 100% cotton patchwork fabric.

★ 25cm x 86.5cm (10in x 34in) main patterned fabric (body, inner legs)

★ 12.5cm x 86.5cm (5in x 34in) coordinating patterned fabric (hooves, ears)

★ 10cm x 7.5cm (4in x 3in) stripe fabric (horn)

★ 5cm x 7.5cm (2in x 3in) lightweight fusible fleece

★ 2m (2¼yd) each of four coordinating colours of mini ric-rac for mane and tail

★ Two small black buttons for eyes, and matching thread

★ Good-quality polyester thread (if cotton thread is used, your seams could break during stuffing)

★ Good-quality toy filling

FINISHED SIZE: 28cm (11in) tall

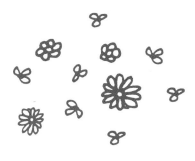

CUTTING YOUR FABRICS

Note: Trace the Yumi the Unicorn templates (see Templates) onto tracing paper or template plastic, transferring all of the markings, and cut them out along the traced lines. When using these templates to trace the pattern pieces onto your fabric, do ensure that the marked grain line on the template matches the fabric grain line (the direction of the fabric parallel with the selvedge).

FROM YOUR COORDINATING PATTERNED FABRIC:

Cut one strip measuring 5cm x 86.5cm (2in x 34in).

Cut one piece measuring 7.5cm x 10cm (3in x 4in).

Fold the remaining fabric in half with right sides together. Trace the hoof base template twice onto the folded fabric and cut out along the traced line to give you four hoof pieces.

PREPARING TO SEW

1 Interface one half of the 7.5cm x 10cm (3in x 4in) piece of your coordinating patterned fabric with your piece of fusible fleece.

2 Set your sewing machine to a small stitch length of approx. 1.5 for stitching the toy and use a good-quality polyester thread for strong seams.

MAKING THE UNICORN

Note: A 6mm (¼in) seam allowance is included in all pattern pieces unless advised otherwise. Read through all instructions before beginning to avoid surprises.

1 Take your main patterned fabric piece measuring 25cm x 86.5cm (10in x 34in) and your strip of coordinating patterned fabric measuring 5cm x 86.5cm (2 x 34in); place the fabric pieces on top of each other with right sides together, and then stitch to join along one long edge to make the body/hoof fabric panel. Press the seam open. Fold your fabric panel in half widthways with right sides together so that the short edges meet and fabrics and seams meet evenly.

2 Place the body template and the inner leg template onto the folded fabric panel, making sure to line up the bottom (straight) edge of both templates with the raw edge of the coordinating patterned (narrower) fabric strip, which will become the unicorn's hooves. Trace around each template once, then cut out along the traced lines to give you two body pieces and two inner leg pieces.

3 Take one body piece and the matching inner leg piece and place them on top of each other with right sides together. Referring to **Fig. 1**, sew the inner leg to the body ensuring that you start sewing right at the raw edge of the fabric at the top of the inner leg piece and then gradually turn into a 6mm (¼in) seam. ***Do not*** sew the bottom straight edges of the hooves together. Very carefully snip the inner leg curves. ***Do not*** turn through to the right side. Repeat to join the remaining body and inner leg pieces.

4 Sew the darts in place on the wrong side of each of the inner leg pieces as indicated on the template.

5 Take one of the hoof base pieces and ease this into place along the bottom raw edge of one of the legs, right sides together. It is essential to tack (baste) or pin well, and, when you are happy with the fit, sew the hoof base into place at the end of the leg. To ensure there is no puckering, it will help after each small section is sewn if you stop stitching, with the needle down, and rotate and smooth the leg fabric underneath before continuing. Complete all four legs.

6 Take your four lengths of mini ric-rac and place together evenly to form a bundle. Cut the bundle into eight 23cm (9in) lengths to form eight individual bundles, one for the tail and seven for the mane.

7 To make the unicorn's tail, take one of your ric-rac bundles and fold it in half. Place the bundle onto the tail end of one of your joined body/inner leg pieces so that the folded end rests just outside the raw edge of the fabric (see body template for position). Machine tack (baste) the tail in position (see **Fig. 2**).

8 To make the unicorn's mane, fold your remaining seven ric-rac bundles in half and place them evenly along the unicorn's head (see body template for position) so that the folded ends rest just outside the raw edge of the fabric. Machine tack (baste) the mane in position (see **Fig. 3**).

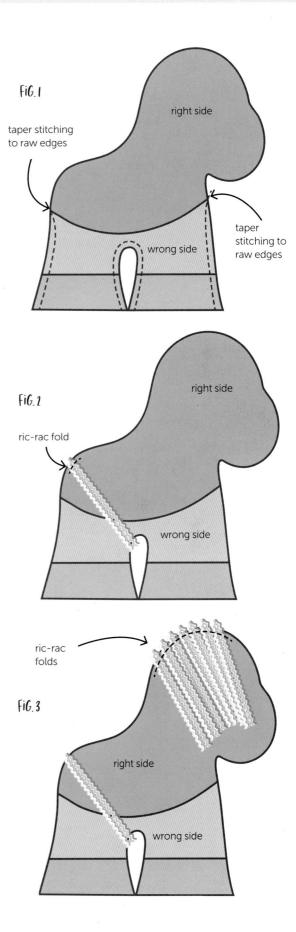

FIG. 1

right side

taper stitching to raw edges

wrong side

taper stitching to raw edges

FIG. 2

right side

ric-rac fold

wrong side

ric-rac folds

FIG. 3

right side

wrong side

9 Place one body piece on top of the other with right sides together, with the inner legs in between. Tack (baste) together starting from one end of the turning gap to the other as marked on the body template. When you reach the inner leg section, ensure that you are tacking (basting) the top straight edges of the inner legs together, right sides facing. You may find it easier to do this by folding the legs up against either side of the body (see **Fig. 4**).

FIG. 4

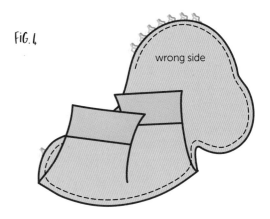

wrong side

Handy Tip

When tacking (basting), make sure that the mane and tail are well clear of the edges so that they do not get caught in your stitching.

10 Sew the body together leaving the turning gap open. Carefully snip any curved and angled edges along the seam before turning the unicorn right side out.

11 Stuff the unicorn very firmly with toy filling making sure that the legs in particular are well stuffed to ensure the unicorn can stand up by itself. Using strong polyester thread, ladder stitch the opening closed (see Stitching Techniques), stuffing in a little more as you go to avoid leaving a dimple.

12 Carefully trim the unicorn's mane and tail to neaten and shape as desired.

Handy Tip

To keep the ric-rac neat, paint a little fray stopper or fabric glue on the end of each length.

13 Now to make the ears. Take your small piece of fleece-backed coordinating patterned fabric and fold in half, right sides together, so that one side is interfaced and the other is not. Trace the ear template twice onto the interfaced side, and then sew along the traced lines leaving the turning gaps open as indicated by the broken line on the template. Cut out each ear approx. 3mm (⅛in) outside your sewn line; snip corners, turn through to the right side and press.

14 Using strong polyester thread, ladder stitch an ear onto either side of the unicorn's head (see Stitching Techniques : Attaching Parts). I chose to ladder stitch the ears in place in a folded shape as shown in the photograph.

15 To make the horn, take your piece of stripe fabric and fold in half with right sides together. Trace the horn template once onto the folded fabric, and then sew along the traced line, leaving the end unstitched as indicated by the broken line on the template. Cut out the horn approx. 3mm (⅛in) outside the sewn line and turn right side out. Fold the raw ends of the turning gap in by approx. 6mm (¼in) and finger press in place. Stuff the horn firmly with toy filling.

16 Position the horn where desired on your unicorn's head or refer to the photographs as a guide to positioning. Hold the horn in place by pinning through the horn and into the head, much like a pin cushion. Using strong polyester thread, ladder stitch the horn in place on the head working the ladder stitch in a circle (see Stitching Techniques: Attaching Parts). When you get approx. three-quarters of the way around, stuff the horn a little bit more to make sure it is nice and firm. I recommend you stitch around at least twice to ensure the horn is firmly attached.

17 Using black thread, sew the button eyes into place on the unicorn's face. If desired, pull the thread to indent the eyes. If you are making this toy for a small child, substitute a small piece of black wool-felt for the buttons, or create the eyes with satin stitch (see Stitching Techniques).

Fifi THE FAIRY

Flying daintily from rose bush to rose bush, you simply cannot miss Fifi the Fairy. She has fabulous pink floral hair swept up into buns atop her head, and with her delicate rosebud print top and sweetly gathered polka dot miniskirt, she is a fashion trendsetter in the fairy world. Her cheeky grin will capture any child's heart as she flies into their bedroom. Even better, Fifi is created without any buttons or small attachments, so is perfect for even the littlest of hands.

CUTTING YOUR FABRICS

Note: *Trace the Fifi the Fairy templates (see Templates) onto tracing paper or template plastic, transferring all of the markings, and cut them out along the traced lines. When using these templates to trace the pattern pieces onto your fabric, do ensure that the marked grain line on the template matches the fabric grain line (the direction of the fabric parallel with the selvedge).*

FROM YOUR PINK FLORAL-PRINT FABRIC:

Cut one piece 18cm x 18cm (7in x 7in) for hair.

Cut one piece 7.5cm x 30.5cm (3in x 12in) for bottom wings.

Trace the head template once for the head back and the hair bun template twice onto the remaining fabric and cut out along the traced lines.

FROM YOUR AQUA PATTERNED FABRIC:

Fold fabric in half with right sides together. Trace the body top and body bottom templates once each onto folded fabric and cut out along the traced lines to give you two body tops and two body bottoms.

Unfold remaining fabric and trace the body base template once; cut out along the traced line.

FROM YOUR PINK SPOT-PRINT:

Cut one strip 9cm x 56cm (3½in x 22in) for the skirt.

Cut one piece 7.5cm x 35.5cm (3in x 14in) for the top wings.

FROM YOUR PLAIN (SKIN-COLOURED) FABRIC:

Cut one piece 18cm x 18cm (7in x 7in) for the face.

Fold the remaining fabric in half with right sides together. Trace the arm and leg templates twice each onto the folded fabric, but **do not** cut out (these will be sewn on the traced line).

PREPARING TO SEW

1 Interface one half only of each of your wing fabric pieces with fusible fleece.

2 Trace the hairline template onto the paper side of the fusible web and roughly cut out close to the traced line. Fuse this hairline piece to the wrong side of your piece of pink floral-print fabric for the hair measuring 18cm x 18cm (7in x 7in), positioning it centrally along the bottom edge.

3 Set your sewing machine to a small stitch length of approx. 1.5 for stitching the toy and use a good-quality polyester thread for strong seams.

MAKING THE FAIRY

Note: *A 6mm (¼in) seam allowance is included in all pattern pieces unless advised otherwise. Read through all instructions before beginning to avoid surprises.*

1 Take your pink floral-print fabric for the hair (with fusible web attached) and cut along the traced line from the bottom edge of the hairline only, so that you have a piece remaining as shown in **Fig. 1**.

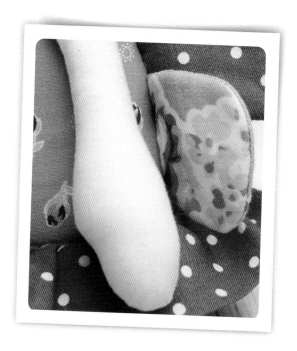

2 Peel the backing paper away from the fusible web on this hair piece, then position it onto your piece of plain (skin-coloured) fabric for the face, making sure there is adequate plain (skin-coloured) fabric below the hairline to be able to fit in the doll's face template. Fuse in place. Machine appliqué the bottom hairline edge onto the plain (skin-coloured) fabric – I used machine buttonhole stitch.

3 Take the head template and trace this onto the hair/face fabric panel created in step 2, so that the appliquéd hairline meets the hairline on the template. Cut the head out along the traced line. Cut away any excess plain (skin-coloured) fabric (above fused section) from the wrong side of the front head. Put aside for now.

4 Take your folded piece of plain (skin-coloured) fabric with the arms and legs traced onto it and, keeping the fabric folded, sew along the traced lines of the arms and legs, leaving the straight ends unstitched as indicated by the broken line on the templates. Cut out limbs approx. 3mm–6mm (⅛in–¼in) outside your sewn lines, and then turn right side out.

5 Firmly stuff the limbs to the very ends with toy filling, leaving the last 2cm (¾in) unstuffed. Tack (baste) the open ends closed.

6 Take one of the body top pieces and place it right side up on your work surface. Place the arms on top of the body top piece aligning the raw edge of the arms with the raw edge of the neckline and positioning the arms approx. 3–6mm (⅛–¼in) in from the sides; machine tack (baste) in position close to the raw edge (see **Fig. 2**).

7 Take your set-aside front head and front body top with arms and place on top of each other with right sides together so that they are aligned at the neckline. Pin in place, and then sew along the neckline. This is the joined front piece.

8 Take your remaining body top and head back pieces and place on top of each other with right sides together, aligned at the neckline. Pin in place, and then sew along the neckline, leaving the middle section open for turning and stuffing as indicated by the broken line on the body top template. This is the joined back piece.

FiG. 1

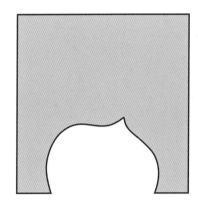

FiG. 2

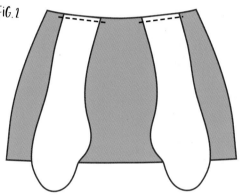

Handy Tip

Crisp edges on your turning gap makes stitching it closed in step 20 a little easier, so press the seam and turning gap allowance open after joining the body and head back pieces together.

9 Take your pink spot-print wing piece and fold it in half, right sides together, so that one side is interfaced and the other is not. Trace the top wing template twice onto the interfaced side, flipping the template for your second tracing. Then sew along the traced lines leaving the turning gaps open as indicated by the broken line on the template.

10 Repeat step 9 with your pink floral-print wing fabric piece and your bottom wing template. Cut all of the wings out approx. 3mm (⅛in) outside the sewn lines, turn right side out and press.

11 Place the joined front piece right side up on your work surface and then position the wings on top of this, right sides together, so that the straight edges of the wings meet the raw edges of the body top: first place the bottom wings, then the top wings so that they overlap by approx. 1cm (⅜in) and machine tack (baste) into place (see **Fig. 3**).

12 Take the fairy front with wings and the fairy back piece and place on top of each other, right sides together. Sew together along the sides of the body top and around the head (you will be securing the wings in place as you stitch) leaving the bottom edge of the body top open. **Do not** turn the body top right side out. To make the forthcoming steps a little easier, fold the arms up to sit inside the head section at this stage.

FIG. 3

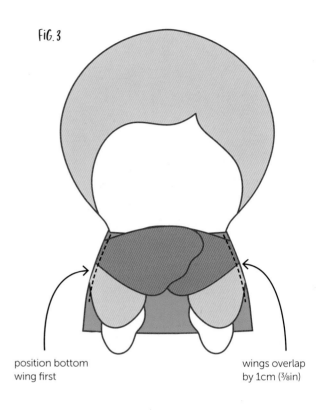

position bottom wing first

wings overlap by 1cm (⅜in)

Handy Tip

When sewing body front and back together make sure the arms and wings are well clear to avoid catching them in your stitching.

13 Take your strip of pink spot-print skirt fabric and fold in half lengthways with wrong sides together, so that the strip measures 4.5cm x 56cm (1¾in x 22in). Press well. Unfold the strip, join the short ends with right sides together to create a ring, and sew. Refold the fabric along the previous fold line, wrong sides together, and press once again.

14 Take a long length of doubled polyester thread and securing the start point with a knot, take small to medium hand running stitches all the way around the raw edge of your folded fabric ring, and when you reach your start point, pull up your thread to gather the top edge to begin to gather the skirt. Gather the top edge of the skirt evenly until it measures the same circumference as the bottom edge of the body top, then tie off your thread end securely so that the skirt ruffles cannot loosen.

15 Take the inside-out body top and place the gathered skirt inside the open bottom edge, so that the raw edge of the gathered skirt aligns with the raw edge of the body opening, right sides together. Machine tack (baste) in place all the way around the body opening approx. 3mm (⅛in) from the raw edges.

16 Take the two aqua patterned body bottom pieces, place on top of each other with right sides together, and sew along the short side edges only. Now take the body base piece and ease this evenly into position along the bottom raw edge of the body bottom (still inside out) with right sides together. (You may find this is easier to do by marking the quarter points on your base and body bottom and then matching these up.) It is essential to tack (baste) or pin well first.

17 When you are happy with the fit, sew the body base into place, leaving the leg gaps open at the front as indicated by the broken lines on your body bottom template. To avoid puckering, it will help after each small section is sewn if you stop stitching, with the needle down, and rotate and smooth the fabric underneath before continuing. Turn the joined bottom body/base right side out.

18 Take your still inside-out body top and fit the body bottom inside the opening over the gathered skirt, right sides together. Make sure that the leg opening side of the body bottom is facing the body front and that all the raw edges are evenly aligned. You should now have the bottom raw edge of the body top, the raw edge of the gathered skirt and the top raw edge of the body bottom meeting evenly together. Pin or tack (baste) well and then sew the three layers into place. *Do not* turn through to the right side.

19 Still working on the inside-out body, insert one of the legs, raw edges first, through the turning gap on the back of the neckline. Guide the raw edges into one of the leg gaps on the body bottom, making sure that the raw edge of the leg aligns with the raw edge of the leg gap and that the toe is facing outwards. Following the stitching line on the body base, sew the leg in place. Repeat to sew the second leg in the remaining leg gap.

20 Carefully and methodically turn the completed fairy right sides out through the gap in the neckline, and then stuff firmly with toy filling. Ladder stitch the opening closed (see Stitching Techniques) stuffing a little more as you go to avoid a dimple.

Handy Tip

When turning limb-laden toys, always start by turning though the stuffed limbs, beginning with those closest to the turning. Once the limbs are neatly through the rest of the fabric will follow naturally.

21 Take one of your pink floral-print bun circles and securing the end of your thread with a knot, make small hand running stitches all the way around the raw edge (see Stitching Techniques). When you reach your start point, pull the thread to gather the circle. When it is half gathered, place a little stuffing into the centre, then gather it up all the way, securing the gathers with a knot. Referring to Stitching Techniques: Attaching Parts, ladder stitch the bun in a circle to the side of the fairy's head (see photograph for positioning). I recommend you sew around the circle twice for added strength. Repeat for the second bun.

22 Mark the eyes and mouth onto Fifi's face. Sinking your knots before you start (see Stitching Techniques), create the eyes with satin stitch using two strands of dark grey embroidery thread (floss), then continue with the same thread to backstitch the eyelashes. Using two strands of pink embroidery thread (floss), backstitch the mouth. Using the pink pencil, draw and colour in the cheek circles using the head template and photographs for their size and position.

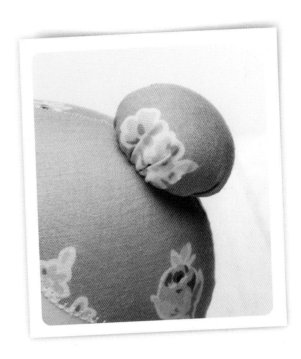

SUPER SCOTTY

Is it a bird? Is it a plane? No, it's Super Scotty! Able to leap tall bunk beds in a single bound, this boy of steel is ready to fight the battle for toy box justice. Take off his cape and his mask and you may mistake him for any ordinary boy, but in one quick change he becomes a superhero who will be sure to keep any child's bedroom full of adventure and action.

YOU WILL NEED

Note: Use 100% cotton patchwork fabric.

★ 18cm x 35.5cm (7in x 14in) brown dot-print fabric (head back, hair)

★ 30.5cm x 38cm (12in x 15in) green patterned fabric (body, legs, arms)

★ 38cm x 38cm (15in x 15in) red spot-print fabric (boots, pants, cape)

★ 25cm x 25cm (10in x 10in) plain (skin-coloured) fabric (head front, hands)

★ 100% wool-felt: red 15cm x 15cm (6in x 6in) for mask and star

★ 100% wool-felt: white 5cm x 5cm (2in x 2in) for chest circle

★ 25cm (10in) of 5mm- (¼in-) wide elastic for mask

★ 30cm (12in) of 1.3cm- (½in-) wide red ribbon for cape ties

★ 18cm x 28cm (7in x 11in) fusible web

★ Six-strand embroidery thread (floss): brown, red

★ Good-quality polyester thread (if cotton thread is used, your seams could break during stuffing)

★ Good-quality toy filling

FINISHED SIZE: 33cm (13in) tall

CUTTING your FABRiCS

Note: *Trace the Super Scotty templates (see Templates) onto tracing paper or template plastic, transferring all the markings, and cut them out along the traced lines. When using these templates to trace the pattern pieces onto your fabric, do ensure that the marked grain line on the template matches the fabric grain line (the direction of the fabric parallel with the selvedge).*

FROM YOUR BROWN DOT-PRINT FABRIC:

Cut one piece 18cm x 18cm (7in x 7in) for hair.

Trace head template once onto the remaining fabric and cut out along traced line to give you one head back.

FROM YOUR GREEN PATTERNED FABRIC:

Cut two strips 7.5cm x 25cm (3in x 10in) for the arms and legs.

Cut two pieces 7.5cm x 5cm (3in x 2in) for the body base.

Fold remaining fabric in half with right sides together. Trace the body template once onto the folded fabric and cut out along the traced lines to give you two body pieces.

FROM YOUR RED SPOT-PRINT FABRIC:

Cut one strip 10cm x 25cm (4in x 10in) for boots.

Cut one piece 12.5cm x 15cm (5in x 6in) for the pants (front and back).

Cut one piece 7.5cm x 5cm (3in x 2in) for the pants gusset.

Fold remaining fabric in half, right sides together. Trace cape template twice onto the folded fabric. *Do not* cut out.

FROM YOUR PLAIN (SKIN-COLOURED) FABRIC:

Cut one piece 18cm x 18cm (7in x 7in) for face.

Cut one piece 6.5cm x 25cm (2½in x 10) for the hands.

PREPARING TO SEW

1 Trace the hairline template onto the paper side of the fusible web; roughly cut out close to the traced line. Fuse this hairline piece to the wrong side of your brown dot-print fabric measuring 18cm x 18cm (7in x 7in), positioning it centrally along the bottom edge.

2 Trace the chest circle and star templates onto the paper side of the fusible web and roughly cut out. Fuse the chest circle to the white felt and the star to the red felt, and then cut out along the traced lines.

3 Trace the pants shape from the body template twice onto the paper side of the fusible web, roughly cut out, and then fuse to the red spot-print fabric piece measuring 12.5cm x 15cm (5in x 6in). Cut out along the traced lines.

4 Set your sewing machine to a small stitch length of approx. 1.5 for stitching the toy and use a good-quality polyester thread for strong seams.

MAKING SUPER SCOTTY

Note: A 6mm (¼in) seam allowance is included in all pattern pieces unless advised otherwise. Read through all instructions before beginning to avoid surprises.

1 Take your brown dot-print fabric for the hair (with fusible web attached) and cut along the traced line from the bottom edge of the hairline only, so that you have a piece remaining as shown in **Fig. 1**.

2 Peel the backing paper away from the remaining fusible web on the wrong side of the brown dot-print fabric, then position and fuse the hair piece onto your piece of plain (skin-coloured) fabric for the face, making sure to position it so that there is adequate plain (skin-coloured) fabric below the hairline to be able to fit in Scotty's face template. Machine appliqué the bottom hairline edge onto the plain (skin-coloured) fabric: I used two lines of raw edge appliqué.

3 Take your head template and trace this onto the hair/face fabric panel created in step 2, so that the appliquéd hairline meets the hairline on the template and cut out along the traced line. Cut away any excess plain (skin-coloured) fabric (above fused section) from the wrong side of the front head piece. Put aside for now.

4 Take one of the green patterned fabric strips and the plain (skin-coloured) fabric strip each measuring 25cm (10in) long and place them on top of each other, right sides together. Sew together along one 25cm (10in) edge, open out the joined panel and press. Fold the panel in half widthways, so that the short edges meet and right sides are together, making sure that the fabrics and seam line are perfectly aligned. Place the arm template onto the folded fabric panel making sure that the marked hand line matches up with the seam in the fabric. Trace around the template twice, flipping the template for the second trace. *Do not* cut out (see **Fig. 2**).

5 Referring to step 4, make a fabric panel for the legs from your remaining green patterned fabric strip and the red spot-print strip, each measuring 25cm (10in) long. Fold the panel in half widthways, so that the short edges meet and right sides are together, making sure that the fabrics and seam line are perfectly aligned. Place the leg template onto the folded fabric panel so that the marked boot line matches up with the seam in the fabric and draw around the template twice, flipping the template for the second trace. *Do not* cut out.

FiG. 1

FiG. 2

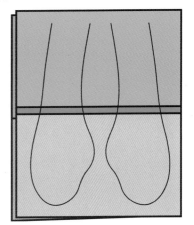

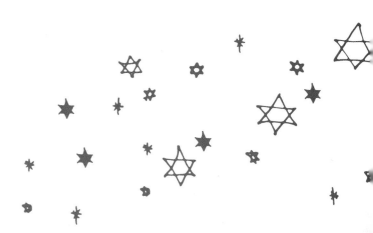

6 Keeping each of the fabric panels folded, sew along the traced lines of the arms and the legs, leaving the straight ends unstitched as indicated by the broken line on the templates. Cut out each limb approx. 3mm–6mm (⅛in–¼in) outside your sewn lines and then turn the limbs right side out. Firmly stuff the limbs to the very ends with toy filling, leaving the last 2cm (¾in) unstuffed. Tack (baste) the open ends closed.

7 Take your front body and back body green patterned fabric pieces and fuse a red spot-print pants shape to the bottom edge of each, and machine appliqué in place. Take the front body piece, then fuse and machine appliqué the white felt circle to the chest, positioning it approx. 6mm (¼in) above the top edge of the pants. Fuse and machine appliqué the red felt star in the centre of the white circle.

8 Place the front body piece right side up on your work surface. Place the arms on top aligning the raw edge of the arms with the raw edge of the neckline and positioning the arms approx. 1.3cm (½in) in from the sides. Machine tack (baste) in position close to the raw edge (see **Fig. 3**).

9 Take the front head and the front body with arms pieces that you set aside and place these on top of each other with right sides together so that they are aligned at the neckline. Pin in place, and then sew together along the neckline.

10 Take the remaining back body and back head pieces and place on top of each other with right sides together so that they are aligned at the neckline. Pin in place, and then sew along the neckline, leaving the middle section open for turning and stuffing as indicated by the broken line on the body template.

11 Take your front body/head and your back body/head and place on top of each other, right sides together. Sew together along the sides of the body and around the head, leaving the bottom edge of the body open. **Do not** turn right side out; to make forthcoming steps a little easier, fold the arms up to sit inside the head section at this stage.

FiG. 3

12 Now take one of the legs and insert it foot first, with toe facing inwards, into the opening at the bottom edge of the body. Centre the leg within one of the side green sections of the front body and align the raw edge of the leg with the raw edge of the bottom edge of the front body. Machine tack (baste) in place to the front body only. Repeat to position the second leg on the other side green section of the front body (see **Fig. 4**).

13 Take the 7.5cm x 5cm (3in x 2in) red spot fabric piece and the two remaining green patterned fabric pieces the same size and sew these together along the 7.5cm (3in) edges to create a panel (see **Fig. 5**). Press the seams open. This is the fabric panel for cutting out the body base template. Working on the wrong side of your fabric, trace the body base template onto the fabric panel so that the marked pants lines match up with the seams, and then cut the base out along the traced line.

14 Take the body base piece and ease this evenly into position along the bottom raw edge of the body (still inside out) with right sides together. You may find this is easier to do by first matching up the pants seams at the body front and back, then continue easing the body base into position around the remaining edges. It is essential to tack (baste) or pin well first, and then, when you are happy with the fit, sew the body base into place. To ensure there is no puckering, it will help after each small section is sewn if you stop stitching, with the needle down, to rotate and smooth the fabric underneath before continuing.

15 Turn the body right sides out through the neckline gap and stuff firmly with toy filling. Ladder stitch the opening closed (see Stitching Techniques) stuffing in a little more toy filling as you go to avoid a dimple.

FiG. 4

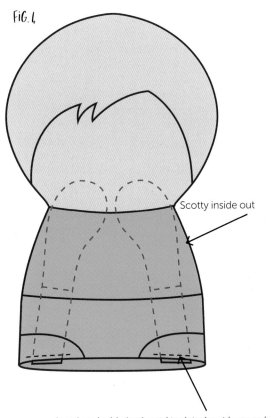

Scotty inside out

place legs inside body and tack to front layer only

FiG. 5

body base fabric panel

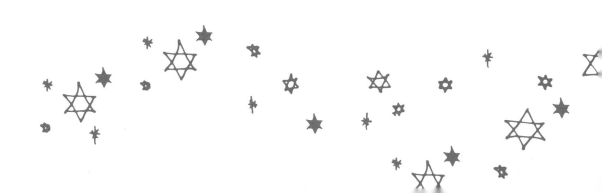

16 Mark the eyes and mouth onto Scotty's face. Sinking your knots before you start (see Stitching Techniques), create the eyes with satin stitch using two strands of brown embroidery thread (floss), and backstitch the mouth using two strands of red embroidery thread (floss).

17 Take the red spot-print fabric with the cape traced onto it and, keeping the fabric folded, sew along the traced line, leaving the top edge open as indicated by the broken line on the cape template. Cut out approx. 3mm (⅛in) outside the sewn line, snipping the corners. Turn right side out and press. Leaving the top edge open, topstitch along the three sewn edges.

18 Take your ribbon trim and fold it in half lengthways with wrong sides together. Press well. Now take the cape and place the open edge inside the folded trim, so that it is centred along the length of the ribbon. Tack (baste) in place. Topstitch along the full length of the trim catching the cape securely in your stitching (see **Fig. 6**). Fit the cape around Scotty's neck and tie at the front.

FIG. 6

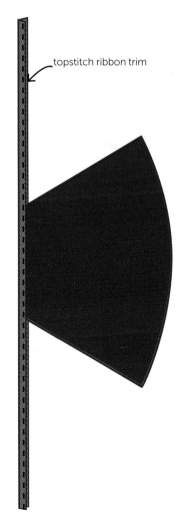

topstitch ribbon trim

19 To make Scotty's mask, trace the mask template twice onto the remaining red felt. Using small sharp scissors, cut out neatly. Pin or tack (baste) the two mask pieces together and topstitch along the outside edge, leaving two gaps at the sides as indicated by the broken line on the template. Topstitch also around the eye holes, then trim any uneven edges to neaten. Take your elastic and insert one end into one of the gaps at the side of the mask; topstitch to secure. Placing the mask onto Scotty's face, measure how long the elastic needs to be for a good fit; trim as required. Insert the remaining end of the elastic into the gap at the other side of the mask and topstitch in place. Fit the mask on Scotty's face.

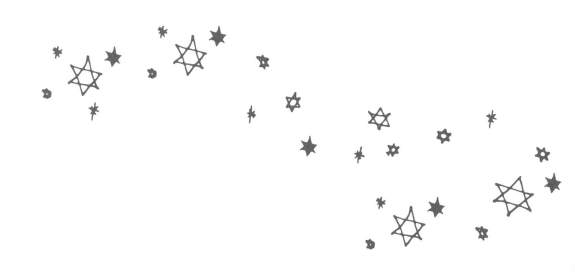

DRAKE THE DRAGON

Stomping around on his hind legs, whipping his powerful tail from side to side, and flapping his wings, Drake the Dragon makes quite an impression. But don't be fooled by his brightly coloured coat, spiky back and impressive red horns. There is nothing to fear. Take a closer look to see a tiny flash of a cheeky grin and you will quickly realize that his huff and puff is all for show.

YOU WILL NEED

Note: *Buttons should be omitted if making this toy for a very small child. Use 100% cotton patchwork fabric with a width of 106cm–114cm (42in–44in).*

★ 28cm (11in) x full fabric width of blue number-print fabric (body, head gusset, arms, legs)

★ 30cm x 10cm (12in x 4in) white spot-print fabric (tummy gusset)

★ 18cm x 18cm (7in x 7in) red dot-print fabric (wings, horns)

★ 12.5cm x 9cm (5in x 3½in) lightweight fusible fleece

★ 50cm (20in) medium to large green ric-rac

★ Four medium/large red buttons for button jointing

★ Six-strand embroidery thread (floss): colour to match buttons

★ Two small black buttons for eyes, and matching thread

★ Dollmaker's needle: 12.5cm (5in) or longer

★ Good-quality polyester thread (if cotton thread is used, your seams could break during stuffing)

★ Good-quality toy filling

FINISHED SIZE: 25cm (10in) tall

CUTTING YOUR FABRICS

Note: *Trace the Drake the Dragon templates (see Templates) onto tracing paper or template plastic, transferring all of the markings, and cut them out along the traced lines. When using these templates to trace the pattern pieces onto your fabric, do ensure that the marked grain line on the template matches the fabric grain line (the direction of the fabric parallel with the selvedge).*

FROM YOUR BLUE NUMBER-PRINT FABRIC:

Fold the fabric, trace around the body template once and cut out along the traced line to give you two body pieces.

Open out the fabric and trace the head gusset template once onto single layer fabric and cut out along the traced line.

Refold the fabric and trace the arm and leg templates twice each onto the folded fabric, flipping the templates for your second trace. **Do not** cut out (these will be sewn on the traced line).

FROM YOUR WHITE SPOT-PRINT FABRIC:

Trace the tummy gusset template once onto fabric and cut out along the traced line.

FROM YOUR RED DOT-PRINT FABRIC:

Cut one piece 12.5cm x 18cm (5in x 7in) for the wings and one piece 5cm x 18cm (2in x 7in) for the horns.

PREPARING TO SEW

1 Interface half of the red dot wing fabric with the fusible fleece piece, and then fold the fabric in half with right sides together, so that one side is interfaced and the other is not. Trace the wing template twice onto the interfaced side, flipping for your second trace. **Do not** cut out (these will be sewn on the traced lines).

2 Take your piece of red dot horn fabric and fold in half with right sides together. Trace around the horn template twice but **do not** cut out (these will be sewn on the traced lines later).

3 Set your sewing machine to a small stitch length of approx. 1.5 for stitching the toy and use a good-quality polyester thread for strong seams.

MAKING THE DRAGON

Note: *A 6mm (¼in) seam allowance is included in all pattern pieces unless advised otherwise. Read through all instructions before beginning to avoid surprises.*

1 Place one of the body pieces right side up on your work surface. Take your ric-rac and, working from one end, pin it into position from the first star marking on the head to the second star marking near the tail. Cut and put aside the remainder of your ric-rac (this will be used in step 2). Machine tack (baste) the ric-rac into place all the way along the edge, making sure that you carefully ease your ric-rac ends to the outside of the body to start and end neatly (see **Fig. 1**). Snip away any excess at the ends.

Handy Tip

When attaching ric-rac to a piece that has yet to be sewn, keep in mind the 6mm (¼in) seam allowance. Be sure to position and attach the ric-rac so that the centre of the ric-rac will be secured when sewn.

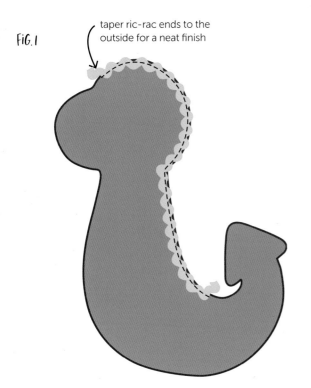

FiG.1

taper ric-rac ends to the outside for a neat finish

FiG.2

2 Attach the remaining ric-rac length in the same way to the right side of the second body piece, from the star marking at the front of the head to the dot marking at the back of the head. Machine tack (baste) in place (see **Fig. 2**). Snip away any excess at the ends. (Note: careful positioning of your ric-rac within the seam line will ensure a line of prominent spikes without any gaps.)

3 Take the head gusset and tummy gusset pieces and place on top of each other, right sides together, and sew together along the straight neckline edge. Then press seam open.

4 Take the joined head/tummy gusset piece and position it on top of one of the body pieces with right sides together as in **Fig. 3**: start by matching up the head/tummy gusset seam with the triangle at the front neckline as marked on the body template (**a**), then tack (baste) the head gusset section into place around the head to the back of the neck (**b**). Finally tack (baste) the tummy gusset section into place towards the tail (**c**). Do not pull either fabric piece but ease generously: note, the gusset will not fit the entire length to the tail – this is intentional. Once tacked (basted) in place, sew the head/gusset and body pieces together, tapering your stitching off the seam allowance at either end of the gusset strip (see **Fig. 3**).

5 Now tack (baste) the remaining side of the head/tummy gusset to the remaining body piece in the same way, but leave a gap along the bottom edge for turning as indicated by the broken line on the body template and continue your tacking (basting) all the way around the back and tail to join the body pieces. Both sides of the gusset need to be evenly distributed within the body with no gathering or pulling – if you are unhappy with the fit, start again, and this time be more generous with the side that was too long.

6 Before turning the dragon through to the right side, snip the corners at the tail triangle and carefully snip the seam allowance at the front neckline. Turn right side out and then stuff the dragon firmly with toy filling. (Be sure to stuff the dragon's tail to the very ends for a nice firm shape.) Ladder stitch the opening closed (see Stitching Techniques) filling with a little more stuffing as you go to avoid a dimple.

FIG. 3

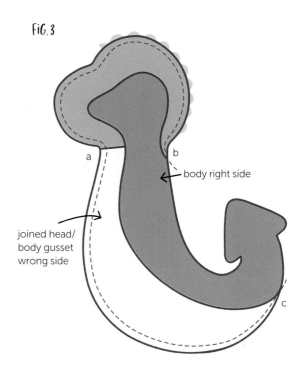

a

b

→ body right side

joined head/body gusset wrong side

c

Handy Tip

When snipping into your seam allowances, take care not to get too close to the stitching line, or you risk weakening your seams.

7 Take the folded piece of interfaced red dot-print fabric with the wings traced onto it and, keeping the fabric folded, sew along the traced lines, leaving the straight ends unstitched as indicated by the broken line on the wing template. Cut out the wings approx. 3mm (⅛in) outside the sewn lines, and then turn the wings right side out. Press well, then topstitch all the way around the wings, turning under the open edges to neaten as you go.

8 Take one of the wings and using strong polyester thread, take small hand running stitches along the straight edge; pull up the thread to slightly gather the edge and continue with the same thread to attach the wing in position on the dragon's back with ladder stitch. (Refer to photographs for a guide to positioning and Stitching Techniques for how to attach parts with ladder stitch.) Repeat to secure the second wing in place.

Handy Tip

I recommend that you ladder stitch along both the front and back edge of the wing, and that you go over your stitching twice to create a strong join.

9 Take the folded piece of red dot-print fabric with the horns traced onto it and, keeping the fabric folded, sew along the traced lines, leaving the straight ends unstitched as indicated by the broken line on the horn template. Cut out the horns approx. 3mm (⅛in) outside the sewn lines, then turn right side out. Fold in the raw edges by approx. 6mm (¼in) and finger press to give a neat edge, and then stuff each horn firmly with toy filling.

10 Position a horn at one side of the dragon's head gusset, referring to the photographs as a guide to positioning. Hold the horn in place by pinning through the horn and into the head, much like a pin cushion. Using strong polyester thread, ladder stitch the horn in place working in a circle (see Stitching Techniques: Attaching Parts). When you get approx. three-quarters of the way around, stuff the horn a little bit more to make sure it is nice and firm. I recommend you stitch around at least twice to ensure the horn is firmly attached. Repeat to place and secure the second horn.

11 Using black thread, sew the small black button eyes into place on the dragon's face. Pull the thread to indent the eyes ever so slightly if desired.

12 Take the folded piece of body fabric with the legs and arms traced onto it and, keeping the fabric folded, sew all the way around the traced lines. Cut the pieces out approx. 3–6mm (⅛– ¼in) outside your sewn line. Do not snip the seams. To turn the limbs right side out, cut the small turning slit as marked on the arm and leg templates on **one side only** of each limb (single fabric thickness).

Handy Tip

If you are making this toy for a baby or a small child, omit the buttons and instead blanket stitch a small piece of black wool-felt in place or create the eyes with satin stitch (see Stitching Techniques).

Handy Tip

Make certain you cut a slit into the correct fabric layer so that you are creating two mirror-image arms and legs.

13 Stuff each limb firmly with toy filling, then whip stitch the opening closed (see Stitching Techniques). As the turning gaps will be hidden against the dragon's body, there is no need to worry about perfect stitching. It is important to stuff the legs very firmly so that they can support the toy's weight.

14 The button jointing technique is used to attach the limbs to the dragon's body and you should start by attaching the legs. First thread the dollmaker's needle with a long length (approx. 150cm/60in) of six-strand embroidery thread (floss) in a colour to match your buttons. Tie a double knot in the end of your length of thread and trim close to the knot.

15 Referring to **Fig. 4**, begin button jointing. Start by threading the needle through one side of the dragon's body at the desired leg location (refer to the photographs), taking it right through the body and out the other side at exactly the same level. Thread the needle through one of the legs, then through one of the buttons, then go back through all of the layers again (button, leg, body) to come back out close to your start point. Here, thread the needle through the remaining leg and button, as shown in **Fig. 4**, and return again through the body to the other side. Continue through all the layers a few times, for a nice, strong attachment, pulling the threads taut after each pass through. Tie off your thread and sink the knot into the leg (see Stitching Techniques).

16 Repeat the button jointing process to attach the arms, referring to the photographs as a guide to their positioning.

FIG. 4

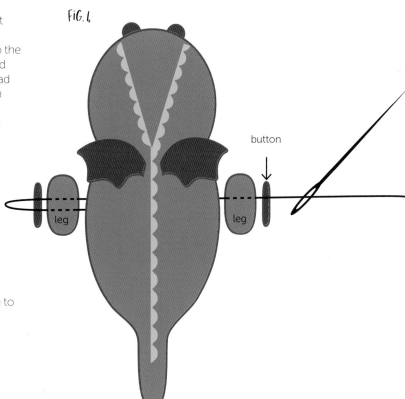

button

leg

leg

Handy Tip

To make a toy suitable for a small child you can joint the limbs in the same way but omit the buttons. Just remember to sink the thread knots at start and finish.

PRINCESS PENELOPE

With her shiny crown and demure smile, you could be forgiven for thinking that Princess Penelope spends her days cooped up in the palace, but nothing could be further from the truth. She loves bug hunting in the palace gardens – she keeps her hair in plaits and her gown short so she can run around with ease. She is a firm believer that just because she is a princess she doesn't have to behave like one!

YOU WILL NEED

Note: *Use 100% cotton patchwork fabric with a width of 106cm–114cm (42in–44in).*

★ 15cm (6in) x full fabric width of pink floral-print fabric (hair, peplum)

★ 25cm x 35cm (10in x 14in) blue patterned fabric (body, shoes)

★ 10cm x 56cm (4in x 22in) red patterned fabric (skirt)

★ 23cm (9in) x full fabric width of plain (skin-coloured) cotton/linen blend fabric (head, arms, legs)

★ 100% wool-felt: yellow 12.5cm x 10cm (5in x 4in) for the crown

★ 100% wool-felt: red 2.5cm x 2.5cm (1in x 1in) for the heart decoration

★ 25cm (10in) of small white ric-rac

★ 15 x 18cm (6in x 7in) fusible web

★ Six-strand embroidery thread (floss): black, pink, blue

★ Good-quality polyester thread (if cotton thread is used, your seams could break during stuffing)

★ Good-quality toy filling

FINISHED SIZE: 40.5cm (16in) tall

CUTTING YOUR FABRICS

Note: *Trace the Princess Penelope templates (see Templates) onto tracing paper or template plastic, transferring all the markings, and cut out along the traced lines. Do ensure that the marked grain line on the template matches the fabric grain line (the direction of the fabric parallel with the selvedge).*

FROM YOUR PINK FLORAL-PRINT FABRIC:

Cut six strips each 3.25cm x 18cm (1¼in x 7in) for the plaits.

Cut one piece 15cm x 25cm (6in x 10in) for the skirt peplum.

Trace the head template once and cut out on the traced line for the head back.

FROM YOUR BLUE PATTERNED FABRIC:

Cut one strip 7.5cm x 30.5cm (3in x 12in) for the shoes.

Fold the fabric and trace around the body top and body bottom templates once; cut out along the traced lines to give you two body tops and two body bottoms.

FROM YOUR RED PATTERNED FABRIC:

Cut one strip 10cm x 56cm (4in x 22in) for the skirt.

FROM YOUR PLAIN (SKIN-COLOURED) COTTON/LINEN BLEND FABRIC:

Cut one strip 15cm x 30.5cm (6in x 12in) for the legs.

Trace the head template once and cut out on the traced line.

Fold the remaining fabric in half and trace around the arm template twice. ***Do not*** cut out (these will be sewn on the traced line).

PREPARING TO SEW

1 Trace the hair template onto the paper side of the fusible web, roughly cut out close to the traced line and then fuse this to the wrong side of your remaining pink floral-print. Cut the hair shape out along the traced line and then fuse this to your plain (skin-coloured) cotton/linen blend head piece. This is the head front.

2 Take the pink floral-print fabric for the skirt peplum, fold in half right sides together, and trace around the peplum template twice but ***do not*** cut out. Put aside for now.

3 Trace the heart shape from the crown template onto the paper side of the fusible web and roughly cut out. Fuse the heart to the red felt, cut along the traced line and put aside for now.

4 Set your sewing machine to a small stitch length of approx. 1.5 for stitching the toy and use a good-quality polyester thread for strong seams.

MAKING THE PRINCESS

Note: *A 6mm (¼in) seam allowance is included in all pattern pieces unless advised otherwise. Read through all the instructions before starting to avoid surprises.*

1 Machine appliqué the hairline into place on the head front (I used a small machine blanket stitch).

2 Cut the length of white ric-rac in half. Taking one of the body top pieces, place the ric-rac along the neckline with the right side facing you and machine tack (baste) into place stitching within the seam allowance, approx. 3mm (⅛in) from the raw edge. Attach the remaining length of ric-rac to the second body top piece in the same way.

Handy Tip

When attaching ric-rac to a piece that has yet to be sewn, keep in mind the 6mm (¼in) seam allowance. Be sure to position and attach the ric-rac so that the centre of the ric-rac will be secured when sewn.

3 Take one of the body top pieces and the head front with hair and place on top of each other, right sides together. Ensuring that the placement is central, ease the neckline of the body to the neckline of the head, pinning or tacking (basting) into place before sewing together. Repeat to join the pink floral-print head back to the remaining body top piece.

4 Take one of your pink floral-print fabric plait strips, fold in one short end by approx. 6mm (¼in) and press well. Fold the strip in half lengthways, with wrong sides together, and press. Open out and fold the raw edges of each long edge evenly to the fold line and press along the fold line once again, topstitching the strip along the open edge to secure (see **Fig. 1**). Repeat to prepare the remaining five plait strips.

5 Take three of your prepared plait strips and partially overlapping, secure the raw ends together with a few machine stitches close to the edge. Lay the joined body/head front piece right side up on your work surface and place the three joined plait strips onto the head so that they lay diagonally across the face (see **Fig. 2** for placement) and machine tack (baste) into position. Repeat with the remaining strips on the other side of the head.

FiG. 1

FiG. 2

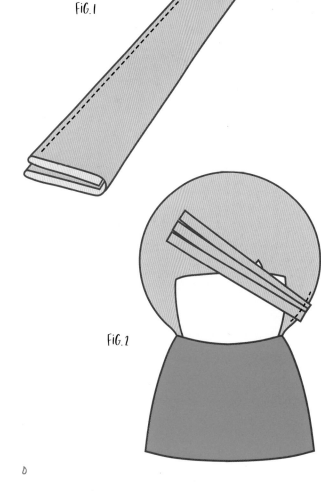

6 Take your folded linen with the arms traced onto it and, keeping the fabric folded, sew along the traced lines of the arms, leaving the straight ends unstitched as indicated by the broken line on the template. Cut out the arms approx. 3mm (⅛in) outside your sewn lines, and then turn the arms right side out.

7 Firmly stuff the arms with toy filling, leaving the last 2cm (¾in) unstuffed. Make small running stitches around the top raw edges of each arm, pulling the thread to gather; secure with tacking (basting) stitches.

8 With the body/head front still right side up on your work surface, place each arm in turn at the top of the body so the raw edges align (see **Fig. 3**) and machine tack (baste) in place. Make sure to position the arms as shown in **Fig. 3**, with the thumbs on the outside – when the doll is complete all will be well and the hands will be the right way around.

9 Take the body/head back and place it on top of the body/head front, right sides together. Pin or tack (baste) these two pieces together ensuring that the neckline seams align and that the plait strips and arms remain clear of your stitching. When you are happy with the fit, sew the pieces together leaving the bottom edge open. Turn through to the right side.

10 Take your red patterned fabric skirt strip and fold it in half, right sides together, so that the short ends meet, and sew in place to make your skirt ring; press the seam open. Neaten one long edge of the skirt ring with a narrow double hem: fold under the raw edge by approx. 6mm (¼in) and press in place, then fold under again to create a neat edge. Press once more before topstitching in place.

11 Take your folded pink floral-print fabric with the peplums traced onto it and, keeping the fabric folded, sew along the traced lines, leaving the top section open as indicated by the broken line on the peplum template. Cut the peplums out approx. 3mm (⅛in) outside your sewn line and turn right side out; press and then topstitch along the sewn edges.

FiG. 3

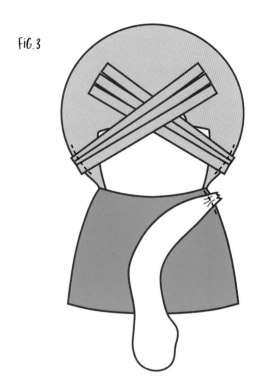

12 Return to your main skirt ring and mark the halfway points along the top raw edge only. Take one of your peplum pieces and centre the top raw edge along one of the halfway points on the skirt ring as shown in **Fig. 4**, and machine tack (baste) in place. Repeat to attach the remaining peplum to the other halfway point on the skirt.

13 The skirt will be gathered to fit, so you need to work two lines of machine stitching at approx. 3mm (⅛in) and 6mm (¼in) from the top raw edge of your skirt (including peplums). Begin by setting your machine to the largest stitch size and make sure not to secure your stitching at the start and finish.

14 Once both stitching lines have been worked, pull the loose bobbin threads to gather the top skirt edge evenly. You are aiming for this to measure the same circumference as the open end of Penelope's body (approx. 24cm/9½in). Adjust your gathers so that the peplums sit nicely and evenly at either side. (I chose to have the peplum sections only very slightly gathered and the front and back skirt sections more heavily gathered.)

15 Fit the gathered skirt over the open end of the body so that right sides are together and the raw gathered edge of the skirt is lined up with the raw bottom edge of the body. Tack (baste) neatly and evenly in place.

16 Take the two body bottom pieces and sew along the short edges with right sides together to create a ring. Keeping the fabric ring inside out, fit the body bottom over the skirt so that what will become the top edge of the body bottom meets the raw edge of the body/skirt layers. Tack (baste) in place. Remembering to re-set your machine stitch to a small stitch length of approx. 1.5, sew these three layers together securely. Fold the skirt and body bottom down into place.

17 To make Penelope's legs, start by making your leg panel fabric: take the linen leg strip and blue patterned fabric shoe strip and sew with right sides together along one long 30.5cm (12in) edge. Open out and press. Fold the fabric panel in half widthways, so that the short edges meet and right sides are together, making sure that the fabrics and seam line are perfectly aligned.

FIG. 4

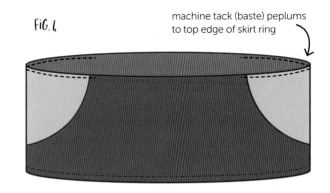

machine tack (baste) peplums to top edge of skirt ring

18 Place the leg template onto the folded fabric panel making sure that the marked shoe line matches up with the seam in the fabric. Draw around it twice, flipping the template for the second trace. Keeping the fabric panel folded, sew along the traced lines, leaving the straight ends unstitched as indicated by the broken line on the template. Cut out each leg approx. 3mm (⅛in) outside your sewn lines and turn the legs right side out. Firmly stuff the limbs to the very ends with toy filling, leaving the last 2.5cm (1in) unstuffed. Tack (baste) the open ends closed.

19 Fold the bottom edge of the body in by 6mm (¼in) and press in place. Take the legs and, ensuring that the toes are facing inwards, position them between the folded edges of the body so that the left leg is at the left side seam and the right leg is at the right side seam, and tack (baste) in place. There should be a gap between the legs as in **Fig. 5**. Topstitch the legs into place as close to the body edge as possible and through all layers, leaving the gap between the legs open for stuffing.

20 Now stuff Penelope with toy filling: stuff the head first ensuring that you have a firm fill before starting to stuff the body. When the head and body are firmly stuffed, ladder stitch the opening closed (see Stitching Techniques), stuffing a little more as you go if required.

21 Plait the fabric strips at either side of the head and secure the ends of the plaits with a few stitches. Cover the securing stitches with a bow tied from two lengths of all six strands of blue embroidery thread (floss).

FIG. 5

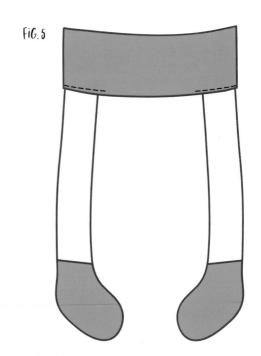

22 Mark the facial details onto Penelope's face (see head template). Using two strands of pink embroidery thread (floss) create the mouth with backstitch and the cheek circles with running stitch. Using two strands of black embroidery thread (floss), satin stitch the eyes and backstitch the eyelashes.

Handy Tip

If you are intending to give this toy to a baby or very young child, omit the crown as this small part could be a choking hazard.

23 To make Penelope's crown, take the piece of yellow felt and fold it in half. Trace the crown template onto the folded felt and then cut out to give you two crown pieces. Pin the crown pieces together so that they are aligned, and topstitch together all the way around them, as close to the edge as possible. Fuse the red felt heart to the centre front of the crown and machine appliqué in place with standard straight stitch. Fold the crown in half, right sides together, so the short ends meet and sew with a 3mm (⅛in) seam allowance. Turn right side out.

24 Position the crown as desired onto the princess's head and pin in place. Using two strands of strong polyester thread, ladder stitch the bottom edge of the crown into place (see Stitching Techniques: Attaching Parts), going around your stitching at least twice to ensure a strong attachment.

Handy Tip

I chose to position my doll's crown off to one side of the head as she is always running around, but you could place yours centrally if you prefer.

GARDEN QUILT

Wrap your precious little one in this gorgeous quilt to keep them as snug as a bug in a rug. Perfect to brighten up any room, this single bed sized quilt features simple piecing with some lovely appliqué blocks made using motifs from my 'Snug as a Bug' fabric collection. You can make more appliqué blocks, or mix and match the appliqué shapes in any way you choose, to create your own one-of-a-kind Garden Quilt.

YOU WILL NEED

Note: Use 100% cotton patchwork fabrics 106cm–114cm (42in–44in) wide for this project.

★ 46cm (18in) x full fabric width of plain yellow fabric

★ 46cm (18in) x full fabric width of plain pink fabric

★ 30cm (12in) x full fabric width of plain blue fabric

★ 46cm (18in) each of a selection of ten 'Snug as a Bug' fabrics (or other small-scale prints)

★ 46cm (18in) pink binding fabric

★ 2.2m (2½yd) good-quality quilt wadding (batting)

★ 4.4m (5yd) of your chosen fabric for backing

★ 1m (40in) fusible webbing

★ Good-quality cotton thread for hand and machine sewing

★ Six-strand embroidery thread (floss): dark pink, blue and green

FINISHED SIZE: 1.4m (55in) wide x 1.9m (75in) long

CUTTING YOUR FABRICS

Note: Keep your fabric leftovers to be used for the appliqué motifs.

FROM PLAIN YELLOW FABRIC:

Cut two squares 29cm x 29cm (11½in x 11½in).
Cut two rectangles 15.5cm x 29cm (6in x 11½in).
Cut four squares 15.5cm x 15.5cm (6in x 6in).

FROM PLAIN PINK FABRIC:

Cut one square 29cm x 29cm (11½in x 11½in).
Cut three rectangles 15.5cm x 29cm (6in x 11½in).
Cut four squares 15.5cm x 15.5cm (6in x 6in).

FROM PLAIN BLUE FABRIC:

Cut one square 29cm x 29cm (11½in x 11½in).
Cut one rectangle 15.5cm x 29cm (6in x 11½in).
Cut five squares 15.5cm x 15.5cm (6in x 6in).

FROM FIVE OF THE 'SNUG AS A BUG' FABRICS:

Cut one square 29cm x 29cm (11½in x 11½in).
Cut two rectangles 15.5cm x 29cm (6in x 11½in).
Cut three squares measuring 15.5cm x 15.5cm (6in x 6in).

FROM THE REMAINING FIVE 'SNUG AS A BUG' FABRICS:

Cut three rectangles 15.5cm x 29cm (6in x 11½in).
Cut four squares 15.5cm x 15.5cm (6in x 6in).

MAKING THE QUILT

Note: A 6mm (¼in) seam allowance is included in all pattern pieces unless advised otherwise. Read through all instructions before beginning to avoid any surprises.

1 Trace the Garden Quilt appliqué templates (see Templates) onto fusible webbing following the cutting instructions provided. Note, each template is made of several parts that need to be cut individually to make up the appliqué block designs. Use the photographs of the quilt to guide you. Roughly cut the template shapes outside the traced lines.

2 Choose fabrics from your leftover pieces for each of the component parts of your appliqué templates. Make sure there is adequate contrast for touching fabrics in the final layout (see quilt photographs and note that the appliqué blocks are made using your plain fabrics as backgrounds). Once you are happy with your choices, iron the fusible webbing shapes to the wrong side of your selected fabric pieces. Cut out all the shapes along the traced lines on the fusible webbing.

3 Working on one appliqué block at a time, peel the backing paper from the appliqué pieces and position them in the correct order onto the plain fabric of your choosing; iron to fuse all pieces in place. You should have four large square flower appliqué blocks (one of each design), four rectangle long, thin flower appliqué blocks (two of each design), five small square flower appliqué blocks, and three small square ladybug appliqué blocks.

4 Using either machine or hand blanket stitch (see Stitching Techniques), appliqué all the pattern pieces into place onto each of your blocks. To complete the ladybug blocks, mark the stitching lines for the antennae and work these in backstitch (see Stitching Techniques) using three strands of embroidery thread (floss).

5 Take two squares measuring 15.5cm x 15.5cm (6in x 6in) randomly chosen from your plain, 'Snug as a Bug' and appliquéd blocks, and place together with right sides facing. Sew together along one edge to create a rectangle (see **Fig. 1**). Make 24 rectangles in this way. Press well, pressing seams to one side.

6 Take two of the pieced rectangles and place together with right sides facing. Sew together along one long edge, ensuring that the centre seams meet, to create a pieced square. This is your 'A block' (see **Fig. 2**). Make a total of 12 'A blocks'. Press well, pressing seams to the darker side, and set aside.

7 Take two rectangles measuring 15.5cm x 29cm (6in x 11½in) randomly chosen from your plain, 'Snug as a Bug' and appliquéd blocks, and place together with right sides facing. Sew together along one long edge to create a square (see **Fig. 3**). This is your 'B block' (see **Fig. 3**). Make a total of 14 'B blocks'. Press well, pressing seams to one side.

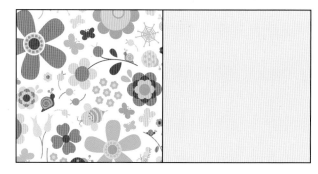

FiG.1

FiG.2   A block

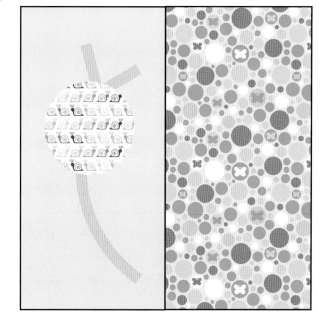

FiG.3   B block

Handy Tip

Make sure the same fabrics do not meet in any of your quilt piecing. Try to have different colours and scales of print alongside each other for best results.

8 Check that the blocks are square and the same size. If not then trim the blocks to size after sewing.

9 Take three of the A blocks and two of the B blocks. Positioning the B block rectangles vertically, sew the A blocks and B blocks together alternately, to create Row 1 of your quilt. Repeat to create Rows 3, 5 and 7, referring to the overhead photograph of the quilt.

10 Take three of the 29cm x 29cm (11½in x 11½in) fabric squares and two of the B blocks. Positioning the B block rectangles horizontally, sew the blocks together alternately to create Row 2 of your quilt. Repeat to create Rows 4 and 6, referring to the overhead photograph of the quilt.

11 Lay your pieced rows out in order on the floor and, once you are happy with the arrangement, sew the seven rows together along the length. To ensure that all seams and blocks meet evenly, you may like to pin your rows together before sewing (I recommend pinning and adding one row at a time). Once the stitching of the rows is completed, press seams to one side.

12 To make a backing for your quilt, cut two lengths of backing fabric, each measuring 2.2m (87in) in length by the full fabric width. Sew together along the 2.2m (87in) edge and press to one side. Your backing will be wider than required so trim the width only of your quilt backing to measure approx. 1.65m (65in).

Handy Tip

For a quicker and more economical way to back your quilt, purchase 2.2m (2 ½ yd) of wide quilt-backing fabric.

Row 1

Row 2

Row 3

Row 4

Row 5

Row 6

Row 7

13 Make your quilt sandwich: place the backing right side facing down on a flat surface. Pull taut and tape the fabric down to your surface to avoid movement. In the same way, lay the wadding (batting) on top, and finally the pieced quilt top, right side facing up. Tack (baste) the layers together using curved basting pins, or by taking large tacking (basting) stitches through all layers at regular intervals.

14 Quilt as desired. I chose a custom quilting design with my longarm quilter but you could just as easily hand quilt or machine quilt using the stitch-in-the-ditch method. Avoid quilting within the appliqué motifs. It is much more effective to quilt an outline around the outside of the shapes to make them really pop out. Once your quilt is fully quilted, trim the wadding (batting) and backing edges to 6mm (¼in) outside of your quilt top edges.

15 Cut seven lengths of your chosen binding fabric each measuring 6.5cm (2½in) by the full fabric width. Take your first two binding strips and place the trimmed ends on top of each other as shown in **Fig. 4**, and sew together at a 45-degree angle. Repeat with all strips to create one long length of binding. Trim the seam allowance and press all seams open. Fold the binding strip in half, wrong sides facing, all the way along its length and press well.

FiG. 4

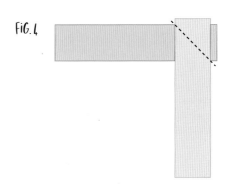

16 Starting 13cm (5in) from the beginning of your binding strip, start sewing the raw edge of your folded binding to the raw edge of your quilt front (**Fig. 5**).

17 When you reach a corner, stop and secure your stitching 6mm (¼in) from the corner edge (**Fig. 6a**). Fold your binding strip up and away from your quilt to create a 45-degree angle (**Fig. 6b**). Holding this fold in place, now fold the binding strip back down to lay neatly against the next edge of your quilt. Continue sewing your binding in place, beginning 6mm (¼in) from the corner (**Fig. 6c**).

18 Continue to sew your binding in place all the way around the quilt, and finish and secure when you are approx. 25cm (10in) from your starting point. Laying the start and the end of your binding strips in place along the remaining quilt edge, trim the ends of your binding strip so that they overlap by 1.3cm (½in). Open the ends out and sew together, right sides facing. Refold the binding strip and sew the remaining section in place.

19 Fold the binding over the raw edges to the back of your quilt, enclosing the wadding (batting). Pin or clip in place. Working by hand, ladder stitch the neat folded edge of the binding to the quilt back (see Stitching Techniques), mitring each corner as you reach it.

Handy Tip

When hand stitching your binding in place, make sure you use a thread colour that matches the binding fabric to make your stitches as invisible as possible.

FIG. 5
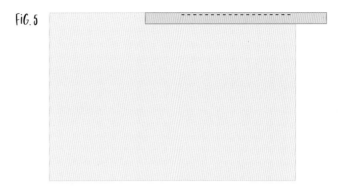

FIG. 6A
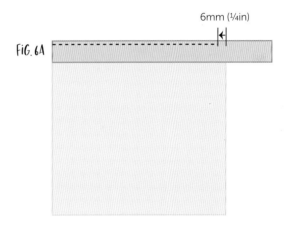

6mm (¼in)

FIG. 6B
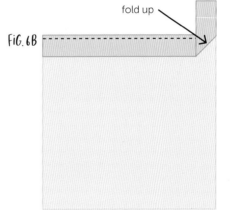

fold up

FIG. 6C
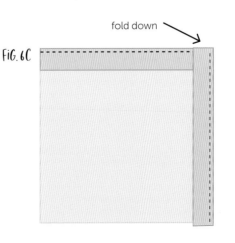

fold down

LADYBUG BAG

Little children love to have their own bag in which to carry around their most important and precious toys. Knowing just how much my little girl adores ladybugs, I had the thought that it would be perfect to combine the two. The Ladybug Bag I have designed is the perfect size for carrying all that the little one in your life needs to go about their busy day. But wait - lift the ladybug's wings to reveal secret pockets...

YOU WILL NEED

Note: *Use 100% cotton patchwork fabric with a width of 106cm–114cm (42in–44in).*

★ 25.5cm (10in) x full fabric width of blue small-scale floral-print fabric (front pocket, handles)

★ 53cm x 65cm (21in x 26in) pink small-scale floral-print (main bag, lining)

★ 10cm (4in) x the full fabric width of white snail-print (bag top)

★ 50cm x 30cm (20in x 12in) raspberry spot-print fabric (wings)

★ 38cm (15in) lightweight fusible fleece

★ 110cm (44in) of 1.8cm (¾in) yellow bias tape

★ Good-quality polyester thread

FINISHED SIZE: 38cm (15in) high x 30cm (12in) wide

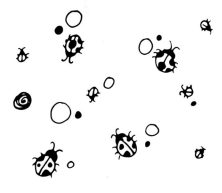

CUTTING YOUR FABRICS

Note: *Trace the Ladybug Bag templates (see Templates) onto template plastic, transferring all the markings, and cut out around the traced lines. Follow the instructions on the templates to make the full pocket and full main bag templates.*

FROM THE BLUE SMALL-SCALE FLORAL PRINT:

Draw around the pocket template once onto folded fabric, right sides together, and cut out along the drawn line to give you two pocket pieces.

Cut four strips 4cm x 38cm (1½in x 15in) for the handles.

FROM THE PINK SMALL-SCALE FLORAL PRINT:

Draw around the main bag template twice onto folded fabric, right sides together, and cut out along the drawn lines to give you two main bag pieces and two lining pieces.

FROM THE WHITE SNAIL PRINT:

Draw around the bag top template twice onto folded fabric, right sides together, and cut out along the drawn lines to give you four bag top pieces.

FROM THE RASPBERRY SPOT-PRINT:

Draw around the wing template twice onto folded fabric, right sides together, and cut out along the drawn lines to give you four wing pieces.

FROM THE FUSIBLE FLEECE:

Draw around the pocket template once, the main bag template twice, the bag top template twice, and the wing template twice (flip the template for the second wing). Cut along the drawn lines.

Cut two strips 4cm x 38cm (1½in x 15in) for the handles.

MAKING THE BAG

Note: *A 6mm (¼in) seam allowance is included in all pattern pieces unless advised otherwise. Read through all instructions before beginning to avoid any surprises.*

1 Iron fusible fleece to the wrong side of the corresponding fabric pieces.

2 Take the two pocket pieces and, working on one at a time, sew the pleats into place by folding the raw pleat edges on top of each other, right sides facing, and sewing into place.

3 Place the pocket pieces together, right sides facing and sew along the top edge only. Turn right sides out and press. Topstitch the sewn edge with two lines of stitching. Tack (baste) the remaining raw edges of the pocket together evenly.

Handy Tip

A single or double line of topstitching gives a neat, professional finish to bag seams and handles.

4 Take the two main bag and two lining pieces and sew the pleats into place as in step 2.

5 Take the main bag front (with fleece) and place the pocket on top right sides facing up. Ensure that the bottom edge and pleats meet and then machine tack (baste) the raw edges of the pocket evenly into place. Topstitch a line of stitching from the centre top to the centre bottom of the pocket, to create a double pocket (see **Fig. 1**).

6 Take the main bag front (with pocket) and the main bag back (with fleece) and place together with right sides facing. Sew together along the side and bottom edges, leaving the top edge open. Turn right side out.

7 Place the bag lining pieces together with right sides facing, and, leaving the top edge unstitched, sew together along the side and bottom edges, leaving a 10cm (4in) gap in the bottom edge for turning. **Do not** turn through at this stage.

8 Take one of the wing pieces with fleece and one without fleece and place together with wrong sides facing. Tack (baste) together all around the edges. Repeat to make the second wing.

9 Take a 56cm (22in) length of bias tape and fold in half along its length with wrong sides facing. Press very well. Bind the raw edge of the sides of the wing (**do not** bind the top straight edge): place the raw edge of the wing into the fold of the bias tape; make sure you catch both sides of the bias tape as you topstitch it in place around the edge, mitring the bottom corner as you go. Repeat for the second wing.

Fig. 1

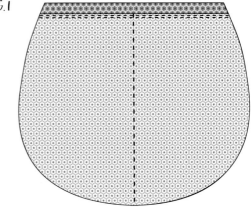

Handy Tip

You can divide one or both pockets further by adding more lines of topstitching, to make, for example, a row of pencil pockets.

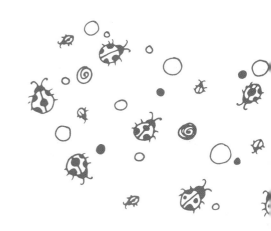

10 With the main bag right side up, position the wings, also right side up, onto the bag front so that they become flaps to cover the pockets. Tack (baste) the top raw edge of the wings to the top edge of the main bag front, as shown in **Fig. 2**.

11 Take one of the handle strips with fleece and one without fleece and place together with right sides facing. Sew along both long edges, turn and press. Topstitch a line of stitching along both sides of the handle strip. Repeat to make a second handle.

12 With the main bag right side up, position one handle onto the bag front. Tack (baste) the raw ends of the handle to the top edge of the main bag front approx. 4cm (1½in) from each side (see **Fig. 3**). Turn the bag over and repeat to attach the second handle to the bag back.

FiG. 2

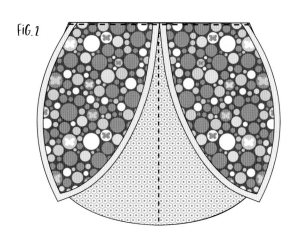

FiG. 3

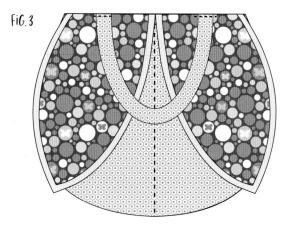

Handy Tip

For a more secure bag opening, insert a magnetic closure into the lining of the bag top (on both sides) before attaching it to the main bag.

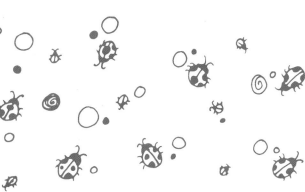

13 Take one of the bag top pieces with fleece and one without fleece and place together with right sides facing. Sew along the top curved edge only; turn and press. Topstitch with two lines of stitching. Repeat to make a second bag top.

14 With the main bag right side up, position one bag top onto the bag front. Tack (baste) the raw ends of the bag top to the top edge of the main bag (see **Fig. 4**). Turn the bag over and repeat to attach the second bag top to the bag back.

15 Place the main bag (right side facing out) into the inside-out lining bag. Make sure that all the layers are lying flat and straight between the two bag layers and that the top edges are aligning, then tack (baste) into place. Sew the bag top together securely.

16 Turn the bag right side out through the gap in the bottom edge of the lining. Fold the lining inside the bag and press the top edge well.

17 Fold the wings up so that they are out of the way, then topstitch all the way around the top edge of the main bag. Slipstitch the gap in the lining closed.

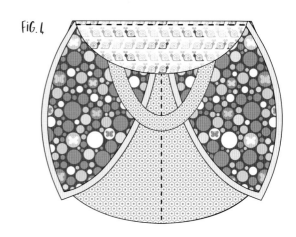

FIG. 4

SEBASTIAN THE SNAIL

Sebastian the Snail, with his spiral shell and tiny antennae, is such a sweet little creature. He goes about his day as silent as can be, crawling amongst the beautiful flowers in the garden, and he would make the perfect companion for any little explorer. After a long day outside, Sebastian likes nothing better than coming indoors to be cuddled tightly in little arms.

CUTTING YOUR FABRICS

Note: *Trace the Sebastian the Snail templates (see Templates) onto tracing paper or template plastic, transferring all of the markings, and cut them out around the traced lines.*

FROM YOUR LARGE FLORAL-PRINT FABRIC:

Fold the fabric in half with right sides together, then trace the main body template once onto the wrong side of the folded fabric, transferring all markings. Cut out along the traced lines to give you two mirror-image pieces of each.

Opening out the remaining fabric to a single layer, trace head and base gusset templates once onto the wrong side of the single layer of fabric. Cut out along the drawn lines.

FROM YOUR SMALL FLORAL-PRINT FABRIC:

Fold the fabric in half with right sides together. Draw around the shell template twice and the shell gusset template once onto folded fabric and cut out along the drawn lines.

Refold the remaining fabric, right sides together, and trace the antennae templates onto the folded fabric but **do not** cut out.

FROM YOUR FUSIBLE FLEECE:

Trace one shell gusset piece and the two shell pieces.

PREPARING TO SEW

1 Set your sewing machine to a small stitch length of approx. 1.5 for stitching the toy and use a good-quality polyester thread for strong seams.

2 From your white wool-felt, draw around the smaller circular eye template twice onto the felt and cut out. Leave aside the blue felt for now – this will be cut out later, when making the eyes.

MAKING THE SNAIL

Note: *A 6mm (¼in) seam allowance is included in all pattern pieces unless advised otherwise. Read through all instructions before beginning to avoid any surprises.*

1 Take the head and base gusset pieces and machine stitch together along the neckline edge as marked, with right sides facing.

2 Take one of the main body pieces and the joined gusset piece. Matching up the neckline seam of the gusset with the neck on the snail's main body, tack (baste) the gusset in place with right sides facing, working from the snail's tail, along the base and all the way around the head. Machine stitch the gusset in place.

Handy Tip

Lock your stitching by starting and ending all machine sewing with a few reverse stitches. This ensures that the seam won't split when you are turning and stuffing your soft toy.

3 Tack (baste) the remaining raw edge of the gusset to the second main body piece with right sides facing. Machine stitch in place and then continue to sew the remaining raw edges of the snail's back together, leaving the turning gap open as indicated.

4 Carefully snip the tail point and the corners. Turn Sebastian right side out, and stuff firmly with toy filling. Ladder stitch the turning gap closed (see Stitching Techniques).

5 Mark the shell spiral onto one shell front piece and one shell back piece. Interface one shell gusset piece and the two shell pieces marked with the spirals with fusible fleece. Hand stitch the spirals with two strands of pink embroidery thread (floss) using small chain stitches (see Stitching Techniques).

6 Tack (baste) the gusset (with fleece) in place between the two hand embroidered shell pieces with right sides together, taking care to match the stars marked on your shell and gusset templates. Once evenly tacked (basted), machine stitch in place. Repeat with the remaining shell and gusset pieces (without fleece) to make the shell lining.

Handy Tip

Snipping into the seam allowance creates a smooth and neat finish after turning, but it can weaken the seams. Snip once or twice only into a corner and ensure that your cut does not reach all the way to your stitching line.

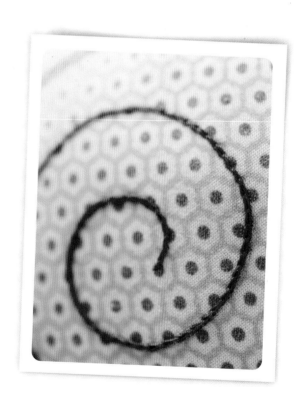

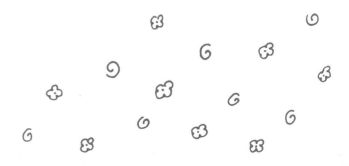

7 Place the main shell and shell lining pieces together with right sides facing, and machine stitch all the way around the raw edges. Snip into the corners and curves. Cut a turning gap in the centre of the shell lining, making sure that you cut the lining layer only, and turn the shell right side out through this gap. Press, then topstitch all the way around the bottom edge.

8 Stuff the shell lightly and then sit this on the snail's back in the desired position. Pin or tack (baste) into place. Ladder stitch the inner bottom edge of the shell onto the snail's back using a double strand of strong polyester thread (see Stitching Techniques : Attaching Parts). When you are approx. 2.5cm–5cm (1in– 2in) from finishing the sewing, stuff the shell firmly through the remaining gap until you are happy with the shape. Ladder stitch the gap closed.

9 Machine stitch the antennae along the drawn lines, leaving the bottom straight edges open for turning. Cut the antennae out approx. 3mm–6mm (⅛in–¼in) outside the sewn lines. Turn right side out and stuff with toy filling, taking care not to damage the seams. To turn small pieces easily, insert a pair of tweezers into your unturned piece, grab the end and pull it through the opening. When stuffing small and fiddly pieces, it can be helpful to use the blunt end of a wooden skewer to push in small pieces of stuffing one at a time. Always work slowly and patiently to ensure that you do not split the seams.

Handy Tip

If the snail is well stuffed, you will find it is much easier to stitch the face details and attach the antennae.

10 Fold the raw edges of the antennae to the inside, then stitch them in place on the snail's head by ladder stitching along the folded bottom edge (see Stitching Techniques: Attaching Parts). Sew around the base of each antenna twice to make sure they are securely stitched on.

11 Position the white wool-felt pupils onto the blue wool-felt, making sure there is adequate space around each one. To appliqué the white pupils in place, blanket stitch by hand or machine (see Stitching Techniques). Mark the eye dot inside each pupil and work a French knot with six strands of grey embroidery thread (floss). Draw the larger eye template onto the blue felt and cut out the completed eyes along the drawn lines.

12 Position the eyes onto the snail's face and use fabric glue to tack (baste) into position. Using two strands of blue embroidery thread (floss), blanket stitch the eyes to secure in place. Mark the stitching line for the snail's mouth between the eyes, and sew with chain stitch using two strands of dark grey embroidery thread (floss) (see Stitching Techniques).

Handy Tip

You could scale the templates down by varying degrees on a photocopier, to create a whole family of snails.

FLUTTER MOBILE

Butterflies are so peaceful, so beautiful, and bring wonder to all. A butterfly mobile, hanging above the cot, is the perfect way to capture the imagination of a newborn baby. Little ones will be enthralled, watching these dancing butterflies flutter by, as they settle into a sweet sleep. You could make up more little butterflies as the perfect take-along toys for babies on the go.

YOU WILL NEED

Note: *Use 100% cotton patchwork fabric.*

★ 25.5cm x 25.5cm (10in x 10in) each of a selection of six 'Snug as a Bug' (or other small-scale print) fabrics

★ 2m (2⅛yd) of 1.8cm- (¾in-) wide bias tape to match your fabrics

★ 10cm (4in) lightweight fusible fleece

★ One 20cm- (8in-) diameter wooden embroidery hoop

★ Wooden beads: one 40mm (1½in) and one 25mm (1in)

★ Small scraps of fabric to cover beads

★ 1m (40in) fine 2mm aqua cord (antennae)

★ Approx. 4m (4⅜yd) fine white 2mm cord (for hanging strings)

★ Fabric glue

★ Six-strand embroidery thread (floss): black

★ Good-quality polyester thread (if cotton thread is used, your seams could break during stuffing)

★ Good-quality polyester toy filling

★ Drill fitted with a 2mm–3mm drill bit

★ Large-eyed dollmaker's needle

Finished size: 50cm (20in) high x 20cm (8in) wide

CUTTING YOUR FABRICS

Note: Trace the Flutter Mobile templates (see Templates) onto tracing paper or template plastic, transferring all of the markings, and cut them out around the traced lines.

FROM YOUR SIX 'SNUG AS A BUG' SQUARES OF FABRIC:

Take each of the pieces of fabric measuring 25.5cm x 25.5cm (10in x 10in) and cut into two pieces measuring 25.5cm x 15.5cm (10in x 6in) and 25.5cm x 10cm (10in x 4in).

Take each 25.5cm x 15.5cm (10in x 6in) piece of fabric and fold in half with right sides facing. Draw around the butterfly body template onto the folded fabric, but ***do not*** cut out.

Take each 25.5cm x 10cm (10in x 4in) and iron a piece of fusible fleece measuring 13cm x 10cm (5in x 4in) to the wrong side of half of this. Fold the fabric in half with right sides facing, and draw around the wing template onto the fleece side, but ***do not*** cut out.

PREPARING TO SEW

1 Put aside all the scraps of fabric for later; these will be used to cover the beads.

2 Set your sewing machine to a small stitch length of approx. 1.5 for stitching the toy and use a good-quality polyester thread for strong seams.

MAKING THE MOBILE

Note: A 6mm (¼in) seam allowance is included in all pattern pieces unless advised otherwise. Read through all instructions before beginning to avoid any surprises.

1 Take one of the prepared 25.5cm x 15.5cm (10in x 6in) pieces of folded fabric (right sides facing). Machine stitch the body around the drawn line, leaving the antennae gaps open as indicated on the template. Cut out the butterfly body approx. 6mm (¼in) outside the sewn line and snip the corners.

2 Measure two 7.5cm (3in) lengths of aqua cord and, to keep it from unravelling, secure at either end with a little tape before cutting. Insert the cords into the antennae gaps, so that all but the very ends of the cords sit within the head. Sew the ends of the cord in place securely.

3 Snip a small slit as marked on the template on one side only of the butterfly, then turn right side out through this gap (note, the turning gap will be hidden by the wings later). Stuff the butterfly firmly with polyester toy filling.

Handy Tip

When choosing fabrics, use fun contrasting colours to make the mobile really eye catching.

4 Tie a knot in the ends of the antennae; trim to the desired length. Mark the eyes and mouth onto the front of the butterfly (the back of the butterfly is the side with the turning gap). Using two strands of black embroidery thread (floss), stitch the eyes with satin stitch and the mouth with chain stitch (see Stitching Techniques).

5 Measure a 1m (40in) length of white cord and secure at either end with a little tape before cutting to prevent it from unravelling; tie a knot at one end and thread the unknotted end in the dollmaker's needle. Take the threaded needle from the inside of the butterfly (access through the turning gap in the back of the butterfly) and come out on the back of the butterfly's head marked with an 'X' on the template. The knot should catch inside the butterfly's head to give you a long hanging cord (see **Fig. 1**). Slipstitch the turning gap closed.

6 Repeat steps 1–5 to make five more butterfly bodies, but in step 5 use a 50cm (20in) length of white cord.

7 Take one of the fleece-backed 25.5cm x 10cm (10in x 4in) pieces of folded fabric (right sides facing). Machine stitch the wings around the drawn line.

8 Cut out the wings approx. 3mm (⅛in) outside the sewn line, and snip the corners. Snip a small slit (see template) on one side only of the wings, then turn right side out through this gap. Press then topstitch the edges.

9 Repeat steps 7 and 8 to give you six sets of butterfly wings in total.

FiG. 1

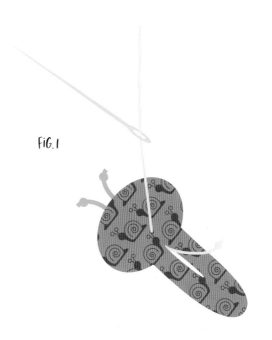

10 Take one of the butterfly body pieces and one of the butterfly wings. Work a line of medium-sized running stitches (see Stitching Techniques: Attaching Parts) in the centre of the back of the wings, from top to bottom, alongside the turning gap, and gather slightly. Now ladder stitch the centre line of the wings onto the back of the butterfly (see Stitching Techniques), covering both turning gaps in the process. Go over the stitching twice to make sure the wings are securely fastened. Repeat this step to give you six finished butterflies.

11 Take the 20cm- (8in-) diameter embroidery hoop; separate the rings and put aside the screw mechanism ring as this is not required for this project. Evenly mark the ring into sixths. Working with a drill fitted with a 2mm–3mm drill bit, drill a hole into the ring at each marked interval (see **Fig. 2**).

12 To cover the ring with fabric, use fabric glue to fix the end of the 2m (2⅛yd) length of bias tape on the inside of the ring, then wind the tape around the ring fixing it in place with glue as you go. Make sure to finish on the inside of the ring and secure the end well. Set-aside the unused bias tape (note, you will need a small piece at least 2.5cm/1in long in step 19), and allow to dry completely.

13 Take one of the butterflies and thread the loose end of its cord into the dollmaker's needle. Thread the cord through one of the holes in the ring working from the outside to the inside of the ring. Repeat to string all of the butterflies through the ring.

FIG. 2

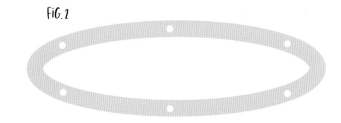

Handy Tip

When you cover a drilled hole on the hoop, make sure glue does not go inside the hole, and mark the position of the hole with a small dot for easy reference later.

14 When all the butterflies have been strung through the ring, adjust the ends of the cords until they are all even, intersecting at the desired length where the bead will be threaded on to hide the cord ends (note, the longer cord will become the hanging cord for the mobile).

15 Where the cords intersect, secure them together with a tied piece of thread, then carefully machine stitch over the intersection several times to ensure a strong join. Neatly trim back the shorter cord ends, leaving the longer one in place.

16 To cover your beads with fabric you first need to cut a small strip of fabric that is approx. 1.3cm (½in) longer than the circumference of your bead by half this length. Snip into the top and bottom edges of your fabric strip about every 6mm (¼in) as shown in **Fig. 3**.

17 Coat the middle unsnipped section of the wrong side of your fabric strip with glue. Wrap the glued fabric strip around the circumference of your bead ensuring it lays neatly and smoothly, and that the overlapped sections are well secured with glue. Working on the top edge of your bead first, and gluing one fringe piece at a time, secure each fringe piece straight up over the top edge of the bead, pushing the end neatly into the bead hole using a knitting needle or other round-ended tool. Repeat for the bottom edge of the bead. Allow your bead to dry completely before using.

18 Once the beads have completely dried, thread the cord first through the large bead, then through the small bead. Slide the beads down to cover the meeting point of the cords; secure the beads in place with glue if you choose to.

19 You may need to trim the long cord to give you the desired length for hanging the mobile. Fold the end of the cord onto itself by approx. 2.5cm (1in) and secure well before trimming the end. Take a small piece of the remaining bias tape and wrap this around the join, folding under the end to neaten, and sew in place. The finished mobile is ready to be hung.

FiG. 3

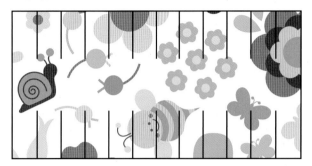

Handy Tip

As an alternative to covering with fabric, the ring and beads could be painted. Sand before painting and allow them to dry really well before continuing.

BUG IN A RUG

I will always remember how attached my little one was to her 'blanky' when she was a baby. By combining a cute toy with a soft and snuggly blanket, my Bug in a Rug is the perfect comforter for your child. For a gorgeous themed nursery, this sweet and cuddly Bug in a Rug has been made in colours to match the Garden Quilt.

YOU WILL NEED

Note: *Use 100% cotton patchwork fabric unless otherwise instructed; one fat-quarter measures 56cm x 46cm (22in x 18in)*

- ★ 53cm x 53cm (21in x 21in) pink, soft blanket fabric (I used minky)
- ★ One fat-quarter yellow web-patterned fabric (binding, head)
- ★ 15.5cm x 35.5cm (6in x 14in) aqua spot-print fabric (wings, antennae)
- ★ 10cm x 10cm (4in x 4in) pink shaded-fabric (face)
- ★ 15.5cm x 10cm (6in x 4in) lightweight fusible fleece
- ★ 10cm x 10cm (4in x 4in) fusible webbing
- ★ Six-strand embroidery thread (floss): pink and turquoise
- ★ Good-quality polyester toy filling
- ★ Good-quality polyester thread in a colour to match your blanket fabric

Finished size: 50cm (20in) square

CUTTING YOUR FABRICS

Note: Trace the Bug in a Rug templates (see Templates) onto tracing paper or template plastic, transferring all of the markings, and cut them out around the traced lines.

FROM YOUR SOFT BLANKET FABRIC:

Cut into a neat, even square 50cm x 50cm (20in x 20in).

FROM YOUR FAT-QUARTER OF YELLOW WEB-PATTERNED FABRIC:

Cut four strips 6.5cm x 52cm (2½in x 20½in) for the binding strips.

Take the remainder of the fat-quarter fabric and fold in half with right sides facing. Draw the head template twice onto the folded fabric and cut out along the drawn lines, to give you four head pieces. Transfer the pleat markings to the wrong side of the head pieces.

FROM YOUR AQUA SPOT-PRINT FABRIC:

Cut a piece 15.5cm x 15.5cm (6in x 6in). Fold in half with right sides facing. Draw around the antenna template twice onto the folded fabric, making sure to leave plenty of space in between. ***Do not*** cut out.

Take the remaining spot-print fabric and iron the fusible fleece measuring 15.5cm x 10cm (6in x 4in) to the wrong side. Fold the fabric in half with right sides facing, and draw around the wing template twice onto the fleece side of the folded fabric, leaving space in between. ***Do not*** cut out.

FROM YOUR PINK SHADED-FABRIC:

Iron the fusible webbing to the wrong side of the 10cm x 10cm (4in x 4in) piece. Draw around the face template onto the fusible webbing side and cut out along the drawn line.

PREPARING TO SEW

1 Set your sewing machine to a small stitch length of approx. 1.5 for stitching the toy and use a good-quality polyester thread for strong seams.

MAKING THE SNUGGLE BLANKET

Note: *A 6mm (¼in) seam allowance is included in all pattern pieces unless advised otherwise. Use a very small stitch on your sewing machine, and read through all instructions before beginning to avoid any surprises.*

1 Take one of the binding strips and place it on an ironing board, right side facing down. Fold in the short ends by 6mm (¼in) and press in place; now fold in the long raw edges by 6mm (¼in) and press in place (see **Fig. 1**). Fold the whole strip in half along the length with wrong sides facing, and press. Repeat to make three more binding strips.

2 Take one prepared (folded) binding strip and place it over one side edge of the soft blanket fabric square. Tack (baste) or pin into place ensuring that the strip is evenly positioned over both sides of the blanket fabric and that the ends meet the corners of the fabric square. Topstitch the inside edge of the binding strip onto the blanket, making sure that the stitching is securing both sides of the fabric as you go. Repeat to attach a binding strip on the opposite side of the blanket square.

Fig. 1

Fig. 2

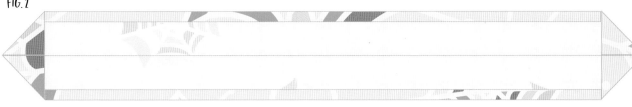

Handy Tip

If you are using minky or another stretch fabric, take care not to stretch the fabric as you sew or the blanket may be distorted out of shape.

Fig. 3

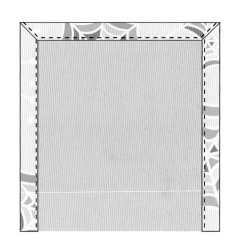

3 Take a third binding strip, open the main fold, and place the strip on the ironing board, right side facing down. Now fold in the corners to create triangles (see **Fig. 2**). Press well, then fold the strip in half along the length once again. Press well once more.

4 Fit the prepared binding strip over the edge of one of the unbound sides of the blanket so that the points of the triangle meet the corners of the blanket. Tack (baste) or pin in place, then topstitch the inside edge of the binding strip, and into the corner angles (see **Fig. 3**), to secure in place. Repeat to attach the final binding strip on the opposite side. Put the blanket aside.

5 Using a small machine stitch, sew the pleats in place on the wrong side of the head pieces and trim excess fabric.

6 Place two of the head pieces together, with right sides facing, so that the pleats and edges meet. Again using a small stitch, sew together along the centre front seam. Repeat for the remaining two head pieces. You now have a head front and a head back.

7 Place the head front and head back together with right sides facing, and sew together along the side and top edges only, leaving the antennae gaps open as indicated. The straight neckline edge at the bottom remains open but **do not** turn through yet.

8 Machine stitch around the drawn lines of the antennae fabric, leaving the bottom straight ends open as indicated on the template. Cut each antenna out by cutting approx. 3mm–6mm (⅛in–¼in) outside the sewn line. Turn the antennae right side out, then stuff firmly with small pieces of the polyester toy filling. When fully stuffed, tack (baste) the raw ends closed.

9 Insert the antennae into the gaps at the top of the head, so that the raw tacked (basted) edges of the antennae meet the top edge of the gaps and the antennae curve outwards; sew the gaps closed, following the curve of the head, to secure the antennae in place. Now turn the head right side out.

Handy Tip

To make turning the thin antenna quick and easy, insert a pair of tweezers, grip the end and pull through.

10 Machine stitch the wings fabric around the previously prepared drawn lines, leaving the straight ends open as indicated. Cut out the wings approx. 6mm (¼in) outside the sewn lines. Turn through and press well. Topstitch the wings approx. 3mm (⅛in) in from the seam edge. Take one of the wings, fold the raw straight edge onto itself and tack (baste) in place (see **Fig. 4**) to give the wing its distinctive 'fluttering' shape. Repeat for the second wing.

11 Take one of the wings and place it onto the side seam of the bug's head, making sure that the wing is facing forwards. It should be centred over the head's side seam, and the raw edges of the wing and head neckline should meet. Sew the wing onto the head along the fill line. Repeat on the other side with the remaining wing, again making sure that it is facing forwards.

12 Stuff the head firmly to the fill line with polyester toy filling; fold in the remaining raw edges of the head and wings and push inside the head.

13 Take the blanket and fold in half and half again to mark the centre point. Position the head at the centre mark on the right side of the blanket, and using a double thickness of strong polyester thread, ladder stitch the head in place (see Stitching Techniques Attaching Parts). Make sure that the raw seams are enclosed within the head and that the stitching is roughly at the level of the fill line. Ladder stitch in a circle following the natural shape of the neckline, then go around again to attach the head securely.

14 Peel the paper backing from the fusible webbing previously ironed onto the face fabric, and iron the face onto the front of the head. Using two strands of pink embroidery thread (floss), blanket stitch the face in place (see Stitching Techniques). Mark the eyes and mouth onto the face using a pencil, then stitch the face details using two strands of turquoise embroidery thread (floss), working the eyes with satin stitch and the mouth with backstitch (see Stitching Techniques).

FiG. 4

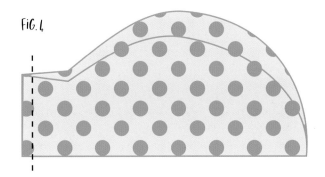

Handy Tip

If you are after a more compact comforter, you can reduce the fabric square to 30cm x 30cm (12in x 12in) and the binding strips to 32cm (12½in) in length.

STITCHING TECHNIQUES

BACKSTITCH

Backstitch creates a continuous line of stitching, so it is ideal for creating facial features on your toys.

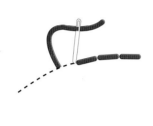

FRENCH KNOT

The double wrap French knot creates a prominent raised dot ideal for small features such as monkey's nostrils or pupils. For a triple wrap French knot, wrap the thread around the needle a third time before pulling through.

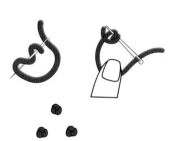

RUNNING STITCH

This simple stitch is used for gathering, as on Fifi's fairy skirt or for adding small features, such as Milo's cheeks.

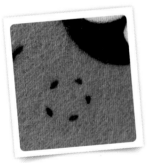

CHAIN STITCH

Chain stitch is great for creating thicker lines and therefore perfect for embroidering Sebastian's shell spiral, as shown here.

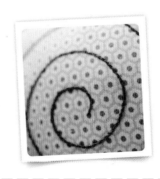

BLANKET STITCH

This edging stitch is used to secure appliquéd fabric pieces such as the lion's nose. If the stitches are functional rather than decorative, choose embroidery thread (floss) in a colour that matches the fabric or felt.

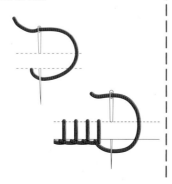

WHIP STITCH

This is used to sew together the edges of a gap where the stitching won't be seen, for example to close the turning slits on the dragon's limbs.

Satin Stitch

This can be used as a substitute for button eyes when making toys for very young children. First backstitch around the outside edge of a circle shape and then work stitches from one side to the other, keeping them close and even.

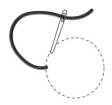 

Sinking a Knot

When button jointing legs, or completing any stitching on a toy that is already stuffed, you will want to avoid any knots being visible where you start and end your stitching, so for a neat finish you will need to sink your knot into the toy.

When you have completed the required sewing, tie a knot in the thread close to where it exits the toy. Take one last stitch into the toy, taking your needle through to an inconspicuous area approx. 2.5cm–5cm (1in–2in) away. Pull the thread through and it will snag when the knot reaches the fabric where you started your stitch. Hold the thread firmly and tug it quickly so that the knot pops into the toy.

Snip the thread end away right where it exits the fabric so that it too sinks into the toy.

Ladder Stitch

CLOSING GAPS

Use ladder stitch to sew turning gaps closed in a neat, strong and nearly invisible way.

ATTACHING PARTS

One of the uses for ladder stitch is to attach parts to soft toys. This method is usually used so that the attachment will either sit flat against, or protrude from, the stuffed toy. Follow the ladder stitch diagram for closing gaps, but make one stitch in the edge of the attachment, then make the next stitch in the body of the toy. The ladder stitches need to be sewn into the body following the shape of the attachment so that the attached part retains its shape.

 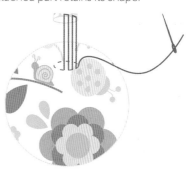

Templates

All templates shown at actual size and include seam allowance.

Petal the Pony

HOOF BASE

fabric grain line

LEG

fabric grain line

turning gap

fabric grain line

BODY

EAR

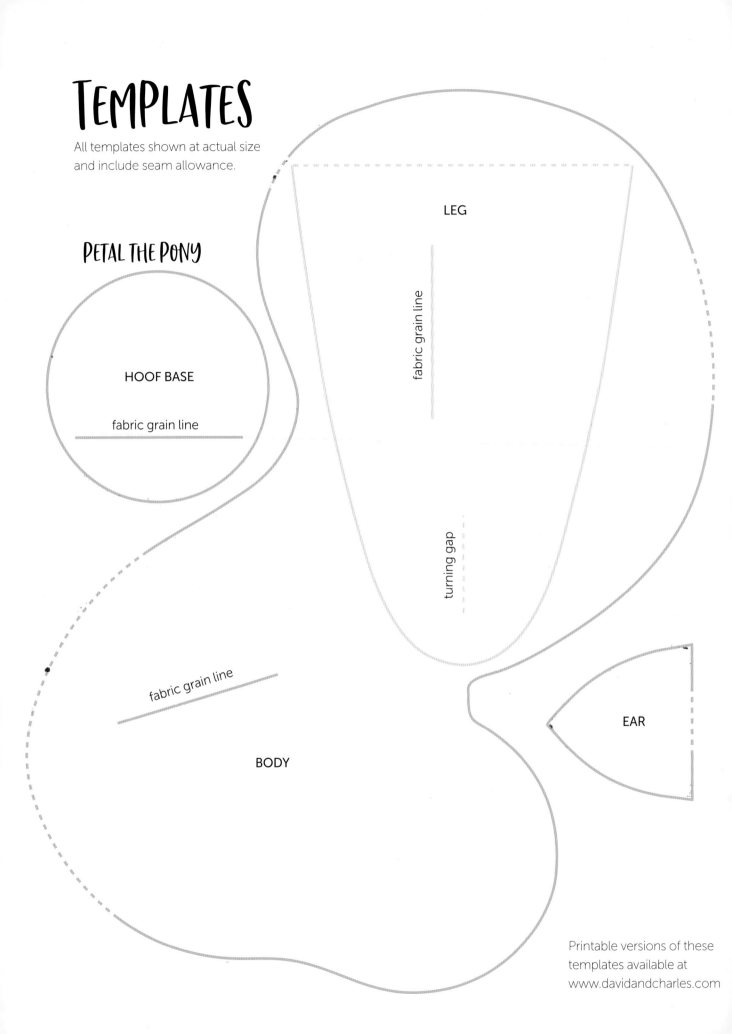

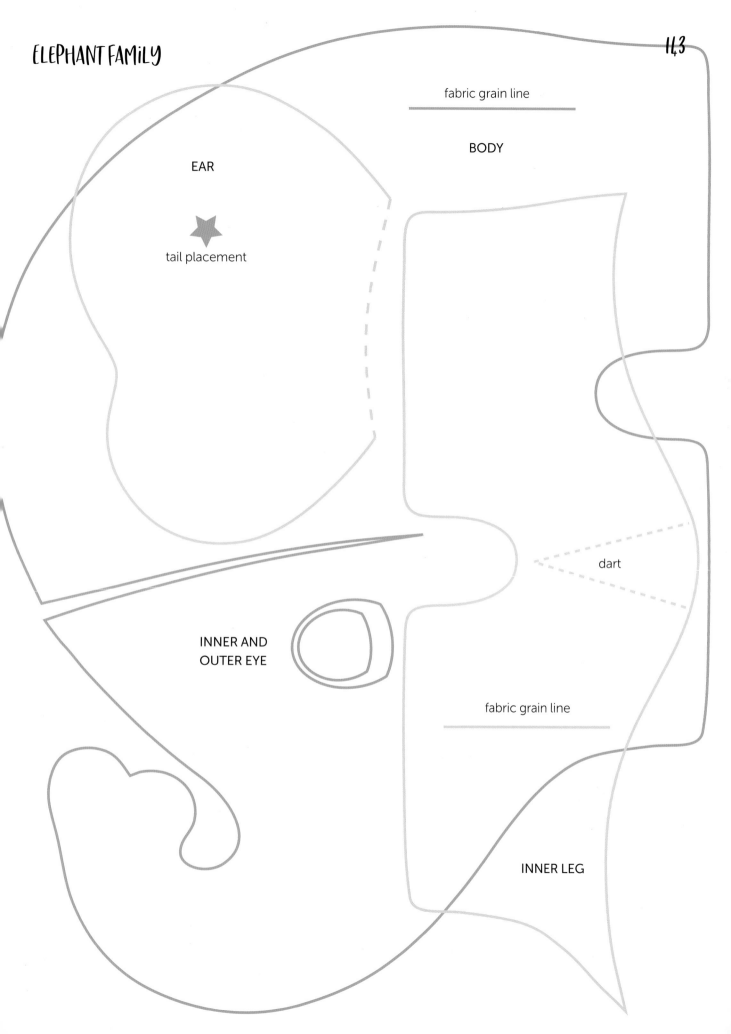

ELEPHANT FAMILY

fabric grain line

BODY

EAR

tail placement

dart

INNER AND
OUTER EYE

fabric grain line

INNER LEG

ELEPHANT FAMILY cont.

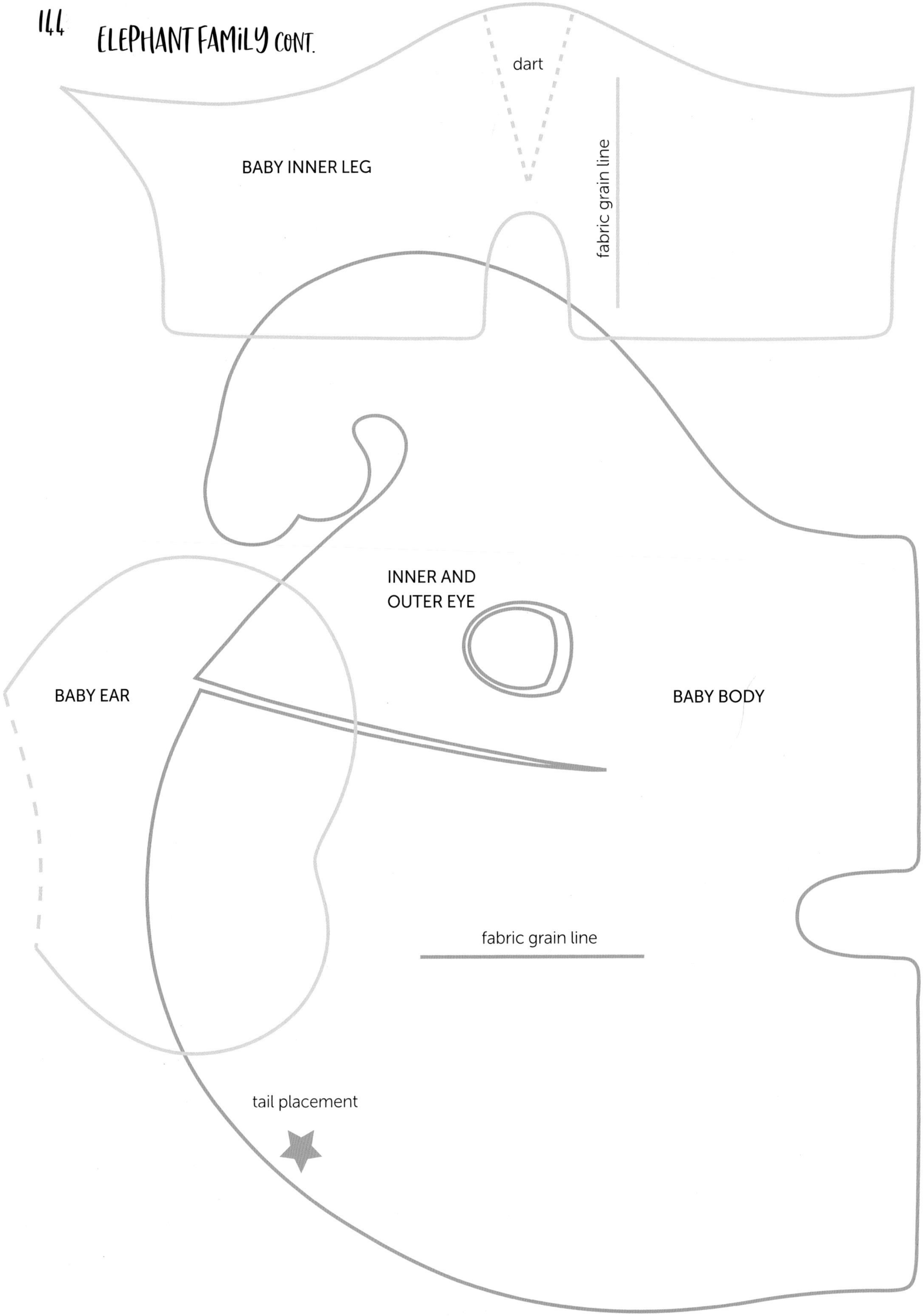

BABY INNER LEG

dart

fabric grain line

BABY EAR

INNER AND
OUTER EYE

BABY BODY

fabric grain line

tail placement

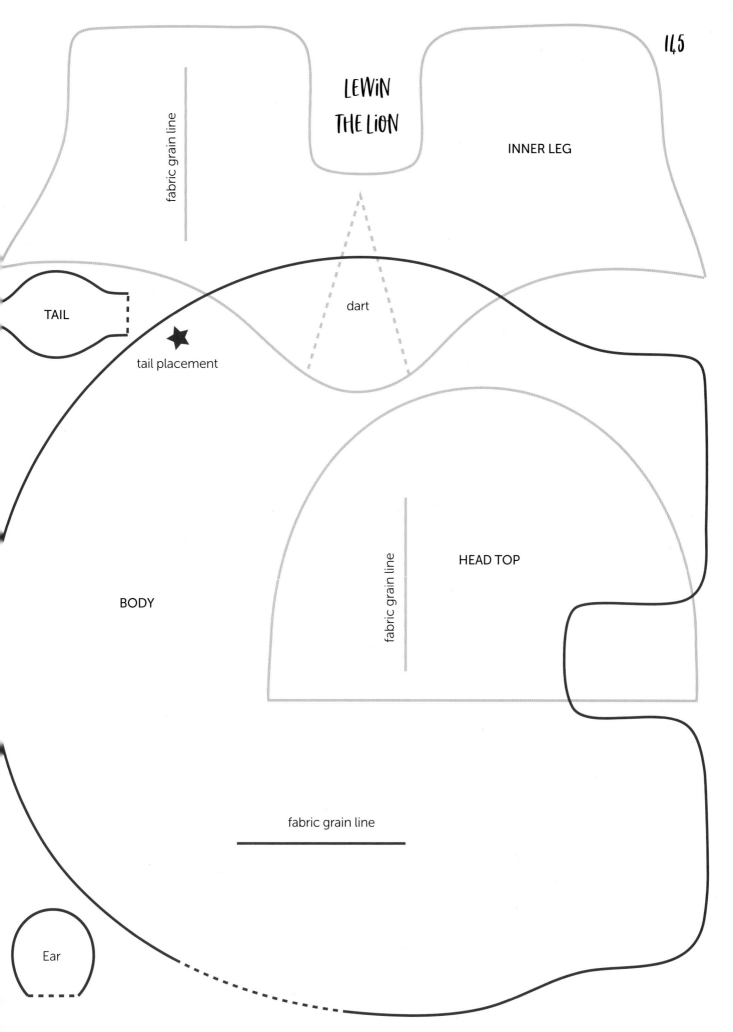

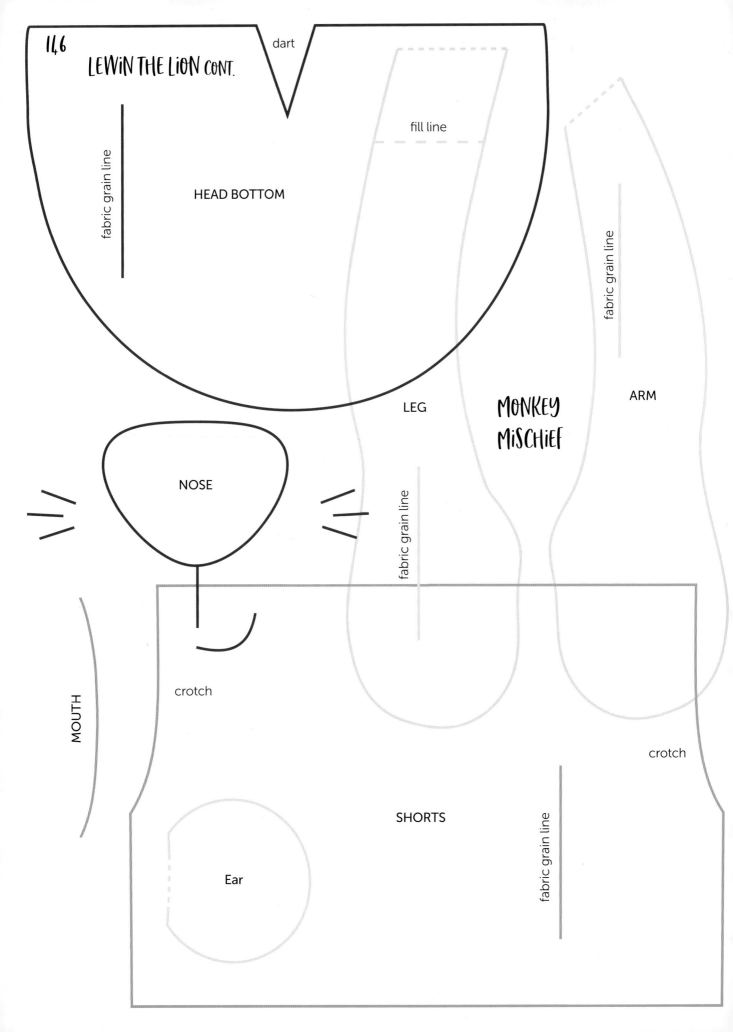

LEWIN THE LION cont.

dart

fill line

fabric grain line

HEAD BOTTOM

fabric grain line

ARM

NOSE

LEG

MONKEY MISCHIEF

fabric grain line

crotch

MOUTH

crotch

SHORTS

fabric grain line

Ear

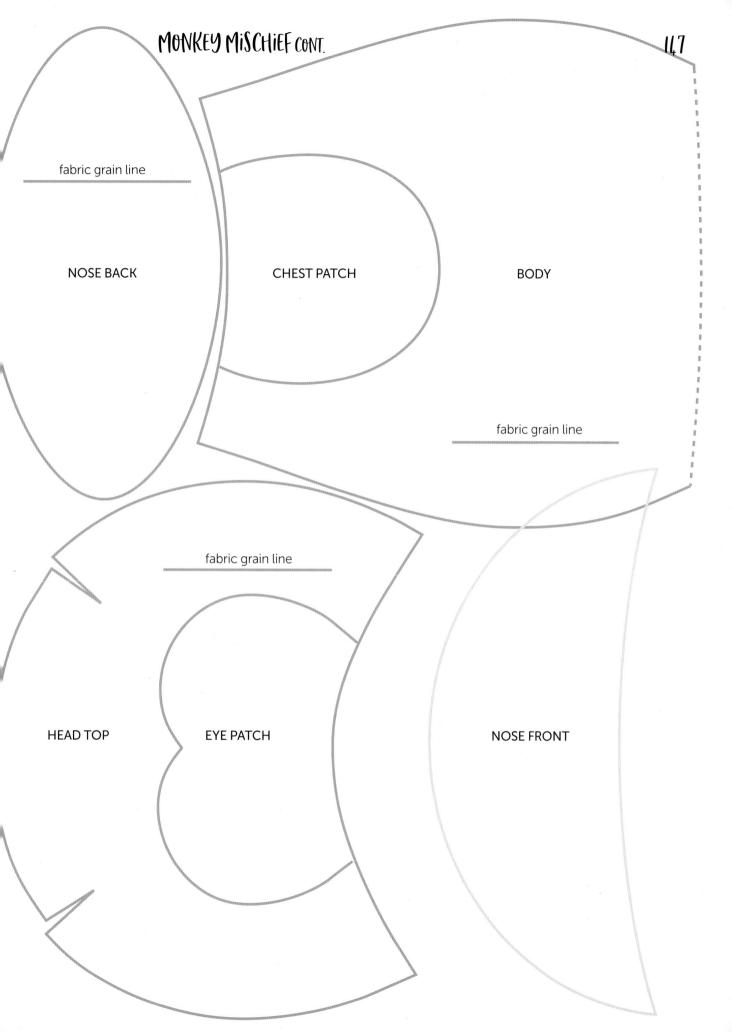

fabric grain line

NOSE BACK

CHEST PATCH

BODY

fabric grain line

fabric grain line

HEAD TOP

EYE PATCH

NOSE FRONT

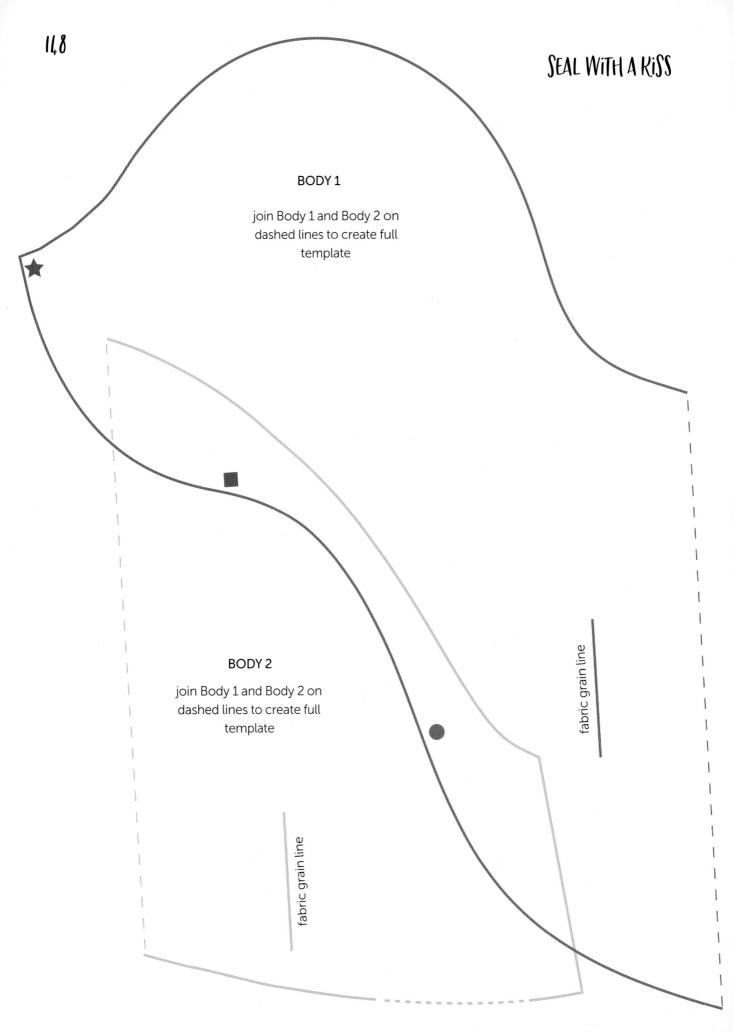

148

SEAL WITH A KISS

BODY 1

join Body 1 and Body 2 on dashed lines to create full template

BODY 2

join Body 1 and Body 2 on dashed lines to create full template

fabric grain line

fabric grain line

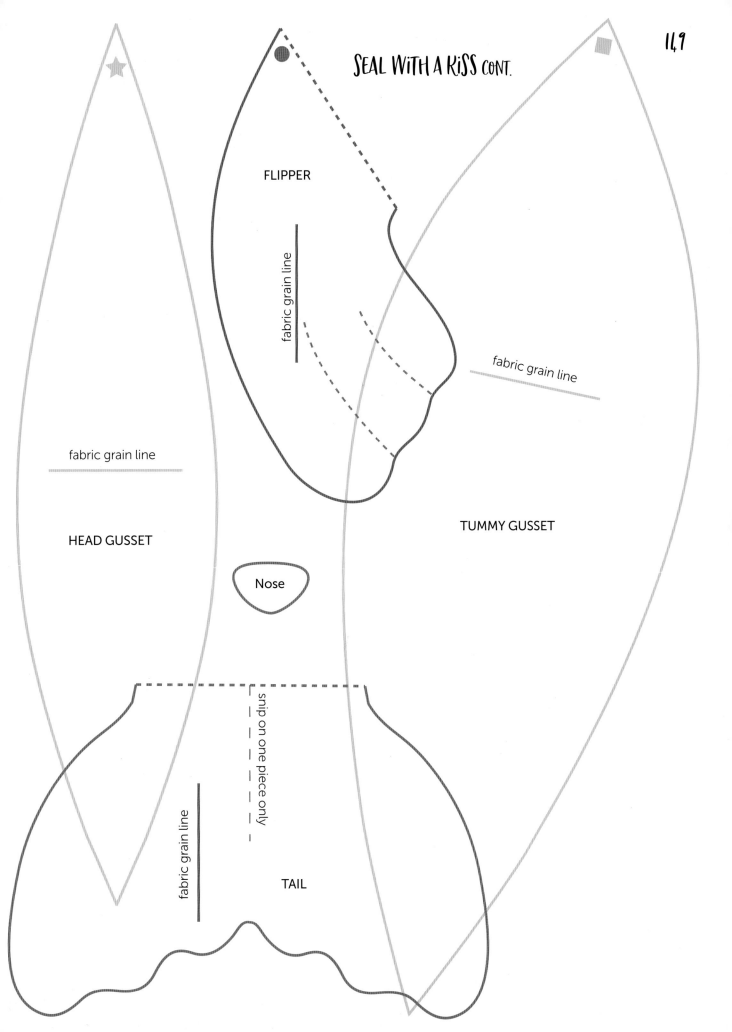

SEAL WITH A KISS cont.

FLIPPER

fabric grain line

fabric grain line

fabric grain line

HEAD GUSSET

TUMMY GUSSET

Nose

snip on one piece only

fabric grain line

TAIL

ARCHIE THE ALIEN

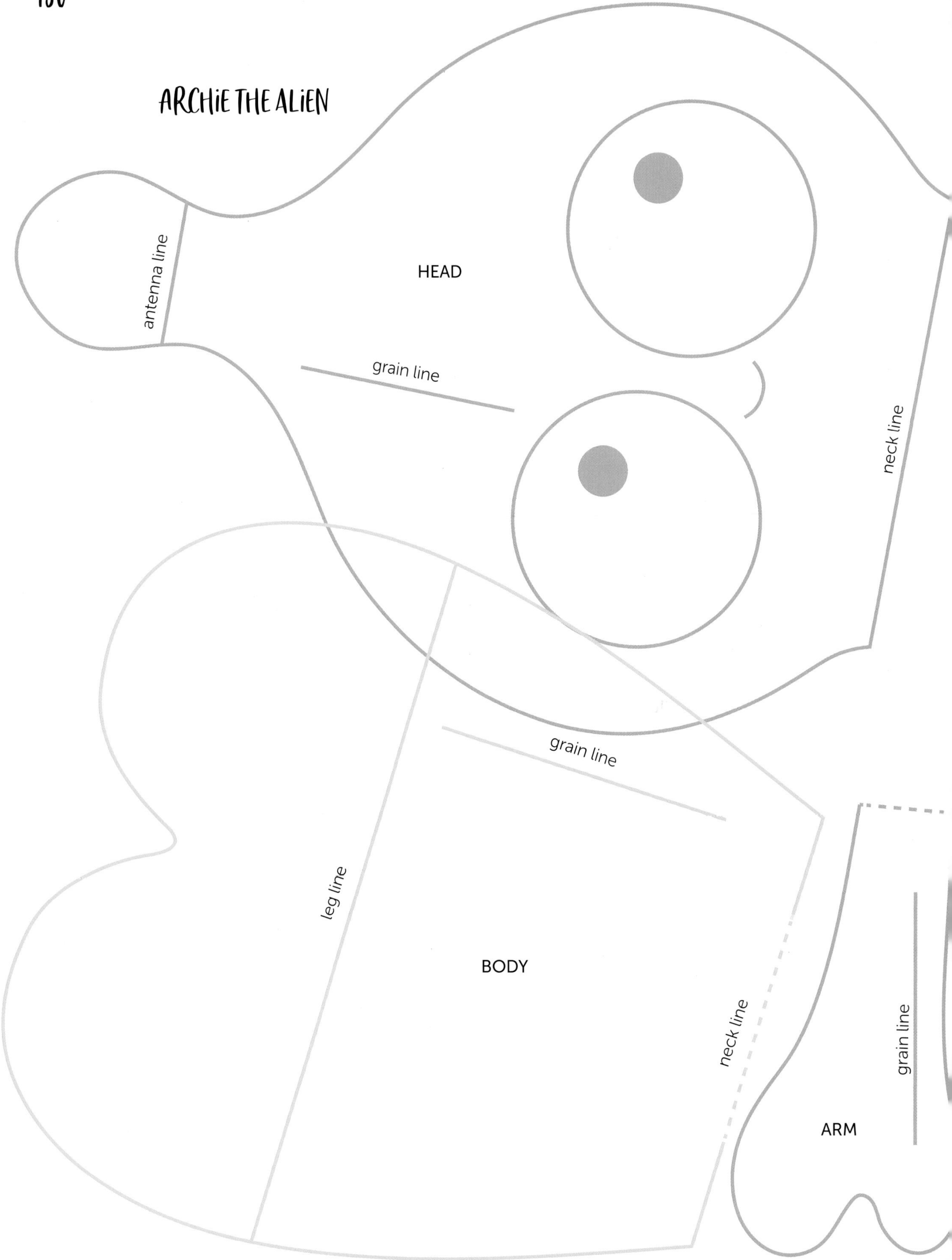

antenna line

HEAD

grain line

neck line

grain line

leg line

BODY

neck line

grain line

ARM

OTIS THE FUN UFO

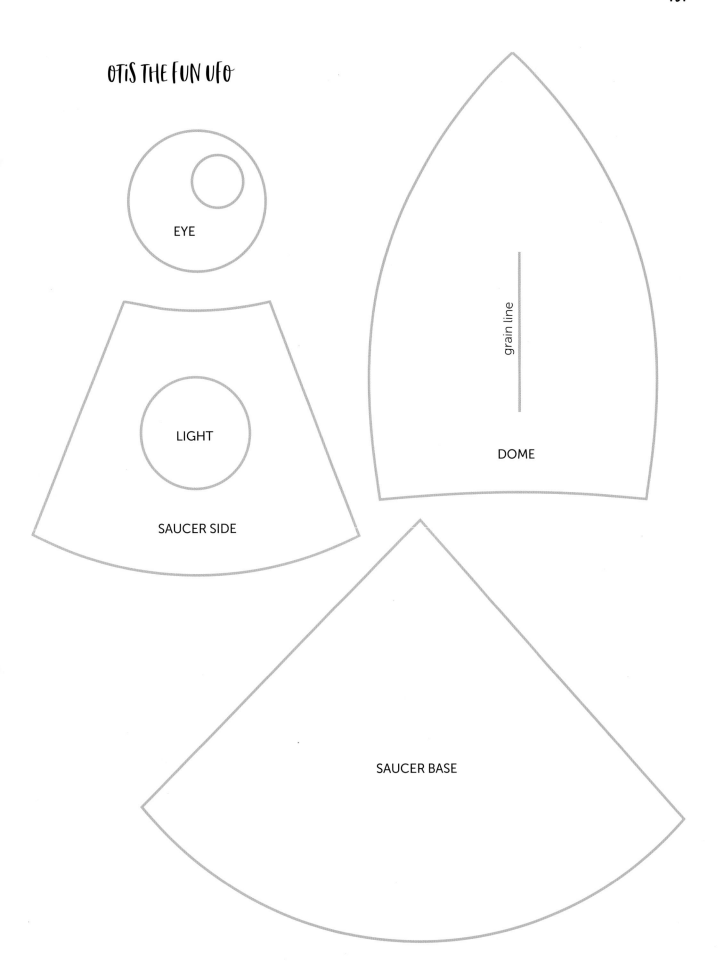

EYE

LIGHT

SAUCER SIDE

grain line

DOME

SAUCER BASE

MiLi AND MiLO

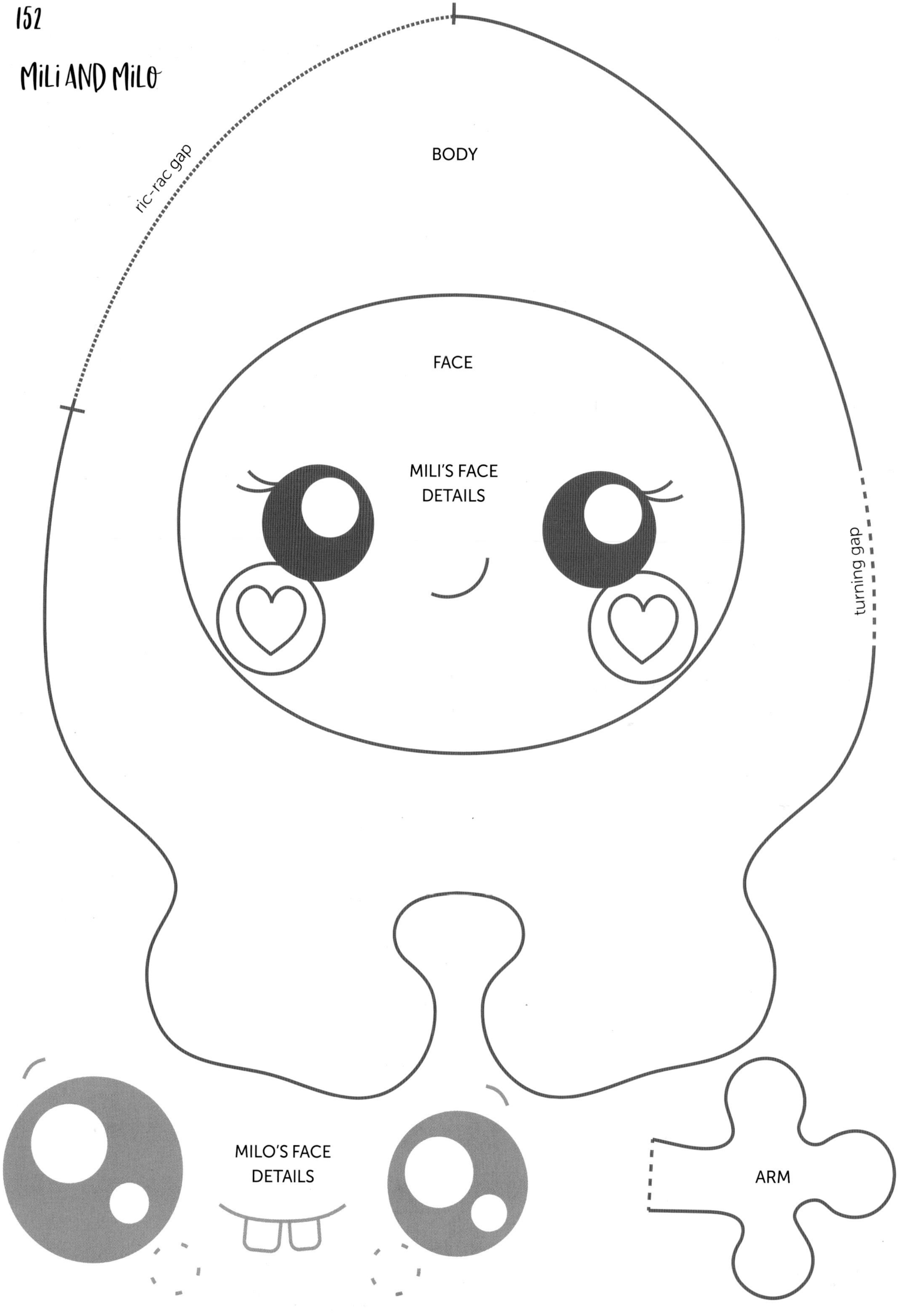

BODY

FACE

MILI'S FACE DETAILS

ric-rac gap

turning gap

MILO'S FACE DETAILS

ARM

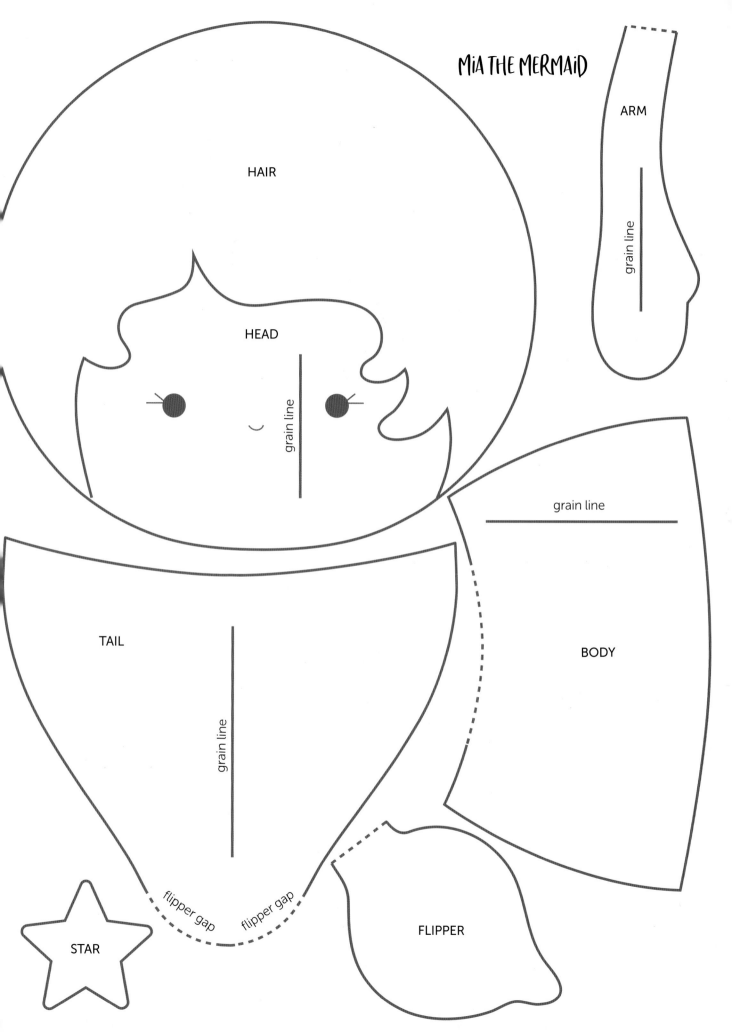

MiA THE MERMAiD

ARM

grain line

HAIR

HEAD

grain line

grain line

TAIL

BODY

grain line

flipper gap

flipper gap

STAR

FLIPPER

154

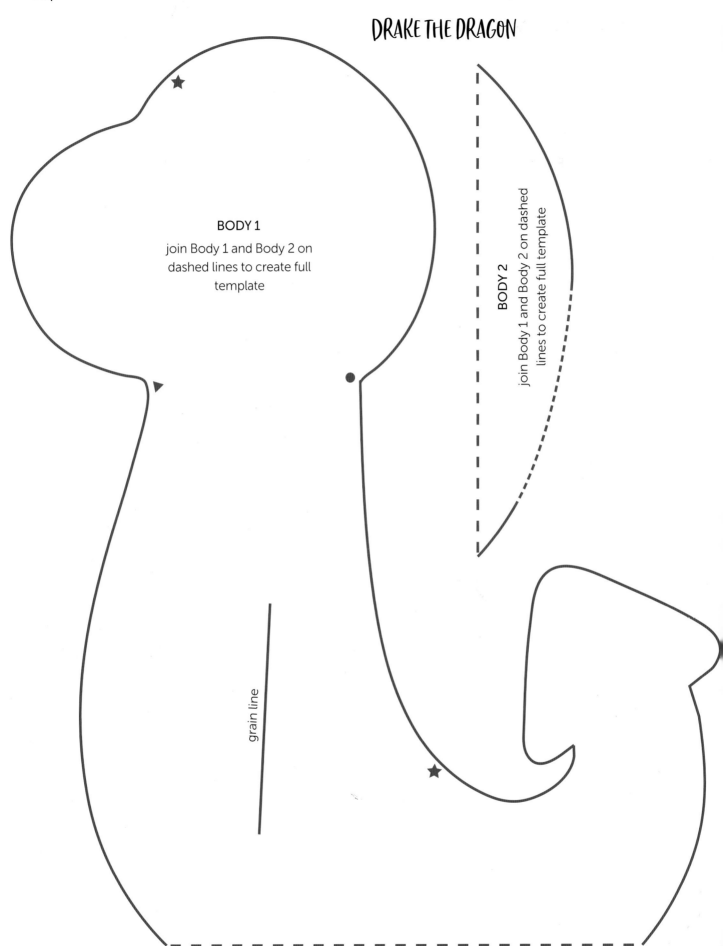

DRAKE THE DRAGON

BODY 1

join Body 1 and Body 2 on dashed lines to create full template

BODY 2

join Body 1 and Body 2 on dashed lines to create full template

grain line

DRAKE THE DRAGON

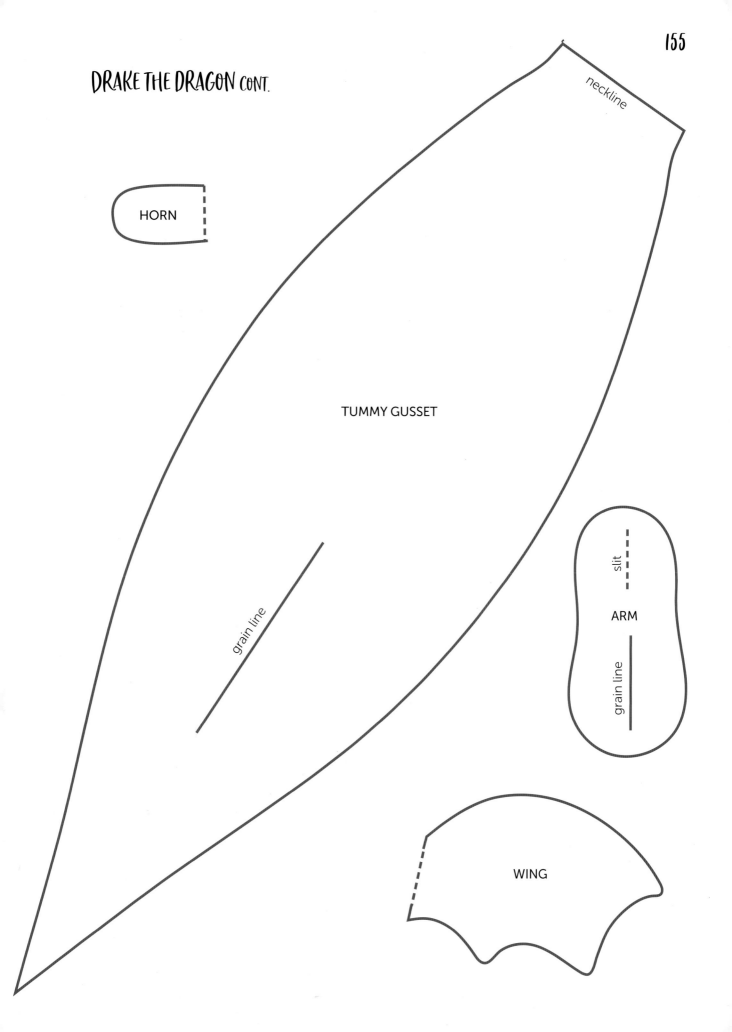

DRAKE THE DRAGON CONT.

neckline

HORN

TUMMY GUSSET

grain line

slit

ARM

grain line

WING

DRAKE THE DRAGON cont.

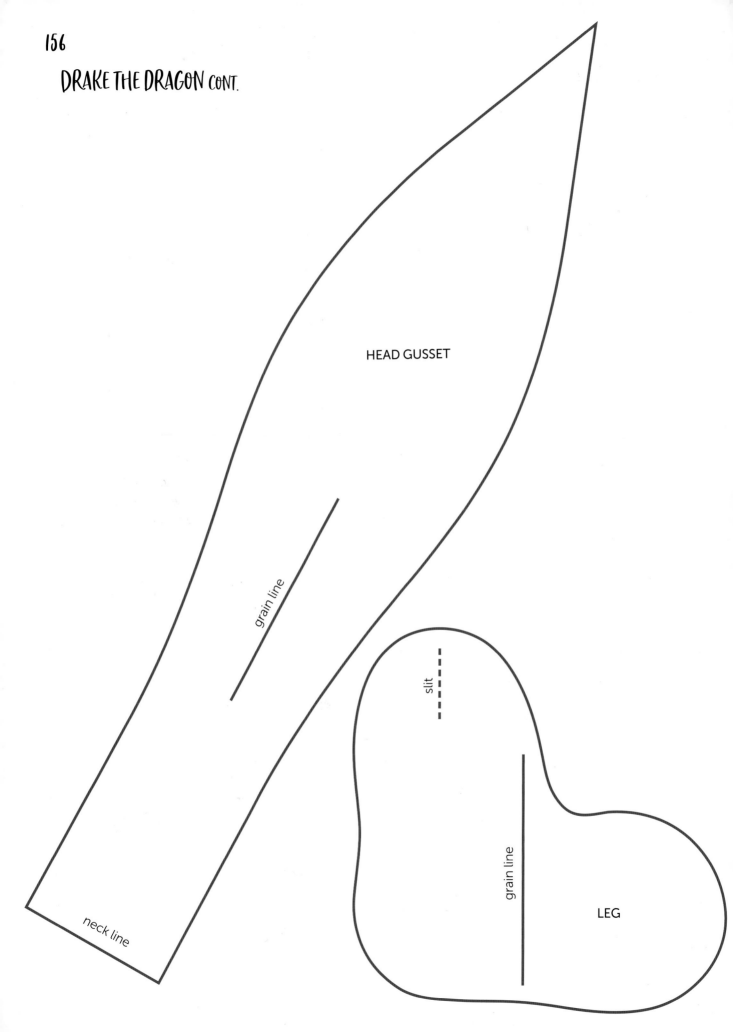

HEAD GUSSET

grain line

neck line

slit

grain line

LEG

YUMI THE UNICORN

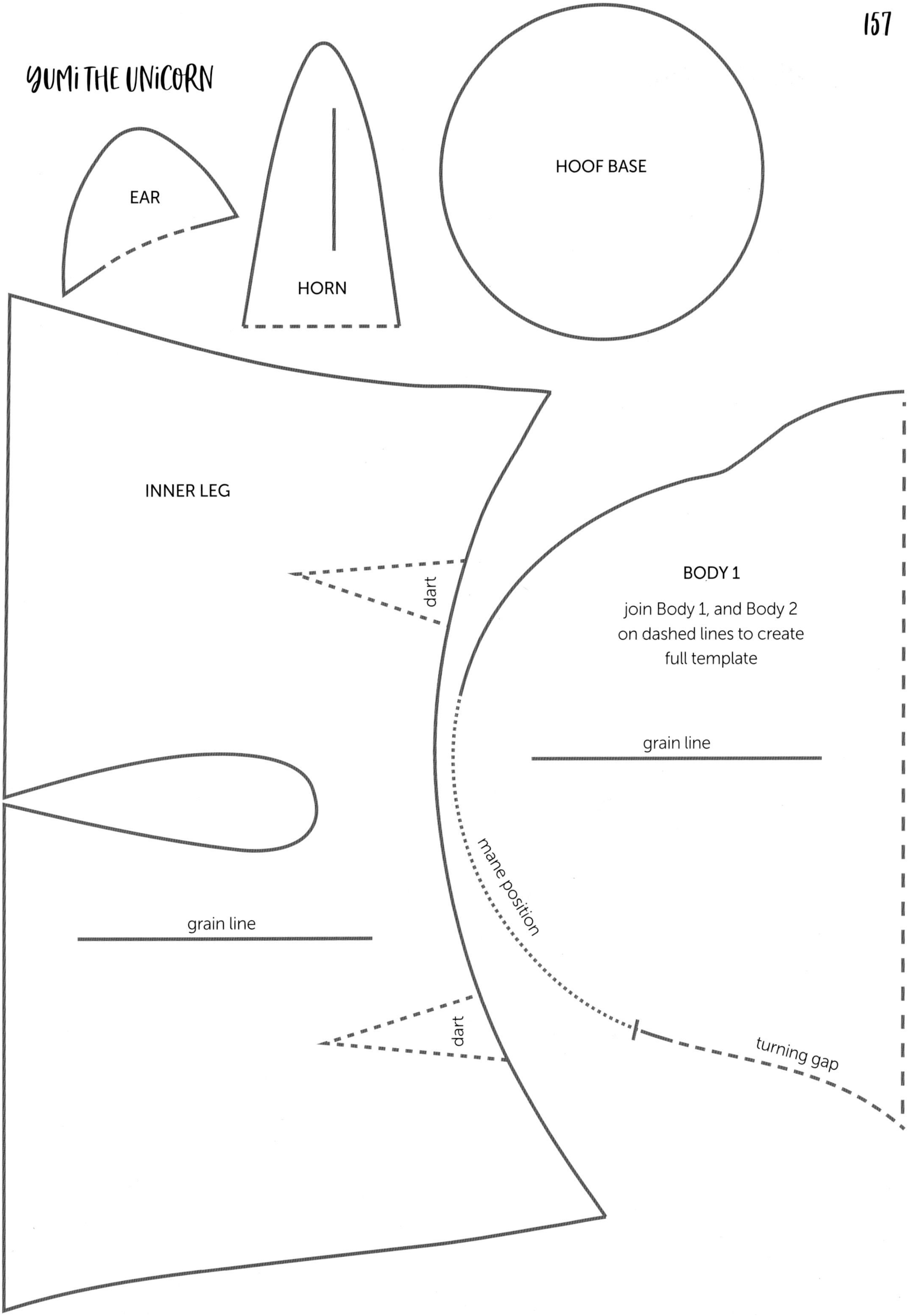

EAR

HORN

HOOF BASE

INNER LEG

dart

dart

grain line

BODY 1

join Body 1, and Body 2
on dashed lines to create
full template

grain line

mane position

turning gap

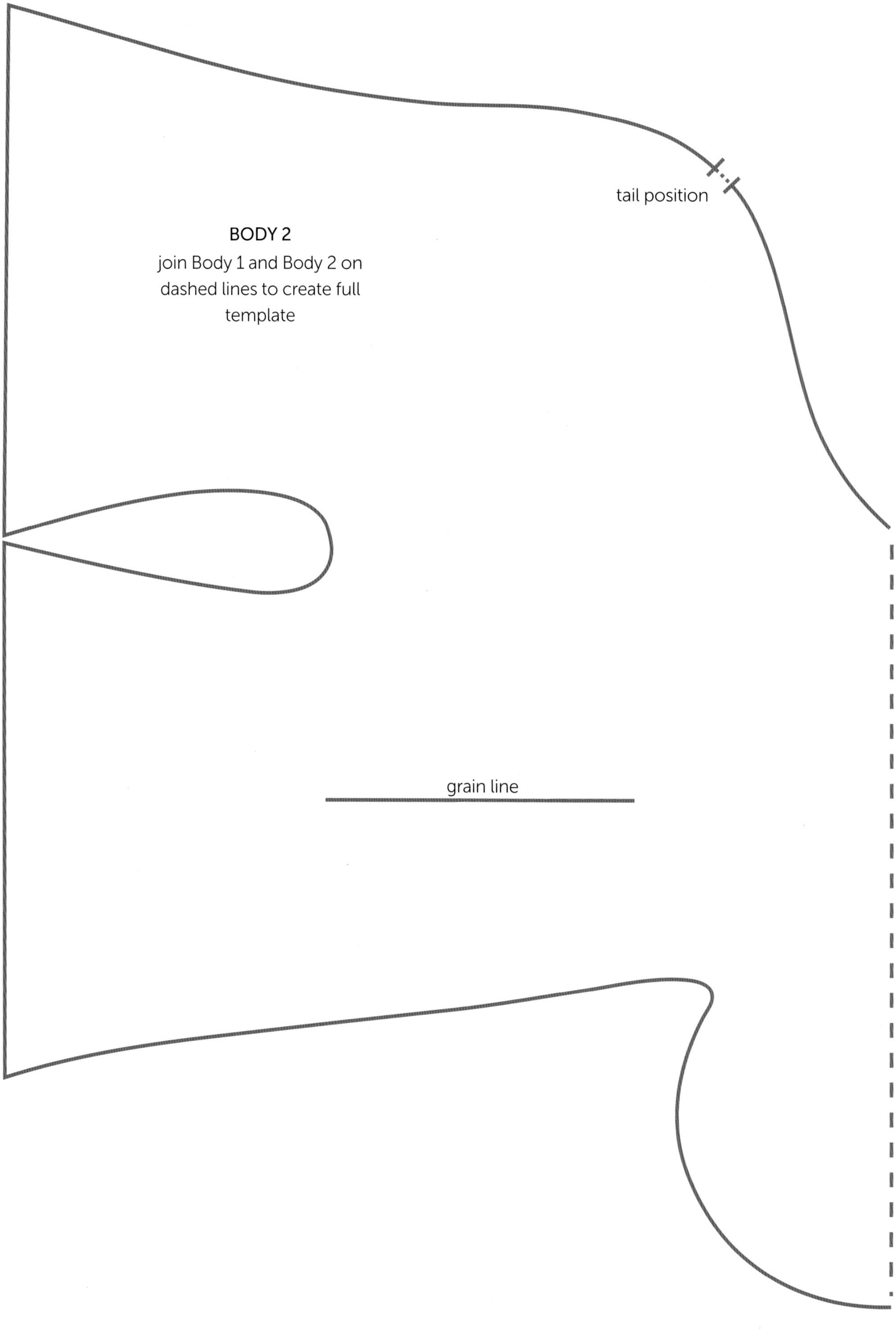

tail position

BODY 2
join Body 1 and Body 2 on
dashed lines to create full
template

grain line

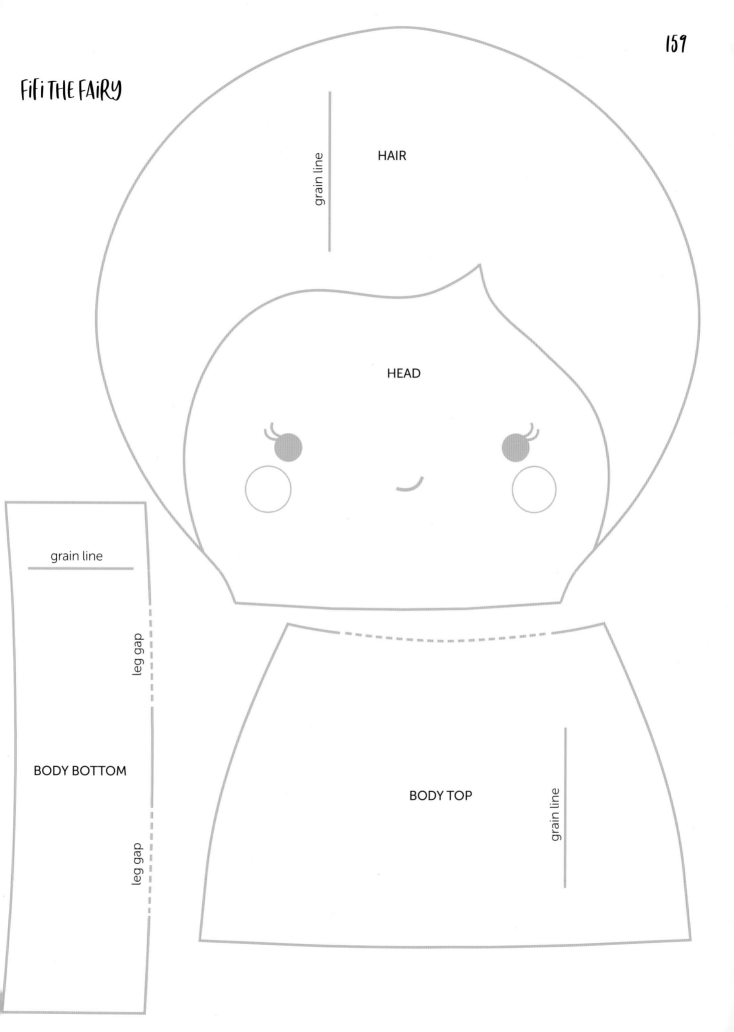

FIFI THE FAIRY

159

HAIR

grain line

HEAD

grain line

BODY BOTTOM

leg gap

leg gap

BODY TOP

grain line

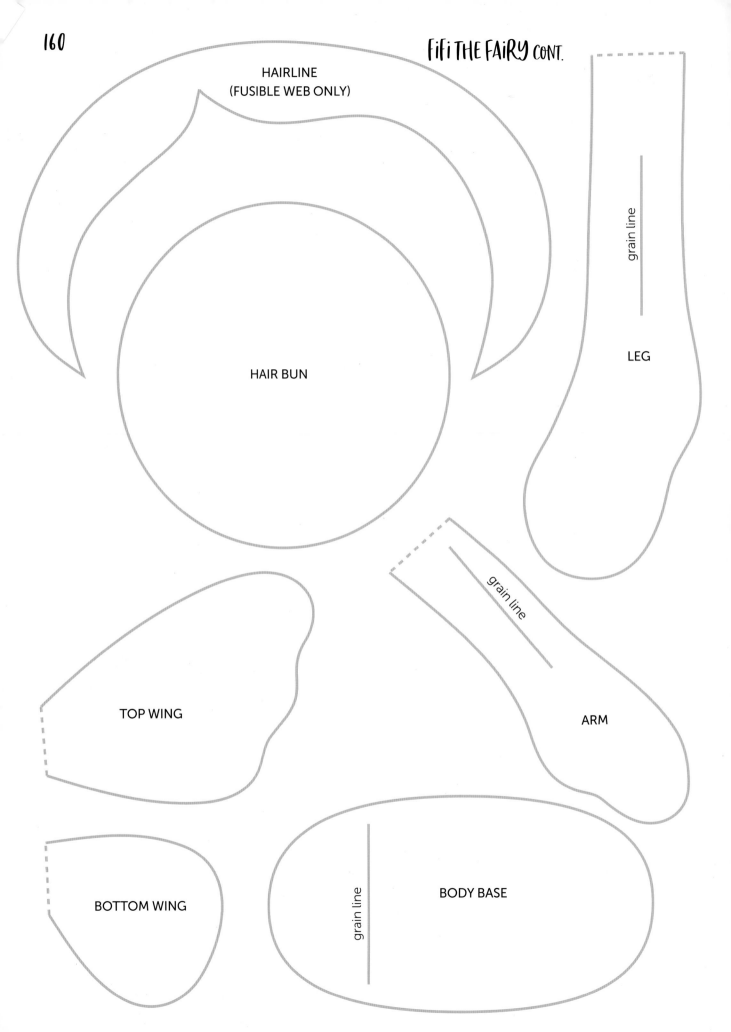

HAIRLINE
(FUSIBLE WEB ONLY)

HAIR BUN

grain line

LEG

grain line

TOP WING

ARM

BOTTOM WING

grain line

BODY BASE

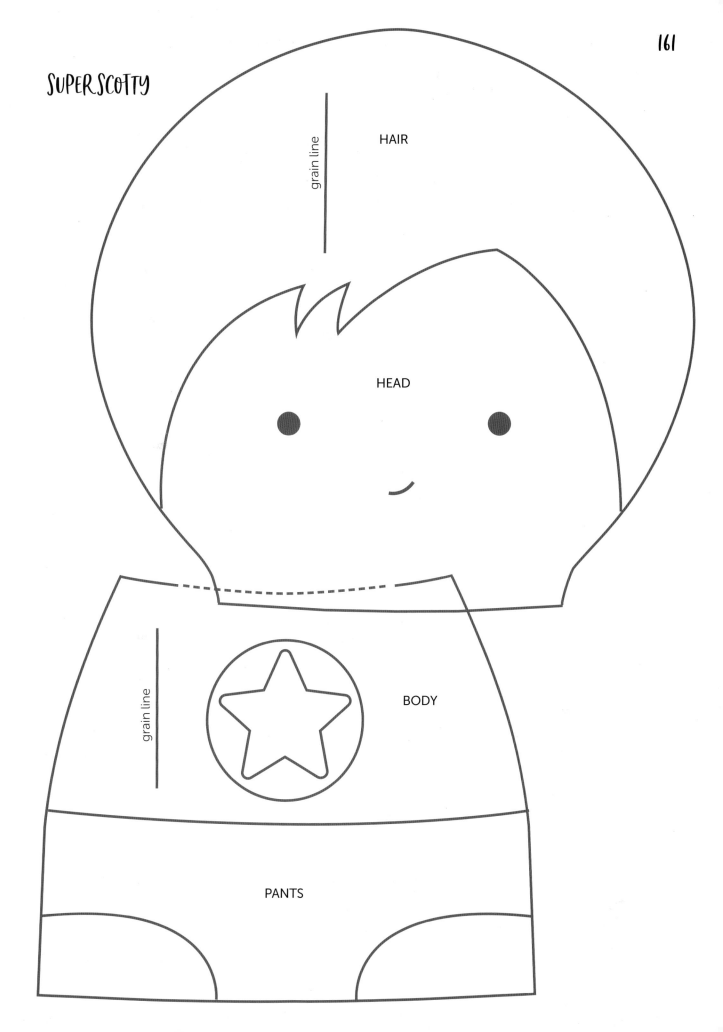

SUPER SCOTTY CONT.

CAPE

grain line

LEG

boot line

MASK

HAIRLINE
(FUSIBLE WEB ONLY)

BODY BASE

grain line

ARM

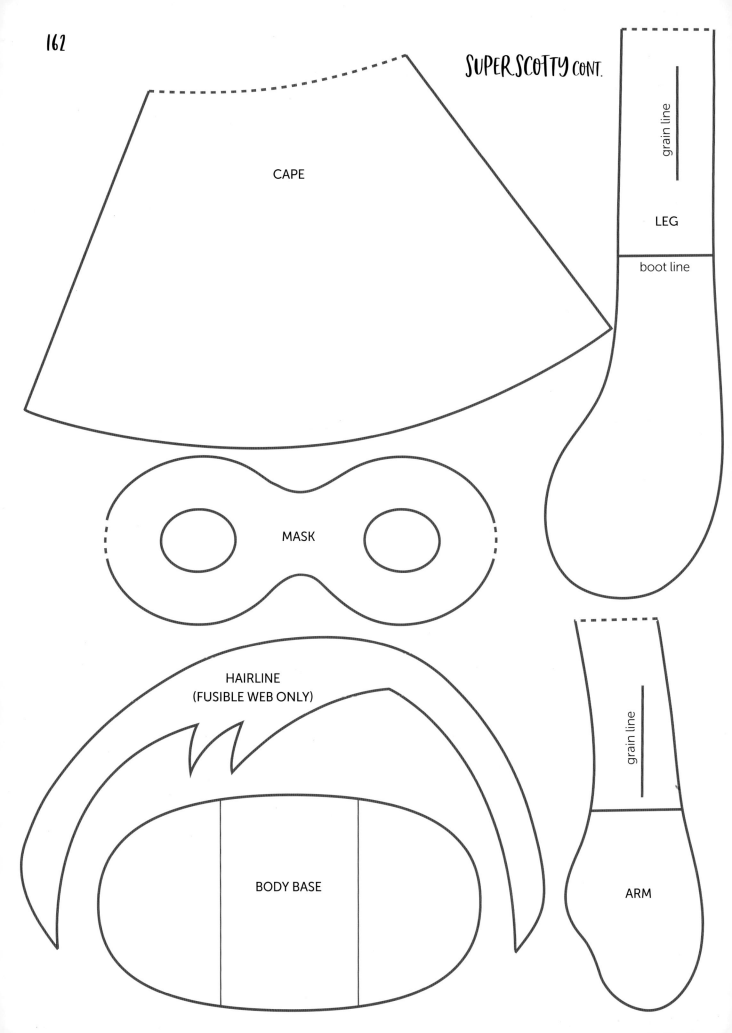

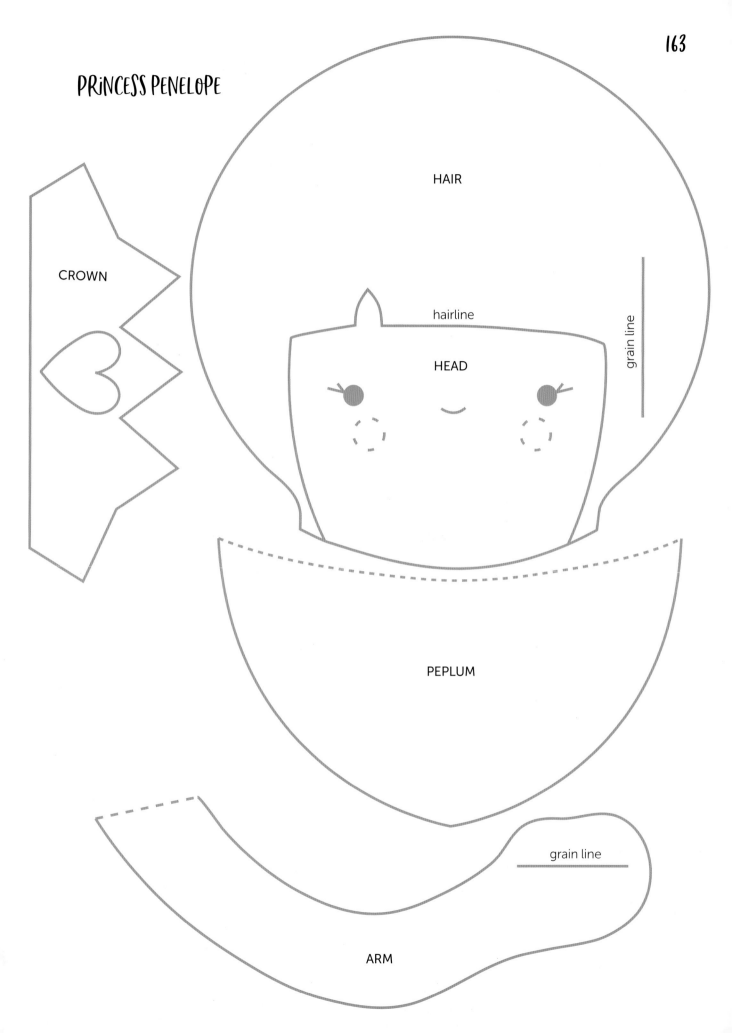

PRINCESS PENELOPE

CROWN

HAIR

hairline

HEAD

grain line

PEPLUM

grain line

ARM

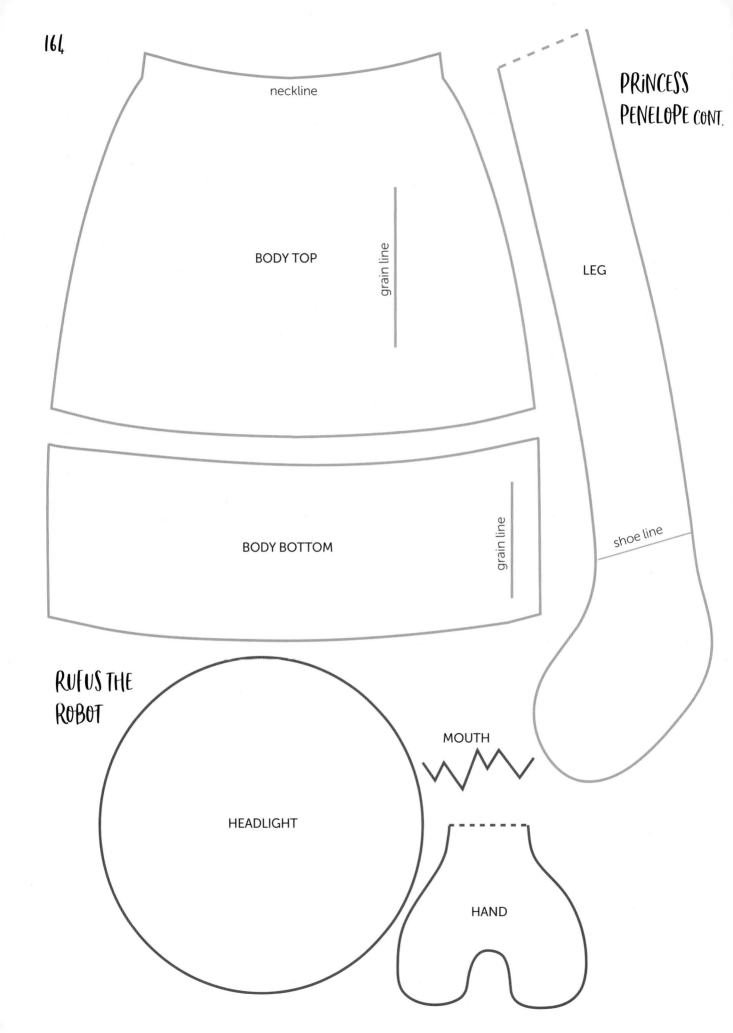

neckline

BODY TOP

grain line

PRINCESS PENELOPE CONT.

LEG

BODY BOTTOM

grain line

shoe line

RUFUS THE ROBOT

HEADLIGHT

MOUTH

HAND

GARDEN QUILT

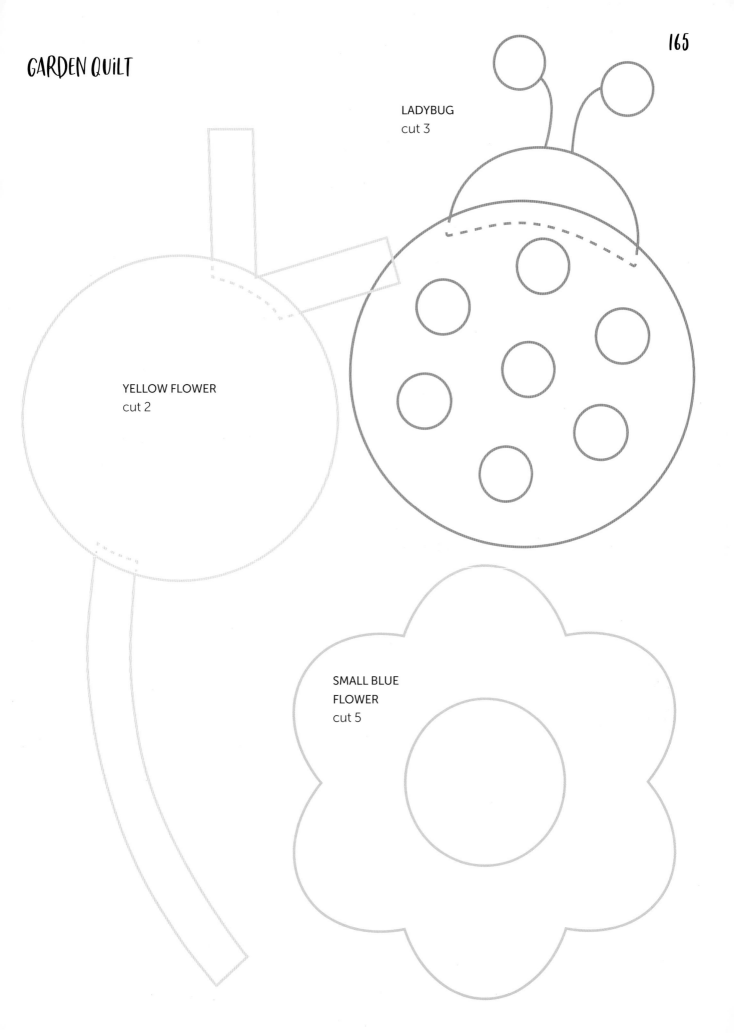

LADYBUG
cut 3

YELLOW FLOWER
cut 2

SMALL BLUE
FLOWER
cut 5

GARDEN QUILT cont.

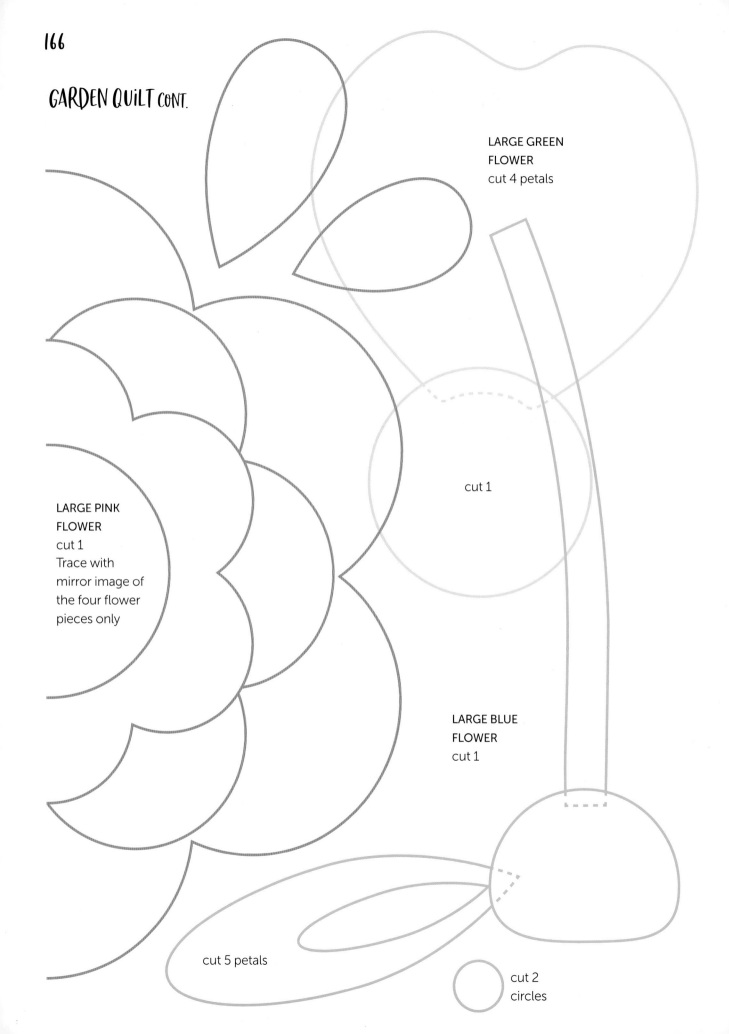

LARGE GREEN
FLOWER
cut 4 petals

cut 1

LARGE PINK
FLOWER
cut 1
Trace with
mirror image of
the four flower
pieces only

LARGE BLUE
FLOWER
cut 1

cut 5 petals

cut 2
circles

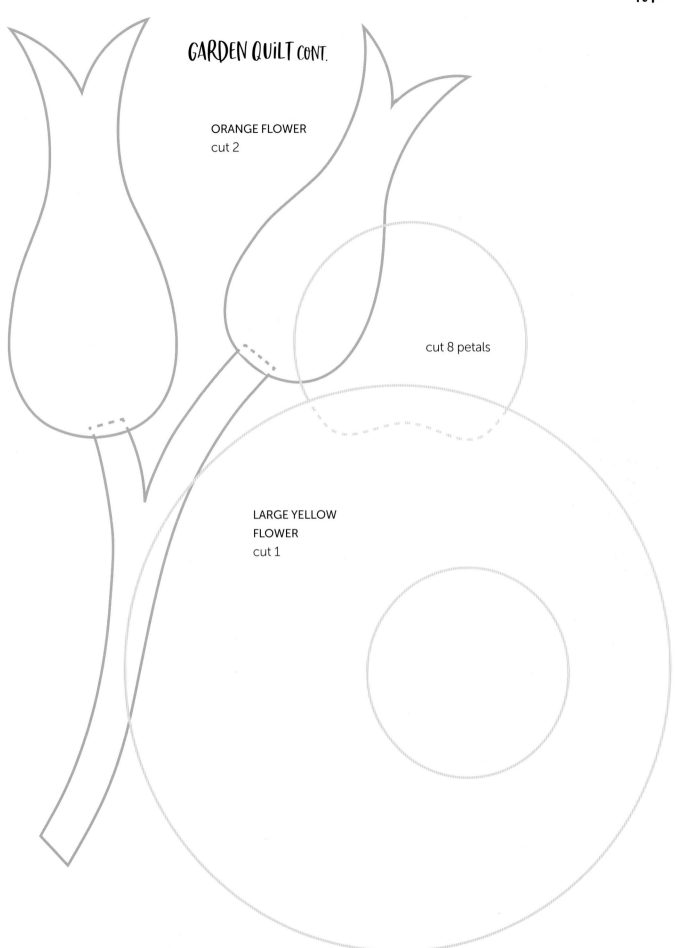

GARDEN QUILT cont.

ORANGE FLOWER
cut 2

cut 8 petals

LARGE YELLOW
FLOWER
cut 1

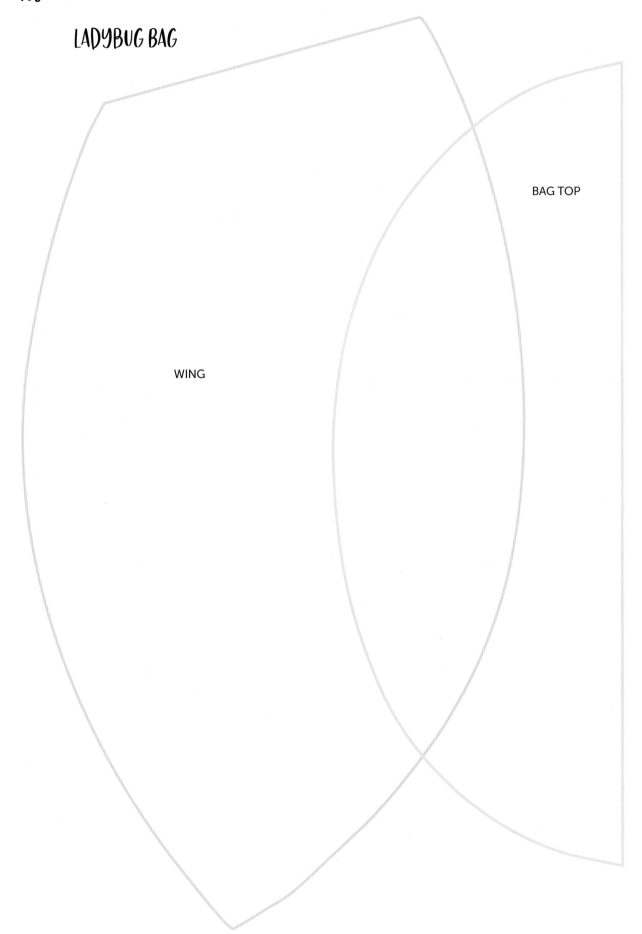

168

LADYBUG BAG

BAG TOP

WING

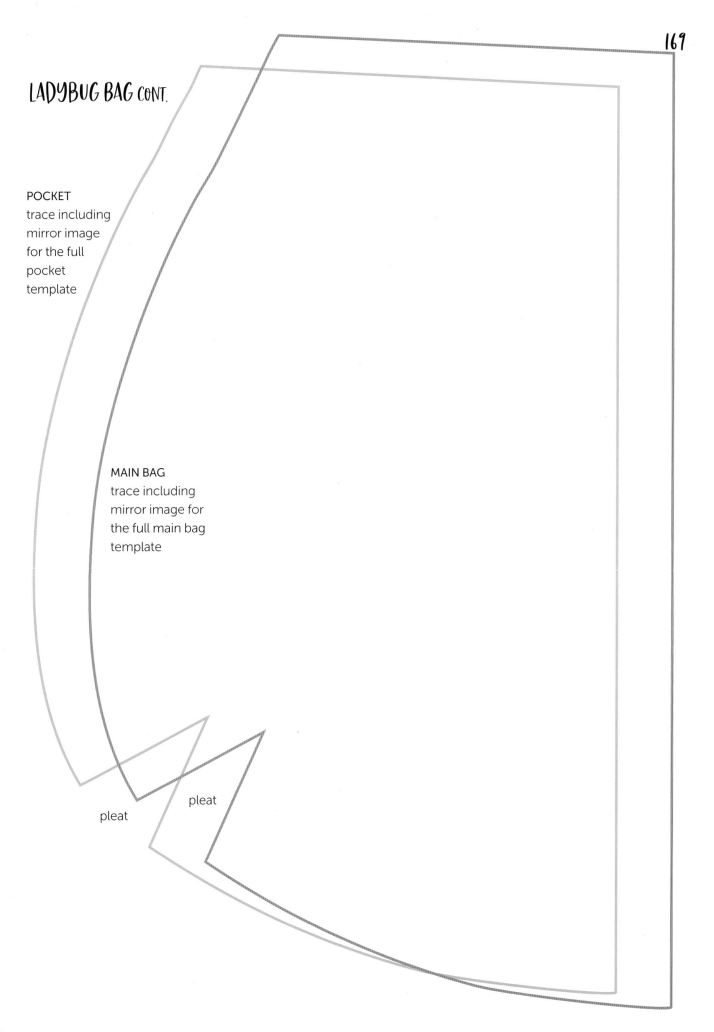

LADYBUG BAG CONT.

POCKET
trace including
mirror image
for the full
pocket
template

MAIN BAG
trace including
mirror image for
the full main bag
template

pleat

pleat

SEBASTIAN THE SNAIL

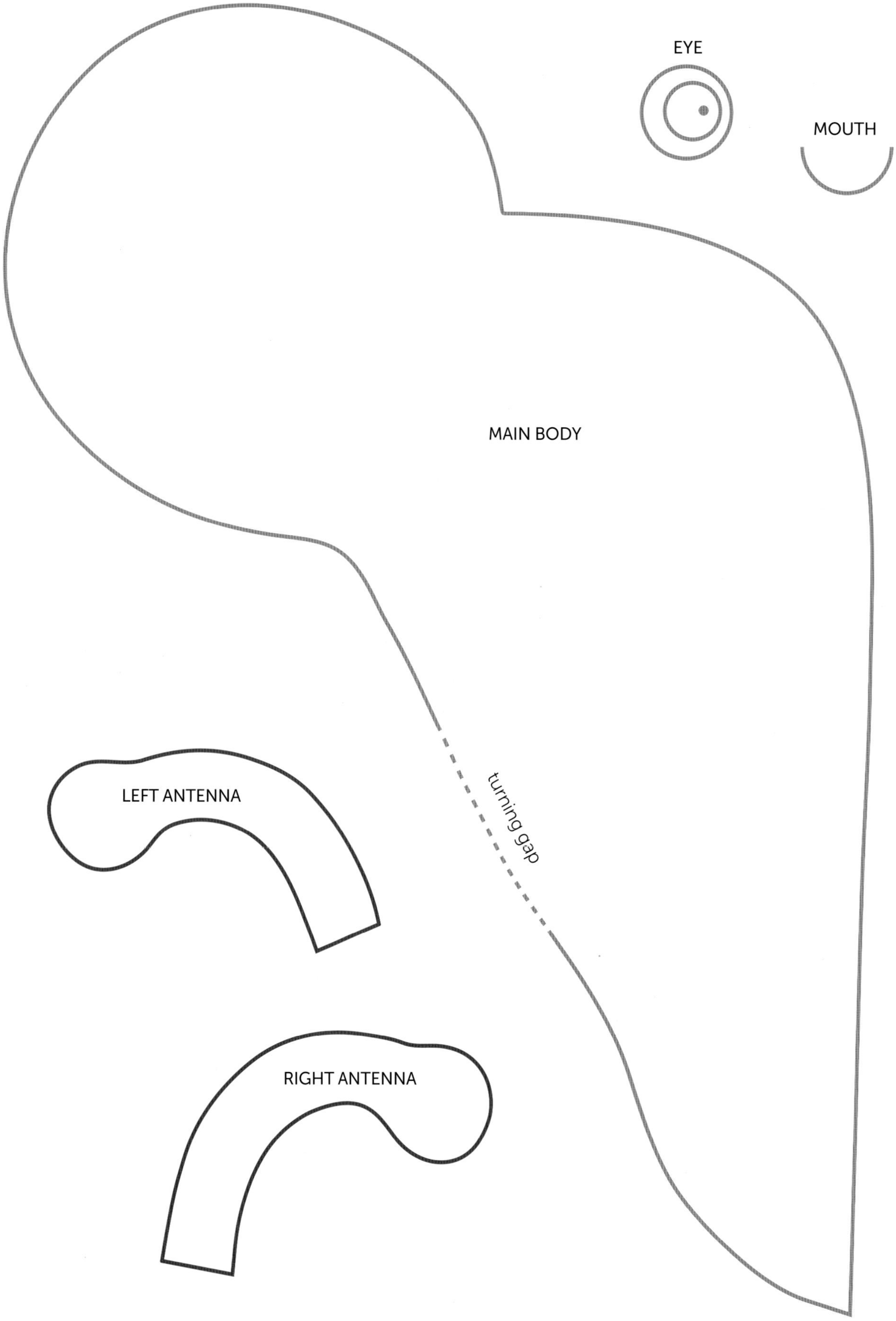

EYE

MOUTH

MAIN BODY

turning gap

LEFT ANTENNA

RIGHT ANTENNA

SEBASTIAN THE SNAIL CONT.

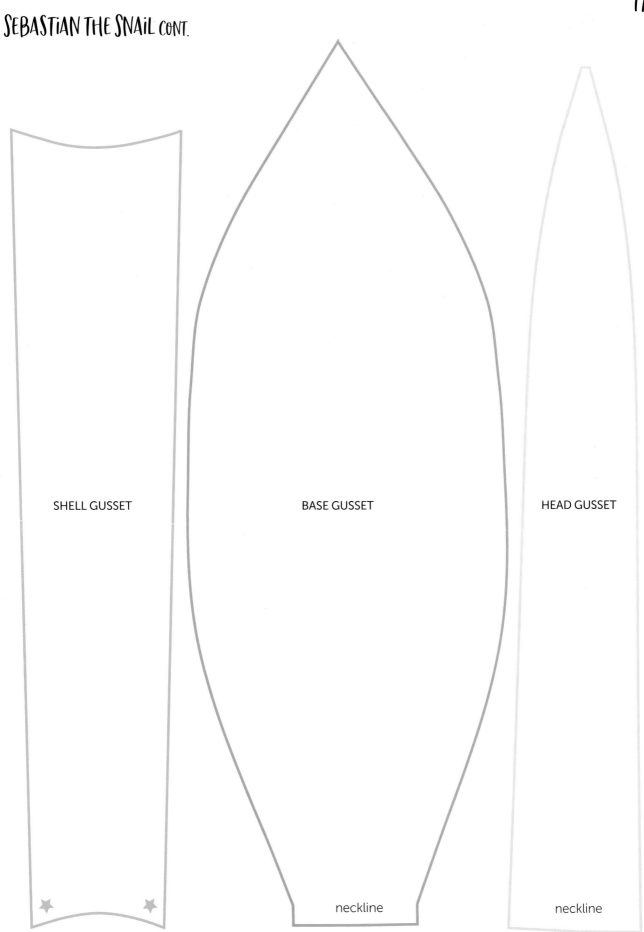

SHELL GUSSET

BASE GUSSET

HEAD GUSSET

neckline

neckline

SEBASTIAN THE SNAIL cont.

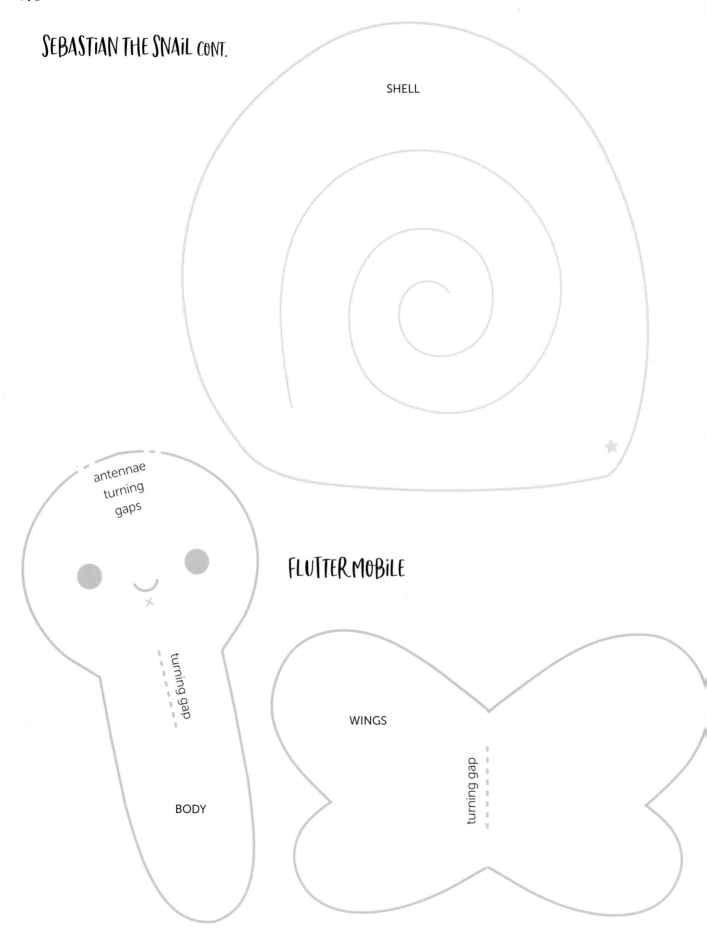

SHELL

antennae
turning
gaps

FLUTTER MOBILE

turning gap

WINGS

turning gap

BODY

BUG iN A RUG

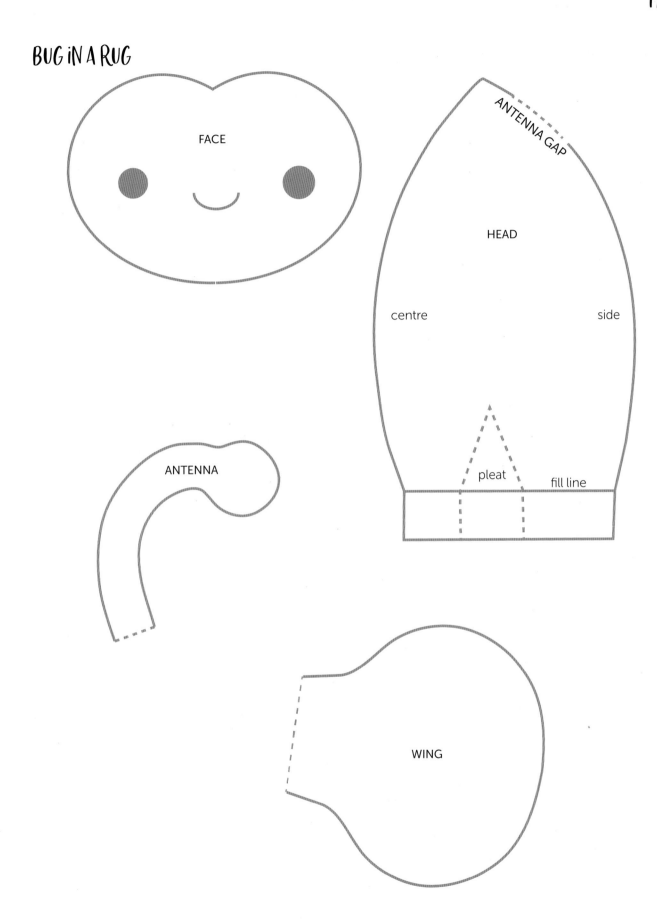

FACE

ANTENNA GAP

HEAD

centre   side

pleat   fill line

ANTENNA

WING

MEET THE AUTHOR

Melanie McNeice is an Aussie pattern designer based in the leafy outskirts of Melbourne, Australia. Melly's adventures in sewing began after she found herself a stay-at-home mum with the desire to still be productive. Melly's passion for sewing grew quickly after her sister encouraged her to give it a try, and only 12 months after beginning to sew, she tried her hand at design under the pattern label Melly & me.

Melly's design goals are to create a range of contemporary sewing patterns that include bright and quirky toys, wearable purses, and fun, modern quilts. She aims to design items that are original and fun, achievable in a day, and completely practical for everyday life! Melly & me has grown to appeal to a worldwide audience, and Melly has designed more than 100 patterns, published five books - *Kaleidoscope*, *Sewn Toy Tales*, *Snug as a Bug*, *Sew Cute to Carry* and now *Supercute Sewing*, and teaches across Australia. In 2010 Melly also began her journey in fabric design and has released five fabric collections since then.

Melly takes inspiration from her two young children, childhood memories, the beauty of nature, and her love of fun and colour. Visit Melly's website to see more of her fun designs at www.mellyandme.com.

THANKS!

As always, I feel a need to give thanks to those in my life who continually inspire, motivate and encourage me. Firstly, to my very own 'Super Scotty' who continually believes in and encourages me in everything I put my hand to – love you. Secondly, to my gorgeous children Zak and Kiki, who are my test subjects and always tell me when something is 'awesome!'. The rest of my wonderful family, especially my sister Rosie and my parents for their continual support and for starting me on my design journey.

Thanks to the team at David & Charles for their enthusiasm and support, and for making this book happen.

I would also like to thank Riley Blake for their partnership in bringing my fabric collection 'Snug as a Bug' to life, Sue Daley from Mill House Collections for supplying Riley Blake fabrics for the book and Anita Ellis from Hillside Quilting for the stunning custom quilting work on the Garden Quilt.

And lastly, but most importantly, to all of the Melly & me fans out there who send me ideas and encouragement, share their work with me and constantly bring smiles to my day.

SUPPLIERS

AUSTRALIA

Melly & Me
www.mellyandme.com
mellyandme@bigpond.com

The Oz Material Girls
www.theozmaterialgirls.com

Fabric Patch
www.fabricpatch.com.au

Patchwork with Gail B
www.patchworkwithgailb.com

Creative Abundance
www.creativeabundance.com.au

USA

ilovefabric
www.ilovefabric.com

Pine Needles
www.pineneedlesonline.com

Heartsong Quilts
www.heartsongquilts.com

UK

Hulu Crafts
www.hulucrafts.co.uk

Prints to Polka Dots
www.printstopolkadots.co.uk

Sew Hot
www.sewhot.co.uk

INDEX

Italic page numbers indicate templates

A DAVID AND CHARLES BOOK
© David and Charles, Ltd 2021

David and Charles is an imprint of David and Charles, Ltd
Suite A, Tourism House, Pynes Hill, Exeter, EX2 5WT

Text and Designs © Melanie McNeice 2021
Layout and Photography © David and Charles, Ltd 2021

First published as part of Snug as a Bug in 2013; Fun of the Fair in 2014 & Sew Fantasy Toys in 2015

This edition first published in the UK and USA in 2021

Melanie McNeice has asserted her right to be identified as author of this work in accordance with
the Copyright, Designs and Patents Act, 1988.

A catalogue record for this book is available from the British Library.

ISBN-13: 9781446308400 paperback
ISBN-13: 9781446380987 EPUB

This book has been printed on paper from approved suppliers and made from pulp from
sustainable sources.

Printed in China by Asia Pacific for:
David and Charles, Ltd
Suite A, Tourism House, Pynes Hill, Exeter, EX2 5WT

10 9 8 7 6 5 4 3 2 1

Senior Commissioning Editor: Sarah Callard
Managing Editor: Jessica Cropper
Project Editor: Jenny Fox-Proverbs
Designer: Sarah Rowntree
Pre-press Designer: Ali Stark
Photography: Jason Jenkins
Production Manager: Beverley Richardson

David and Charles publishes high-quality books on a wide range of subjects. For more information
visit www.davidandcharles.com.

Layout of the digital edition of this book may vary depending on reader hardware and
display settings.